Reluctant Regulators

Reluctant Regulators

How the West Created
and How China Survived
the Global Financial Crisis

Leo F. Goodstadt

香港大學出版社
HONG KONG UNIVERSITY PRESS

Hong Kong University Press
14/F Hing Wai Centre
7 Tin Wan Praya Road
Aberdeen
Hong Kong
www.hkupress.org

ISBN 978-988-8083-25-1

British Library Cataloguing-in-Publication Data
A catalogue record for this book is available from the British Library.

10   9   8   7   6   5   4   3   2   1

Printed and bound by Liang Yu Printing Factory Ltd. in Hong Kong, China

Contents

Preface

It would be hard to find a better vantage point from which to survey the international financial crisis of 2007–09 than Hong Kong. The unparalleled global economic growth that preceded the disaster had followed three decades of a worldwide trend towards the liberalisation of trade and finance at both the national and international levels. Protectionism and state-planning went out of favour, even in a nation previously wedded to the most anti-capitalist ideology as China had been — with astonishing growth as its reward.

Thus, laissez-faire, Hong Kong's long-ignored formula for self-generated, sustained growth, became a global fashion. Its own economic performance had several claims to fame starting with the fastest rise from poverty in Asian history. Thanks to its industrial take-off after World War II, it had become the world's largest supplier of light industrial products by the mid-1960s. Its dominance of the world garment trade continued till the end of the century despite the relocation of virtually all its manufacturing facilities to southern China in response to Deng Xiaoping's 1978 liberalisation policies.

Less well known is its role as Asia's leading international finance centre. For much of the previous century, Hong Kong was the location for Asia's freest financial markets and provided the region's most liberal environment for international banks. Between 1950 and 1971, it had also been the base from which China could safely carry out international financial and commercial transactions despite the economic embargoes of the Cold War. After the nation adopted its 'open door' policies in 1978 and embarked on economic liberalisation, Hong Kong grew in stature as an international financial centre. Yet, until 1986, financial crises were a recurrent feature of the business landscape, aggravated by the mounting vulnerability of the Hong Kong dollar from the mid-1970s. The susceptibility of its financial markets to asset bubbles — especially in the property sector — was a major feature of Hong Kong's history.

The colonial administration of that period was extremely reluctant to accept responsibility for financial stability and introduced regulatory reforms to halt illegal and imprudent banking behaviour piecemeal and as minimally as possible. The United Kingdom, although constitution- ally responsible for the good government of Hong Kong, preferred not to get involved. Nevertheless, despite the crises and scandals, the finan- cial sector went from strength to strength, attracting an influx of major foreign banks and an expansion of Chinese state banks' activities. By 1985, however, the case for regulation had become irresistible as bank failures could be traced to the gross professional incompetence of bank owners and executives as well as to their illegal activities. The govern- ment was now forced to abandon its preference for the lightest touch regulation and its aversion to intervention in the markets as mounting public outrage at the regulators' failures made further bank bailouts too expensive politically.

From a personal point of view, I benefitted from an ample supply of excellent 'mentors' as a young member of the *Far Eastern Economic Review*'s editorial team from 1966 to 1976. Political leaders, officials and businessmen around Asia were willing to explain events and poli- cies to me principally out of an awareness that if journalists are misin- formed, their output can undermine depositor and market confidence. Thereafter, access to policy-makers and industry leaders expanded when I reported for *Euromoney* and *Asiabanking* on financial developments in Hong Kong and the Chinese Mainland, which were of growing interna- tional interest.

One group of bank executives deserves to be identified individu- ally. The speed of China's emergence as a major participant in global financial as well as export markets can be attributed to the personal qualities of its bankers throughout the first 30 years of the People's Republic. From 1949 to 1978, the 'capitalist' world and its ways were targets for relentless condemnation by the Chinese Communist Party, and contacts with foreign firms and individuals could be politically per- ilous. Nevertheless, managers from China's state banks in Hong Kong, many of them from the Shanghai business élite whose relatives on the Mainland were being punished for their 'class origins', followed the line of Prime Minister Zhou Enlai and maintained connections with their foreign counterparts. As a result, China's links with the world's banking system were never severed completely, and thus the obstacles to normalising financial relations with the outside world in the 1970s were less daunting than would later be the case for the former Soviet Bloc. Among those involved in preserving this access to 'capitalism' to whom I am personally indebted were: Li Tsu-tsan (Nanyang Commercial Bank), P. L. Chen (Kincheng Banking Corporation), C. S. Yao (China

Development Finance and Sin Hua Trust & Savings Bank), Nelson Tsao (also Sin Hua), Shu Tse-wong (Bank of China and Nanyang Commercial Bank) and Wang Deyan (Bank of China).

The constraints and the attractions of a rising Anglo-American culture — a major focus of this book — were a regular theme for my editors. Among the key issues were the 'globalisation' of HSBC as it struggled successfully to acquire an American presence and tried but failed in its first bid to gain direct entry to British banking; the speed with which the American money centre bank became the model for the rest of the industry; the threat perceived by New York and London from the burgeoning Japanese banks; the constant complaints from American bankers about Asian discrimination; and the prolonged indifference to Asian opportunities of British bankers.

I also had extensive but usually unanticipated access to banking failures. Several of those who were happy to be interviewed were later ruined in the financial crises of those decades. Among them were men who brought down respected Chinese family banks in scandalous circumstances and prominent executives from British, German, French and Malaysian financial institutions who went to prison or fled from justice. There were colonial officials investigated for corruption and, very occasionally, successfully prosecuted. These acquaintances did not encourage optimism about the self-correcting character of financial markets or the avoidance of self-destructive behaviour by bank owners and executives.

I was fortunate to have developed a consultancy practice as a private sector economist until 1989 with long-term clients who included, among others, Hang Seng Bank, Standard Chartered Bank, N. M. Rothschild & Sons Ltd and County NatWest Securities. I then joined the Hong Kong Government's Central Policy Unit. Here, we had no direct responsibility for either monetary affairs or financial regulation. But it was impossible to avoid all involvement in these areas because of the Unit's role in drafting the annual Budget Speech. We also helped in monitoring and managing the business community's concerns. We dealt with Bank of England and other foreign officials in search of reassurance about Hong Kong's post-1997 prospects and the viability of its financial markets after China's resumption of sovereignty. The Unit contributed to the decision to establish the Hong Kong Monetary Authority (HKMA) as a separate statutory central banking institution staffed by professionals rather than civil servants.

Since 1997, my interest in banking and monetary affairs has been predominantly academic, and I have focused on researching the financial foundations of modern Hong Kong first under the auspices of Trinity College Dublin and subsequently at the University of Hong

Kong's former Centre of Asian Studies and the Hong Kong Institute for Monetary Research. No previous client or employer has been consulted or otherwise involved in the preparation of this book, and none of its contents has been discussed with, reviewed, or approved by officials of any government.

My research trips to Hong Kong have been made all the more pleasant by the kindness and hospitality which my friends and former colleagues at the Central Policy Unit so generously offer me. Among those I must acknowledge here with gratitude are Barry Cheung, Helen Cheng, T. L. Tsim, Dr Rikkie Yeung, Professor Cecilia Chan and their families, who have gone to endless trouble to look after me. I am especially indebted to Roger Luk for his help, direct and indirect, with this book. It is a pleasure to record my thanks to Dr Christopher Munn of Hong Kong University Press who has been the best kind of editor: patient, pleasant and in possession of special professional expertise in the academic field covered by this book.

Hong Kong
March 2011

Acknowledgements

I am happy to acknowledge the considerable assistance from the Hong Kong Institute for Monetary Research (HKIMR) towards the research on which this book is based. This included the award of research fellowships in 2009 and 2011 and publication of three Working Papers which are used extensively in the chapters that follow. I was particularly fortunate that among the other Fellows during my tenure were distinguished American and British academics whose comments on my initial efforts to identify an Anglo-American regulatory culture were invaluable. I must record my indebtedness to Dr Hans Genberg, who as Executive Director (Research Department, Hong Kong Monetary Authority) was then responsible for the HKIMR. I have benefited considerably from his personal support and encouragement during the last six years, which I deeply appreciate. My work has also been greatly facilitated by the interest and assistance which has been shown to me by Dr Dong He, the Executive Director of Hong Kong Monetary Authority currently responsible for the HKIMR. I am also most grateful to Mr Hongyi Chen, the HKIMR's Senior Manager, and his team who have been untiringly helpful during my visits.

The Hong Kong Institute for the Humanities and Social Sciences (incorporating the Centre of Asian Studies) at the University of Hong Kong provided me with generous use of its facilities in the course of drafting this book during 2010–11. Professor Wong Siu-lun, SBS, JP, has been outstandingly hospitable over many years, and the current Director, Dr Angela Leung Ki Che, has been most kind and helpful. I must also thank the Institute's staff for the warm support which I received during this project.

The research on Hong Kong financial developments and their Mainland dimensions would not have been possible without the meticulous efficiency of the Government Records Service. Mr Bernard Hui Sung-tak and his colleagues in the Public Records Office once again provided an outstanding quality of service in their efforts to identify relevant materials among unpublished government documents and to make my access to them as convenient as possible.

I am, as always, indebted to the School of Business Studies, Trinity College, University of Dublin, and in particular to Professor Gerard McHugh, for their interest and kindness, as well as for their facilities, throughout my stays in Ireland.

None of the institutions or individuals referred to in these Acknowledgements has any responsibility for any part of the contents of this book or the views which it expresses.

Introduction — Reluctant Regulators

The crisis that overtook the world's financial markets in 2007 was a disaster that ought not to have occurred. Never had the defences against worldwide financial instability and global recession seemed so strong. The world economy was enjoying both rapid economic expansion and a general freedom from inflation. This achievement had reinforced the consensus among advanced and emerging economies that markets were more efficient than governments in fostering sustained and stable growth and in ensuring a better deal for consumers in terms not only of prices but of quality and choice as well. As an additional reassurance, the world's central bankers had reached agreement on the regulatory measures that would minimise the risks of institutional failure and restrain the spread of financial instability from one country to another.

Financial crises frequently start with what appears to be a relatively insignificant and isolated market misfortune.[1] So it was in 2007. At first, the initial tremors seemed minor events that could be comfortably contained. They began with a collapse in confidence among investors holding the US$200 billion of securities issued by the American sub-prime mortgage market. Zhou Xiaochuan, Governor of the People's Bank (China's central bank) observed at the time that there was no reason for general panic because 'it should not be hard for an economy as large as the U.S. to absorb the losses'.[2] Similarly, it seemed very unlikely that a run on the United Kingdom's Northern Rock Bank in the same year could trigger a general collapse in public confidence. It was so minor a player, senior British officials later suggested, that it seemed to be hardly worth saving.[3]

More improbable still were the catastrophic consequences of the American decision to let Lehman Bros fail the following year. The direct losses that this event would cause were described as 'relatively modest'. But the markets went into total panic. 'Banks hoarded liquidity for fear of lending to infected banks', a central banker later lamented, 'and there was an effective boycott of the remaining large US investment banks'. How could such incidents disrupt international financial centres that had been tested to destruction in the previous decade and emerged intact? In the ten years from 1997, the world financial system had 'stood tall … self-regulating and self-repairing' even in the face of 'oil prices shocks, wars and dotcom mania'.[4] Yet, without warning, it seemed, calamity struck on a scale that appeared beyond all normal experience or reasonable expectations.[5] Observers scrambled to find parallels sufficiently apocalyptic.

> Between summer 2007 and early 2009, the global financial system suffered its worst crisis for at least 70 years, indeed in some ways the worst crisis since the emergence 200 years ago of modern industrial capitalism. And this financial crisis — largely the product of developments within the financial system, not events imposed from without — has generated a severe global recession.[6]

End of a golden era

The crisis was global but its origins were very much an Anglo-American affair. The United States and the United Kingdom dominated the financial world and its regulation, and New York and London were the largest international financial centres. On the very eve of the crisis in 2007 financial officials in Washington and London were taking credit for having created a monetary environment that had allowed world GDP to rise by 80 per cent since 1990.[7] They expressed satisfaction at the way their banking systems had displayed an ability to withstand severe strains caused by changing trade patterns, sharp swings in business cycles and direct threats to national survival.

> The last decade has seen some big and unanticipated changes. Since 1999, oil prices have risen from below $20 a barrel to over $70 a barrel, the US Fed funds rate has varied between 1% and 6.5%, and the stock market has experienced its post dotcom boom, bust and recovery, with the FTSE All Share falling from its 2000 high of over 3200 to below 1660 in 2003 before now recovering to over 3400. We have seen 9/11 and the onset of a new form of international terrorism, the explosive growth of new financial instruments and new players to exploit them, and we have seen the emergence of China and India into major forces in the world economy.[8]

Even as they made these boasts, the warning signs of impending disaster were already almost a year old, but American and British officials could not believe that this golden age would wither. In the second quarter of 2006, financial institutions had begun 'to liquidate portfolios to meet margin calls or solvency requirements', which caused significant funding problems. The Bank of England linked this trend to mounting competition in financial markets 'to stay ahead of, or keep up with, the pack [which] stretches risk management systems in the process'. No special response was deemed necessary, it was explained, because officials remained completely convinced that the markets were self-correcting.[9] In addition, officials were to argue later, 'one would need to be endowed with perfect foresight to have been able to predict how the financial crisis would unfold, spilling over from one institution to another, and from one market to another'.[10]

By 2008, market failures and corporate collapses had imposed enormous burdens on American and British citizens as budgets shrank and taxes rose. In the United States, the sums allocated to the Troubled Asset Relief Program (TARP), the government's first rescue package, could be described only in epic terms.

> The $700 billion TARP program alone is worth more, in inflation-adjusted dollars, than the combined cost of the Hoover Dam, the Panama Canal, the first Gulf War, the Marshall Plan, the Louisiana Purchase, and all of the moon missions. Multiply that ninefold, and you have the current running total of the federal government's economic rescue programs.[11]

The effects of the global crisis on the public finances of the United Kingdom were no less dramatic. 'Fiscal deficits have widened sharply and are expected to be about 13 percent of GDP in 2009 and 2010', the IMF reported, 'Gross general government debt is set to double over the next five years to nearly 100 percent of GDP'.[12] The impact on the capitalisation of the British banking industry was catastrophic. The value of its shares had risen by an annual average of 16 per cent from 1985 to 2006 (compared with only 2 per cent a year in the period 1900–84). They then slumped. By March 2009, they had lost 80 per cent of their cumulative value, a bigger fall than even during the Great Crash in 1929.[13] 'The costs of this crisis will be with us for a generation', the Governor of the Bank of England predicted.[14]

Anglo-American Armageddon

This crisis seemed all the more cruel because of the surprise with which it struck the United States and the United Kingdom. The pain they suffered was similar in scale to that of other advanced economies.[15] But for these two countries, 2007 was Armageddon,[16] a disaster in total contrast to the prosperity and stability that they had achieved over the previous 30 years and that had been widely enjoyed by so many other nations which had adopted their economic convictions. What made the 2007–09 market turmoil and the financial trauma truly apocalyptic was the vulnerability uncovered in New York and London, the world's two largest international financial centres. The paradox was that 'financial fragility and occasional financial crises' ought not to have come as a shock because such events were already well-researched side-effects of the liberal financial régimes that American and British policy-makers favoured.[17] They were the price of progress, it had been claimed previously, and would be well compensated for by faster long-run growth.[18] Bank runs and market collapses were supposed to happen to other people, however. The Anglo-American view was that 'systemic financial crises were seen only in history books and emerging markets', Charles Bean, Deputy of the Bank of England subsequently confessed, 'they were unlikely to happen in advanced economies with their developed and well regulated financial markets'.[19]

The arithmetic of the 2007–09 disaster was not extraordinary, nevertheless. The damage seemed well within the parameters for financial crises since 1970, according to IMF calculations. Total losses for advanced countries as a group were sharply lower in 2007–09 than the average costs they had incurred in financial crises between 1970 and 2006. (See Table 1) Total losses for all countries were higher than in the earlier period, but not dramatically so. Thus, the 'Conclusions' will argue, the crisis proved both affordable and manageable for the financial markets themselves, and they made a rapid return to profitability. The New York securities industry, for example, reported record profits in 2009 of over US\$61 billion, 'almost triple the level of three years earlier'.[20] As a result, the impetus for a radical overhaul of financial regulation weakened once governments had successfully intervened to stabilise the markets even though the economic and social costs of the global crisis were painful in the extreme (with the most severe fall in British real wages since the 1920s, for example).[21]

Table 1
Total Costs of Banking Crises, 1970–2009 (direct fiscal costs, increased public borrowings, output lost)[22]

	Percentage of GDP	
	Banking Crises 1970–2006	**Banking Crises 2007–2009**
Advanced Countries	72.8	55.8
All Countries	45.8	53.3

Several of the main features of 2007–09 matched events that had triggered past financial crises — asset price bubbles, for example, and credit booms. The IMF post-mortem reported some novel new features which increased the scale and severity of the 2007–09 crisis: notably, opaqueness as 'securitization and innovative (but complex) financial instruments' proliferated and the effects of globalisation.[23] These were to a large extent the special contribution of New York and London and their light-touch regulators.

Studies of the recent past, with their implicit promise that future growth would bring more than adequate compensation for current losses, were misleading. This article of faith depended on the assumption that American and British financial officials could maintain the stability of their own systems, which had previously seemed a very likely scenario. From the 1990s until 2006, the American and British economies had appeared to have put behind them the previous period's monetary instability when regular inflationary and budgetary setbacks had disrupted growth. The two countries had looked forward to a prospect of unbroken prosperity glowingly described in an official, post-crisis British report.

> The period since the economic downturn of the early 1990s, which affected almost all developed countries, came to be known as the 'great moderation' in the United States and the 'great stability' in the United Kingdom ... characterised by low and stable global inflation, as well as high and stable global real GDP growth over the past decade.[24]

When New York and London turned fragile, the world's two largest financial centres could not avoid exporting contagion on an unprecedented scale. The United States, for example, accounted for 31 per cent of global financial assets and 62 per cent of global reserve currency assets in 2007.[25] Neither the United States nor the United Kingdom could look to a ready external lender of last resort to bail them out, which aggravated the collapse in market confidence.[26] For the Eurozone, by contrast, the European Central Bank could take on this role after its banks suffered a fall in market confidence almost identical with that in the United States.[27] In consequence, the European Central Bank was able to respond to the tests of highly vulnerable economies (notably Ireland) and political unrest that added to the financial turmoil (in Greece in particular) much better than might have been expected, despite a rise in anti-EU sentiment and a loss of popularity by leading political personalities in Europe.[28]

Predictable and preventable?

Almost immediately after the crisis got underway, central bankers and financial regulators were blamed for the mounting disaster. Their attempts to defend themselves were unconvincing. The recently retired Chairman of the Federal Reserve Board, the redoubtable Alan Greenspan, allowed himself to be quoted as admitting: 'I got the impression that there were a lot of very questionable practices going on'. His excuse for not intervening was: 'What basically does the law mean when it says deceptive and unfair practices?'[29] This failure of the officials in charge to take remedial action — specifically in the United States and the United Kingdom — was inspired by what a leading British regulator was later to describe as the 'Greenspan doctrine':

> ... which doubted whether any policy, monetary or regulatory, should or could be used to lean against the wind of irrational exuberance, doubted the ability of the authorities to judge whether asset prices had become irrational, and explicitly assumed that market disciplines and market incentives would control any irrational exuberance before a major crisis was reached.[30]

This book will show that the risks to financial stability were identified well in advance and deliberately discounted by the officials responsible for financial stability in both the United States and the United Kingdom. Deficiencies in regulatory performance were not so much the outcome of erroneous policies or defective legislation. They were the consequences of an Anglo-American regulatory culture which was convinced of the innate and superior wisdom of financial markets.[31] Financial officials believed in 'market self correction, effective market discipline, and that management and boards are better placed than any regulator to identify business system risks'.[32] The culture created an environment in which 'implementation and enforcement of existing regulation was ... too lax, reflecting a steady drift toward a more hands-off supervisory style, where the belief that the private sector "knows best" was permitted to take hold'.[33]

Before the crisis, the impressive performance of global financial markets and institutions had seemed persuasive evidence that the dominant Anglo-American regulatory culture was soundly based.[34] Over the previous three decades, 'the global market economy, which requires a global finance system at its core, [had] for all its faults been a better mechanism for delivering rising prosperity to an increasing number of people', Lord Turner, a leading British regulator has argued, 'than any other system we've ever seen'.[35] And yet American and British monetary officials have since admitted that they failed to recognise the mismatch between regulatory protocols and market realities, and 'the [subsequent] widespread economic damage has called into question the fundamental assumptions ... that have directed our regulatory efforts for decades'.[36]

A principal theme of this book is the conflict between regulation and growth. On this issue, there is no escape from history. The Anglo-American culture had been shaped by the failure of state planning and controls not only in the former Soviet bloc but also in Western Europe and the Third World which had adopted such policies in the first decades after World War II.[37] The deregulation promoted by the Anglo-American culture was followed by an unprecedented surge in international growth and national prosperity. But the limits of this liberalisation were reached, this book will contend, in 2006. The origins of the international financial crisis will be traced to a conviction among American and British regulators that free capitalist markets must be better judges than bureaucrats of businesses, their performance and their prospects. (The crisis has shown how misconceived was this belief and that markets had hopelessly misjudged large numbers of financial institutions.) China is crucial to this debate because its experiences are a reminder of what inspired the movement for deregulation in the first place: market competition drives modernisation and efficiency far more effectively than state planners can ever achieve. But China also highlights how much modern banking and financial services depend on an effective regulatory system to ensure that the funds they raise from the public are managed with professionalism and integrity in the best interests of depositors and investors. Whenever the regulators are pushed aside, China has shown over the last 30 years, banking losses soar at huge cost to the state and the industry.

Culture and consensus

Chapter 1 will review how American and British financial officials — central bankers and regulators alike — shared preconceptions and convictions that shaped their policies and practices. An Anglo-American culture emerged based on a firm belief that free markets were the best guarantee of sustained high growth, stable prices and currencies and the optimal use of resources, including capital. State involvement in economic affairs came to be regarded as mostly misguided and often counter-productive. The market was seen as having an in-built capacity to penalise inferior performance and corporate mismanagement and, very often, was also depicted as self-correcting and self-policing. This intellectual consensus led to what an official United States inquest into the global crisis depicted as a virtual conspiracy to put financial markets and their activities above the law.

> The sentries were not at their posts, in no small part due to the widely accepted faith in the selfcorrecting nature of the markets and the ability of financial institutions to effectively police themselves. More than 30 years of deregulation and reliance on self-regulation by financial institutions, championed by former Federal Reserve chairman Alan Greenspan and others, supported by successive administrations and Congresses, and actively pushed by the powerful financial industry at every turn, had stripped away key

safeguards, which could have helped avoid catastrophe … we do not accept the view that regulators lacked the power to protect the financial system. They had ample power in many arenas and they chose not to use it.[38]

Chapter 2 presents studies of four issues that were to be of special importance in undermining the stability of the international financial system: mismanagement of the aftermath of the 1997–98 Asian financial crisis; official misjudgements about property bubbles in the decade that followed; the miscalculations of the rating agencies; and misconceptions about the banking-insurance industry nexus. In each instance, American and British officials reviewed the risks involved and their possibly destructive consequences. The chapter will show that in both Washington and London, officials chose not to interfere with the market and publicly justified these deliberate decisions with almost identical declarations of trust in market forces.

Their confidence was accompanied by considerable scepticism among policy-makers and financial officials about their ability to comprehend modern global financial markets and the financial engineering that designed complex derivatives and directed automated trading. Central bankers and regulators did not see themselves as entirely unnecessary. But they minimised their functions in a sincere belief that investors and entrepreneurs knew their own business best. Chapters 1 and 2 will illustrate how the Anglo-American regulatory culture became a dominant influence on the international financial system as a whole and was buttressed by a consensus shared by increasing numbers of political and business leaders, opinion-makers and academics in the last two decades of the 20th century.

China joins the consensus

In the early years after World War II, governments assumed direct responsibility for economic and social development especially in the Third World where free trade and foreign investment were attacked as a Western strategy to exploit their colonial populations. But state intervention failed to deliver progress and eventually fell out of favour. China was to provide a striking example of how state control lost its credibility and why markets were given their freedom. In 1978 Deng Xiaoping convinced the Chinese Communist Party to accept economic reforms after central planning had conspicuously failed to deliver a standard of living which would buy off rising worker unrest and pacify the rural population.[39]

Unforeseen was how traumatic the retreat from state controls would be. The general assumption is that Deng Xiaoping and his allies had a clear blueprint for China's future development when the Party endorsed the principles of modernisation, liberalisation and opening up to the outside world. A prominent Beijing economist warned in 1980, however, that there was no general agreement on what the most urgent challenges were and no well-defined strategy for their solution.

> China does not have a complete and mature reform programme. All we have are the views and initial suggestions collected during discussions in various departments and some small-scale, experimental and incomplete reforms.[40]

The managers of industrial plants, especially in heavy industry, found the new situation no less arbitrary and frequently more unrealistic than the central planning of the past, and they were in constant danger of severe censure by Party officials for whatever went wrong. Entire production lines were rendered redundant by the new reform policies, and often factories were abruptly deprived of funds and raw materials.[41] The heavy financial losses involved were transferred almost entirely to the banking system, with disastrous consequences for its solvency (to be discussed in chapter 3).

The task of drafting a comprehensive agenda for a modern banking system and its regulation was made all the more difficult by the political background. In 1978 a campaign by the Finance Ministry to regain control over the financial resources of local authorities and state enterprises was defeated by implacable resistance from lower-level officials who believed that only local enterprises, local initiatives and local autonomy could meet their constituents' needs.[42] Since central planning and state controls were seen as stifling industry and agriculture, it proved virtually impossible to convince the Party and the state bureaucracies that banking was different and that state regulation was essential to its modernisation.[43] The banks, which had kept their accounts in meticulous order throughout the worst excesses of ideological extremism before Mao Zedong's death in 1976, fell victim to the surge in lower-level autonomy in 1978. Bank staff now found themselves deprived of a supervisory role they had managed to retain when the rest of the economic administration had fallen into chaos from 1966 as 'Red Guards' and 'revolutionary rebels' seized power.[44] Fresh attempts at banking reforms in 1983 made matters worse by reducing still further the ability of the People's Bank to oversee the financial system.[45] Chapter 3 reviews the fluctuating fortunes of would-be financial reformers in the decades that followed.

Although China's reform process was to be complex, confused and often chaotic, the retreat from central planning and state controls was accompanied by 30 years of high-speed GDP growth during which the barriers to foreign trade and investment were dismantled. Along with these innovations came a repudiation of the Maoist era's 'self reliance' and other protectionist policies and a new-found sense of common challenges and shared solutions in China's relations with the rest of the world. Attitudes emerged in China that were very close to the consensus described earlier in this 'Introduction', which had led to liberalisation of financial markets worldwide and to the light-touch Anglo-American regulatory culture that became almost universal. This intellectual convergence was highlighted in a remarkably frank 2003 People's Bank presentation to an international audience.[46]

- The Third World — including China — had been at fault for overestimating the extent to which 'the world economic order was discriminatory in nature against the developing countries'. This had led to a misguided retreat into protectionist policies after World War II.
- Endorsed, almost unconditionally, was 'the export-oriented development strategy adopted first by the four "Asian Dragons"'.
- The principle was to be accepted that competition 'brings not only pressure, but also vigor and prosperity'. China's protectionists were criticised for having tried to block imports of electronic goods in the 1980s, for example, the liberalisation of exchange rates in the 1990s and accession to the World Trade Organisation in 2001. They had been proved wrong by the nation's subsequent performance on global markets.

Conflicts and constraints in China

China's direct relevance to the global financial crisis starts with its extraordinary emergence as a major participant in world markets in the first three decades of economic reform.

- In 1978 foreign trade was equivalent to 10 per cent of China's GDP. Foreign exchange reserves totalled US$1.6 billion[47] (equivalent to 6 per cent of Japan's holdings; 10 per cent of the United Kingdom figure; and 27 per cent of the Indian total[48]).
- In 2007 foreign trade was equivalent to 67 per cent of China's GDP. Foreign exchange reserves totalled US$1.5 trillion (the largest in the world from 2006).

The source of these riches was the extraordinary success of China's export industries during the 30 years since Deng Xiaoping introduced the 'open door' policies. Foreign trade had grown by an annual 17 per cent, while the share of industrial products in exports rose from half to 95 per cent over the period. The economy had become integrated into the global economy not just in terms of external market transactions but also through the revival of foreign ownership in this key growth sector.

- In 1978 all external trade and financial transactions were under state control.
- In 2007 firms owned wholly or partly by foreigners accounted for 54 per cent of China's total foreign trade.[49]

China's growth has thus depended on its ability to conform to international practices and procedures, covering banking transactions as well as customs and other formalities, which helps to explain the approach to financial modernisation reviewed in chapter 3. This chapter will also assess Beijing's attempts to use foreign participation as a driving force for the elimination of the 'command economy mentality' and the creation of professional management and corporate governance together with a modern credit culture throughout the banking system. Nevertheless, foreign banks were given a very cautious welcome onshore, as was plain from the central bank's summary of their market access on the eve of the global crisis.

> [Since China's WTO accession in 2001] ... foreign banks are allowed to provide RMB services to Chinese companies in 25 cities ... Under the precondition of ensuring the state's controlling stake and the country's financial safety, foreign capital were allowed to take part in the reform of state-owned commercial banks.[50]

Chapter 3 investigates the marked contrast between the major role played by foreign manufacturers in China and the stringent restrictions imposed on foreign banks.

Cultural converts

For many governments anxious to exploit market forces to reform their economies, financial institutions have proved the most difficult to liberalise. Former Soviet states in Eastern Europe, as well as Latin American nations, found that privatisation and foreign take-overs offered no guarantees of efficiency, let alone profitability.[51] China chose a reform strategy which has been hailed as 'as unique among emerging markets', yet its basic principle was the same as elsewhere in the world: modern financial markets must be open and competitive. Beijing's approach to implementation, however, was very different.[52] The government would turn its four largest banks into free-standing business corporations, accountable to their shareholders and listed on international stock exchanges. This 'transactional model', recent research has concluded, 'facilitated inter-organizational learning that has translated into tangible results'. Its merits have been endorsed by its imitation by sovereign wealth funds from Singapore, and the Middle East in deals with Western banks since 2007.

China's strategy of using entry into global markets as a shortcut to modernisation required its banks and their regulators to adapt to international practices and procedures. They were already familiar with the distinct Anglo-American model of corporate governance, and they were aware of how, since the mid-1990s, there had been 'a trend of convergence' overseas.[53] As the global crisis intensified in 2007, China's financial officials displayed a close knowledge of American and British regulators and their dilemmas. The People's Bank Governor expressed a degree of kinship with these overseas counterparts. He cited examples, for instance, of corporate scandals in China which matched the American Enron and WorldCom collapses both in their fraudulent strategies and in their timing. Zhou also drew directly on China's recent history to identify the key issues which Western regulators would have to tackle. There was even matching rhetoric: his observations at this early stage of the global crisis were to be paralleled in following months by the comments of American and British central bankers and regulators.

Like American and British financial officials, the Governor was an ardent advocate of moral hazard and unenthusiastic about rescuing banks in trouble: they ought to pay the penalty for their business blunders as a warning to the rest of the industry. But he understood as well as Washington and London that central bankers could not stand idly by as the banking system crumbled, and he was vigorous in defending the Governor of the Bank of England for reversing an earlier decision not to bail out Northern Rock Bank. His views were almost indistinguishable from American and British central bankers on the need to avoid 'over-reacting' to the crisis with measures that would stifle future growth of financial services. He rejected the backlash against 'securitized products and other derivatives' from those arguing that 'simpler is better'. He insisted that the fault was not in the technical sophistication of the products but arose from 'problems in information disclosure or the pricing mechanisms'.[54] Significantly, too, the China Banking Regulatory Commission published an assessment of the global financial crisis and its causes which had a great deal in common with the post-mortems conducted by its counterparts in Washington and London.[55]

The invisible hand

Throughout the three decades of sustained growth which started in the 1978, China, in common with other Third World nations, had intended to reform the regulation of its financial system 'in line with prevailing intellectual fashions and following the example of industrial countries'. It shared the same enthusiasm for dismantling administrative controls and fell into the same error of neglecting the regulatory and other institutional systems needed to maintain financial stability.[56] Chapter 3 will demonstrate how reform without regulation was hazardous, all the more so because of the nation's complex political arrangements and the Chinese Communist Party's dominant status. Despite 30 years of economic reform and sustained breakneck growth, market forces had still not taken command of China's economy. 'While the state sector of the economy has shrunk significantly (to approximately 30 percent of the national economy)', Professor David Shambaugh, a distinguished China specialist, has observed, 'This is deceiving as the state remains the "invisible hand" dominating the economy'. It maintains this control, he explained in an article published in an official newspaper, 'through state banks, state assets, state ownership, state manipulated prices, state cadres, and unpredictable state intervention in various economic sectors'.[57] China's financial regulators can never escape from this 'invisible hand', which reduces their capacity to perform effectively. Especially damaging have been the losses which the banks were forced to incur because 'policy' and 'relationship' lending remained rife. The banks have been compelled to provide credit to enterprises in obedience to state directives regardless of the borrowers' creditworthiness, the People's Bank has complained. Similarly, a banker's decision to provide credit facilities often depended less on the borrower's ability to service the loan and far more on the relationship with the applicant, which might be personal, Party-related or corrupt.[58]

As a result, China offers considerable evidence that financial liberalisation without professional and independent regulators is a prescription for financial instability. For the most part, China's leaders have accepted that central bankers and regulators need autonomy as well as technical expertise to do their job, but the Party has felt free to revive the 'command economy mindset' whenever it is politically expedient to do so.[59] Chapter 4 consists of four case studies that illustrate this state of affairs. The first reviews China's experiences during the 1997–98 Asian financial crisis, which became the catalyst for moves towards regulatory autonomy. The analysis examines why the attempts to reform and recapitalise the banking system were only partially successful. The second and third deal with the costly consequences of the government's desperate measures in 2008–09 to finance its US$586 billion economic stimulus package to counter the international financial crisis. What made the situation all the more alarming for China's leaders was that the nation's economic performance had begun to deteriorate even before world demand for China's exports started to fall in the wake of the global downturn.[60] The rules of fiscal and banking prudence were set aside; the banking reforms of the past decade were seriously weakened in consequence; and a property bubble developed. The final case study discusses

Beijing's limited use of Hong Kong as a force for the modernisation of its major banks and its corporate practices.

Hong Kong, where regulation triumphed

Hong Kong has made a unique but often undervalued contribution to China's modernisation. At the end of the first two decades of its 'open door' policies, a national leader sought to put the record straight.

> Over half of China's exports and imports have either gone through or come from Hong Kong [since 1978], and so it is with the capital influx … Without Hong Kong, the Chinese mainland could not have accessed the global market and sent its commodities to every corner of the world as smoothly as it has for the past 20 years.[61]

Those achievements would have been impossible if Hong Kong had not possessed a financial system capable of meeting all demands on it, both from Mainland manufacturers and exporters and from international investors and trading partners.[62] Hong Kong has remained pre-eminent in this role, unmatched by any other city in China. After three decades of financial as well as economic reforms, it was home to the only part of the nation's banking system that operated an efficient and fully competitive market, according to a 2009 IMF report.[63]

In theory, Hong Kong and the ability of its bankers to meet China's needs, were supposed to be a model for the nation to imitate.[64] During the 1980s, Mainland areas scheduled for priority development were frequently encouraged to 'draw on Hong Kong's experience' in seeking, among others goals, greater access to overseas capital.[65] In the next decade, nevertheless, one of China's state-owned banks in Hong Kong lamented the continuing problems with the government's disruptive intervention in the Mainland's financial sector.

> Throughout the reform process China was unable to escape from the vicious circle of "decontrol results in chaos, chaos leads to recontrol, and control is followed by stagnation". The decontrol and recontrol circle keeps returning.[66]

Despite increasingly close working relations between the Mainland's banking institutions in Hong Kong and the rest of the industry, considerable ingenuity was required to devise arrangements that would overcome the nervousness of Mainland officials when authorising Hong Kong borrowings.[67] Nevertheless, Hong Kong propelled southern China into industrial take-off and financed Guangdong province's transformation into China's leading centre of manufacturing growth and foreign trade, a development that considerably exceeded expectations on the Mainland side and was completely unplanned on Hong Kong's part.[68]

A surprising feature of China's efforts to modernise its banking system is how limited has been the use made of Hong Kong as a model in the present century. Shortly before the global crisis, Joseph Yam, Hong Kong's senior central banker, publicly questioned whether the Mainland and Hong Kong 'have a working relationship that maximises the mutual benefits of the two jurisdictions and therefore is in the best interests of the country'. Yet, this experienced official could rightly boast that, despite Hong Kong having a mere 0.5 per cent of China's population and a GDP equivalent to only 8 per cent of the Mainland total, its banking assets equalled 21 per cent of the Mainland figure. Furthermore, its financial system was 'more open, developed, competitive and efficient, by virtue of its long history of market freedom'.[69]

There are clear parallels between the minimalist regulatory environment and its market abuses which led to regular cycles of bank runs and financial panics in Hong Kong before 1986 and the origins of the global crisis of 2007–09.[70] Chapter 5 will discuss Hong Kong in its global context and how it came to discard the fundamental concepts of the Anglo-American consensus and, instead, made financial stability an overriding priority in its official policies. The chapter's most striking conclusion is that strict regulation — including quantitative restrictions abandoned almost everywhere else — did not handicap the financial sector's growth, its creative dynamic or competitive forces. Nor has government intervention encouraged financial institutions to behave recklessly. Chapter 5 investigates allegations that regulatory activism weakened the laissez-faire foundations of Hong Kong's prosperity and argues that pragmatism has counted for more than economic ideology in its economic success.[71] Its rejection of the Anglo-American approach, it will be asserted, ensured that Hong Kong financial system emerged intact from the severe strains generated by the Asian and the global financial crises.[72]

Cultural considerations

Financial policy-makers 'make no explicit concessions to culture', an insightful study of this issue has noted, yet 'cultural factors underlie economic and financial structures to a greater extent than is often realized'.[73] Throughout this book, 'culture' is used as shorthand for a shared outlook or set of attitudes. It is a term of convenience that avoids the baggage that might come with references to the 'political' or 'ideological'. Ideally, quotation marks should be employed to warn that the word is not used in a precise, technical sense, but it appears too frequently for this safeguard to be practical.

'Regulatory culture' is intended to convey the values and attitudes which financial officials share in common across national frontiers and which shape their policies and their practices. It validates for them the preconceptions which they look upon as their principles, both in making policy and in taking action. Culture here includes a pattern of behaviour which is regarded as 'good' in the sense that the officials concerned believe the general public will deem their actions to be both acceptable and appropriate. Although this culture is largely an Anglo-American creation, it is independent of the very significant differences in the two nations' ideology, political institutions, legal systems, public expectations and popular prejudices, as chapters 1 and 2 will indicate.[74]

The Anglo-American culture and the broad intellectual consensus that sustains it are sometimes confused with the 1990 'Washington consensus', which proposed a blueprint for liberalisation in emerging and Third World economies in that decade (although it was less relevant to Asia).[75] American and British officials did not set out to invent regulatory standards for the world's banks. The formal proposals they developed (mainly through the Basel Committee process) were 'initially designed for internationally active banks'.[76] The Anglo-American culture thus preceded the 'Washington consensus' and survived its eventual fall from favour.[77]

For Chinese financial institutions, reform has been described as a cultural process which involves 'the reshaping of sustained collective expectations of key actors in charge of decision-making inside banks, and also of regulators and other policy-makers from the outside'.[78] Since 1978, China's success in generating huge trade surpluses and attracting vast influxes of foreign investment locked it into the global markets whose supervision has been dominated by the Anglo-American culture.[79] Chinese officials themselves show a desire to achieve a cultural transition and refer, for example, to the unfortunate legacy of the 'command economy mentality' and to the need to create a new 'credit culture'.[80]

The convergence between attitudes in Beijing and in Washington and London has already been noted. Initially, the prospects for such a meeting of minds had seemed poor. The Anglo-American culture faced serious opposition in East Asia, Professor Meredith Woo has argued, where politicians were 'outcome-oriented' and believed economic controls were the best guarantee of achieving their goals. Although 'it is still the case that [China] does not provide a legal environment similar to that in Europe or the United States', this well-known Asian development specialist stated, the Anglo-American regulatory culture has won a place in China's modernisation. China was the most 'anti-market' of all Asian states until 1978 when it started to dismantle the legal, planning and financial structures imported from the former Soviet Union. Wholesale borrowing of American legal models from early in the reform era laid the foundations for the Anglo-American culture to become a potent and very visible influence.[81]

Hong Kong's liberal and capitalist cultural characteristics have been enshrined constitutionally in China's Basic Law as the basis for its political, economic and social systems until 2047 but are expressed in pragmatic terms, such as a commitment to free and open markets, fiscal conservatism, non-interventionism and the rule of law. Nevertheless, while its international financial centre has long been a close partner of New York and London, Hong Kong is not a disciple of the Anglo-American regulatory culture.

Regulators in their own words

This book's concern is with regulatory policies, their origins, aims and implementation. The objective is not to provide an analysis of the monetary or economic causes of the global crisis or an account of how financial markets embarked on increasingly self-destructive behaviour. These matters have been dealt with for the United States in 400 pages of lucid detail by the Financial Crisis Inquiry Commission's *Final Report of the National Commission on the Causes of the Financial and Economic Crisis in the United States.*[82] The aim here is to explore the connections between the regulatory culture and regulatory performance. The focus is on delineating the main preconceptions and policy constraints which can be shown to have shaped policy and enforcement. Throughout the text, 'regulation' is used to refer to all forms of government oversight and control of financial markets and institutions, without distinguishing the term from prudential supervision. (A blurring of this distinction reflects usage common among American and British officials themselves.) 'Financial officials' is used to refer to those who carry out such duties without distinguishing between, for example, central bankers and financial regulators.[83]

In seeking to identify the principal features of the dominant Anglo-American culture and their relevance to the global crisis, the analysis relies, almost exclusively, on the public accounts of their stewardship offered by senior American and British monetary officials themselves. It may be objected that this public record must be misleading because it does not cover the internal political, commercial and personal pressures that were involved in the relationships between financial officials and the governments they served. On the other hand, these officials enjoyed considerable autonomy in Washington and London, and the prevailing regulatory culture had won support across the political spectrum. Central bankers and financial regulators were engaged in a constant and extensive dialogue with the financial services industry, the wider business community and opinion makers. They also had to account for themselves in considerable detail before congressional and parliamentary forums.[84] This public record, which embraces discussions of considerable technical sophistication as well as more 'political' presentations, allows the financial officials' outlooks, priorities and responses to events to be examined in considerable detail, both during the global crisis and in the preceding decade. Thus, while reliance on the official record carries a risk of self-censorship or self-serving presentations by leading officials, the chapters that follow will show how, in fact, these officials have revealed with considerable frankness the regulatory failings which created the business environment that led to the global crisis.[85]

As far as possible, the same approach has been adopted in studying China's regulators. For the earlier part of the post-1978 reform era, the discussion relies, almost exclusively, on the information, comment and data published in the official Chinese media. Once China became a major participant in global markets, its financial officials had to establish a dialogue with the world at large.[86] Thus, analysis of events since 1998 has the benefit of material published by China's central bank and regulatory agencies themselves. Wherever possible, this book uses the version of such material (and of articles in the official media for this later period) intended for international consumption. Public and political debate is neither free nor open in China, and the media face severe constraints on the right to investigate and report. Chapters 3 and 4 will demonstrate how detailed, nevertheless, was the information made public about the nation's financial problems even before the death of Mao Zedong in 1976 and the rise of the reformers.

In addition, ample use has been made of the advice, analysis and research published by international 'supervisory' agencies: the International Monetary Fund (IMF) especially but also the Bank for International Settlements (BIS), the Organisation for Economic Co-operation and Development (OECD) and the World Bank. These reports rely very largely on national central bankers and regulators with whom these international agencies' staff have been engaged in dialogue.

1

Global Crisis — Why Regulators Trust Financial Markets

The financial crisis that struck in 2007 was not the result of a downturn in either national business cycles or the international economy. The defaults in the United States sub-prime mortgage market that triggered the crisis were a shock that 'was by global financial standards rather modest', and it followed a decade of 'seeming robustness'.[1] According to Hector Sants, a senior British regulator, its causes could be attributed almost entirely to:

> a series of gaps with regard to the oversight of financial institutions ... a flawed set of prudential rules particularly for capital and liquidity ... [and] a series of governance failures and poor business judgements by the financial institutions themselves.[2]

Most at fault were the policy decisions made by American and British financial officials over the previous ten years. Their banking systems were the first casualties, and disaster hit their economies hardest. Of the 17 banks and brokerages with the largest 'admitted' losses during the crisis, eight were American and four were British. Between them, they accounted for 59 per cent of the total 'admitted' write-offs estimated by an OECD study at US$1.1 trillion.[3]

This chapter will argue that the defects in regulatory performance were not so much the outcome of erroneous policies or defective legislation. The analysis will suggest that criticism should focus on the Anglo-American regulatory culture and its belief in the innate and superior wisdom of financial markets. This culture encouraged a complacent non-interventionism among regulators even in the face of mounting evidence of self-destructive business practices so that 'market discipline' could be used as 'a philosophy to ward off appropriate regulation during good times', to quote an American financial official.[4] The 'free market' consensus was so firmly entrenched that the pre-2007 regulators and their culture were able to survive the global crash. In the absence of any rival regulatory arrangements that seemed capable of creating a business environment that could match the glittering worldwide growth up to 2006, these officials successfully resisted radical changes after 2009.

The intellectual consensus

The Anglo-American regulatory culture began with a common outlook on management of the economy. The key principles it embodied enjoyed overwhelming approval. 'The absolutely dominant intellectual conventional wisdom [worldwide] of the years running up to 2007', Lord Turner, a prominent British official, has explained, was 'confidence in the ideas that markets were self correcting' together with a conviction that 'it was not the role of regulators to interfere with what the market did'. Officials should not be concerned about financial market innovation, for example — no matter how menacing 'the explosion of sub-prime lending' — on the grounds that market excesses are 'self-correcting'.[5]

This world view began with a commitment to financial liberalisation, whose expected dividends appeared to be validated by the available research.

- With financial liberalisation, the economy as a whole enjoys faster growth because constraints on lending are reduced, which gives entrepreneurs easier access to bank finance.
- By definition, the retreat from controls on bank lending encourages risk-taking and increases the danger that financial institutions will fail and bank runs will occur. But gains from faster economic growth will more than make up for the occasional crises even when they have 'severe recessionary effects'.[6]
- In any case, markets are best left to regulate and discipline the banks, and investors are better placed than government regulators to understand how sound or otherwise a financial institution is.[7]
- Economic growth is best promoted by monetary stability, and appropriate monetary policies will keep recession at bay and maximise prosperity.[8] In consequence, inflation targeting will prove 'the best policy framework for promoting wider economic prosperity and stability'.[9]

On the basis of such research findings, minimalism seemed the proper approach to financial regulation. The policy prescriptions that followed included reliance on market forces as a safer and more effective strategy than government oversight and priority for monetary rather than financial stability. The regulators had two further preconceptions about financial crises with important policy implications (both of which were open to question).

- Financial crises are unavoidable, even in advanced economies, 'especially while maintaining a dynamic and innovative financial system'.[10] As a result, regulators cannot be held responsible if a crisis occurs.

- Financial crises tend to have little in common, which makes their occurrence hard to predict and their origins difficult to comprehend.[11] As a result, recent experience is not a sound basis for substantial changes to regulatory policies and protocols.

Endorsement by leading academics of the principles on which the Anglo-American culture was based meant that little attention was given to the limitations of economic theory when applied to financial regulation. Their distinguished sponsors' views were regarded as authoritative even when their research concerns were not primarily with the business of finance. 'Current macroeconomic research has had little to say about bank lending, financial instability and house and asset price bubbles', Professor David Blanchflower, a well-known academic involved in British central banking, later complained, 'Modern macroeconomic research pointed policymakers in the wrong direction'.[12] Economists had reached no clear agreement about what regulatory arrangements would ensure a flourishing banking industry that would achieve an effective balance between risk-taking and institutional stability and that would also supply the funds for maximum economic growth while safeguarding depositors.[13] Nor had there been an agreed view among economists about the contribution which banking makes to the development process.[14] A further complication was that even in 2010, the Bank of England lamented, there was no consensus about what would work best at the level of the financial firm and its markets.

> ... although the style of banking supervision varies enormously across the world, almost nothing seems to have been done to get to the bottom of the question of which approaches are the more effective — having an army of on-site examiners, such as for example in the United States; or relying on offsite analysis, which tends to be the pattern in much of Europe.[15]

Since the start of the global financial crisis, the prevailing intellectual consensus has come under attack. Indeed, 'many people view the financial crisis that began in 2007 as a devastating blow to the credibility not only of banks but also of the entire academic discipline of financial economics'.[16] Yet, whatever the newfound disenchantment with the underlying economic doctrines espoused by the Anglo-American regulatory culture, the consensus has not been overthrown. Its economic principles and its financial and monetary prescriptions have continued to command majority support among political and business leaders and much of the media.

The leading financial officials in Washington and London retained a powerful influence over national policy, and their good standing was reconfirmed in striking terms.[17] In 2009 the new Obama administration was quick to publicly endorse 'the expertise and powers' of the Federal Reserve Board as 'indispensable for preventing and managing financial crises'. Timothy Geithner, the new Secretary for the Treasury, added that 'the programs it has initiated since the onset of this crisis have played a critical role in helping to contain the damage to the broader economy'.[18] The British Parliament had already confirmed the reappointment of Mervyn King as Governor of the Bank of England in mid-2008 in equally fulsome terms. '[His] skills, qualities and experience … will be greatly needed and tested', the House of Commons Treasury Committee declared, 'in facing the challenges … arising from the current market turmoil and from anxieties over inflation'.[19]

'Siamese twins'

This consensus originated in the United States and the United Kingdom and formed the foundation of a common regulatory culture. The two countries' monetary officials had a strong sense that they shared regulatory practices and problems, and they adopted similar public stances on major issues, although for the most part, their consensus was unspoken and went largely unnoticed. In many other fields, it would be tempting to argue that the United Kingdom had no choice but to accept the United States' leadership and adopt its agenda. In the case of financial services, such an explanation will not do. In this business, the two countries competed on relatively equal terms,[20] and only in respect of this industry could a Bank of England official claim in 2007 without sounding totally ridiculous that Americans feared British competition.[21] Scepticism about London's status as a serious rival to New York has inspired an exhaustive comparison of their performance in attracting foreign listings. The results, it was claimed, suggested that London's superior standing 'in policy circles and in the financial press' had been won by not playing fair. Although New York was able to extract a listing premium, this research project concluded, foreign firms were attracted to London by the considerable leeway they enjoyed there in fixing the level of regulation to which they would be subject.[22] The study left no doubt, however, that London was regarded as a significant competitor.

Nevertheless, an occasional commentator has preferred to view the relationship in terms of political and economic dependence.[23]

"The right way of thinking about New York and London is that they are Siamese twins," said Martin Wolf, the economics columnist for The Financial Times … having hitched its wagon to Wall

Street more than a decade ago, the City of London cannot afford to untether itself. It simply has too much at stake ... Britain can't regulate unilaterally anymore — it is simply too dependent on American institutions. Its regulatory response will be to mimic whatever the Obama administration decides to do. "If regulation is transformed in London it is because of what the U.S. does," Mr. Wolf said. "The U.S. will say, 'You are to follow us'. We now have no regulatory autonomy." It's tough being a Siamese twin.

Such scepticism underestimates both the origins and the resilience of this culture. The emergence of a shared American and British approach to financial regulation can be traced to at least the early 1970s. Both countries knew from increasingly costly experience the frustrations that governments faced in trying to dictate to financial markets. In 1968 Washington began a struggle to maintain the convertibility of its currency at a fixed gold price of US$35 per ounce. By 1971 Washington had to yield to irresistible market pressures, and the currency was devalued. In 1973 a fixed exchange rate could no longer be defended, and the era of floating rates had begun.

The United Kingdom had suffered a similar defeat. Despite decades of stringent restrictions on access to foreign currencies for both trade and investment purposes, London in 1967 lost its battle to avoid devaluation of the pound. In 1972 it turned its back on history, reduced the Sterling Area to a rump and abandoned the pound's status as a reserve currency. Nevertheless, despite the long years of exchange controls, the United Kingdom's determination to preserve what it could of its traditional international financial centre had resulted in an offshore market that was free from normal exchange controls. London was home to the most active segment of the Euromarket and by 1974 had attracted 'hundreds of foreign banks'.[24] It had become a haven for multinational financial institutions 'seeking regulatory refuge, particularly from the United States'. The Bank of England became concerned about who would take ultimate responsibility for their oversight and stability. Multiple financial crises that year made an overwhelming case for an international forum to tackle the challenges of the globalisation of financial markets. With the backing of American regulators, a British proposal to establish what was to become the Basel Committee was accepted by the ten leading industrial nations and Switzerland.[25]

In response to the switch to floating exchange rates and a rapid increase in the mobility of capital during the 1970s, the priorities of financial officials at the international level shifted from defending currencies and 'towards safeguards against financial instability', the Bank for International Settlements has recounted. Hitherto, the international financial system had been based on rules devised by governments and enforced by their central banks. Henceforward, financial markets would have control. It was in this environment that the Anglo-American consensus first established its credentials. In the 1980s, a spate of banking scandals in both countries gave the issue of financial regulation a new priority. Washington and London shared much the same policy dilemma: the need for enhanced regulation to maintain public confidence in their financial systems counterbalanced by a fear that tighter regulation would restrict market expansion and competitiveness especially in the global context.

Another impetus to their consensus was alarm among American and British financial officials about a growing threat from Japanese banks. There was a recognition in the two countries of the danger of regulatory arbitrage if they imposed different standards of conduct on their market participants.[26] The incentive for the United States to cooperate was further heightened in 1986, when the United Kingdom introduced a liberal regulatory system and drastically reduced the restrictions on competition between financial institutions and on entry of foreign firms into its domestic markets. The effect of this 'big bang' liberalisation on the global business environment was dramatic. London was driving reform and deregulation around the world as its attractions surged as an international financial centre.[27]

The Basel Accords that emerged during this decade appeared to represent international cooperation at its best. They were a breakthrough in the reconciliation of competing national interests and the establishment of uniform regulatory policies to promote international financial stability.[28] They were also an ingenious arrangement for creating international agreements that lacked any formal binding force and yet would be given legal status at the national level.[29] From the start, American and British regulators, and their mutual understandings, set the agenda for the other participants in the formal discussions.[30] Nevertheless, national interests (small German firms, for example, and Japanese banks) and the demands of business lobbies remained powerful forces especially after negotiations on Basel II began in 1999.[31]

Special relations

The Anglo-American culture consists of a set of shared attitudes and preconceptions which shaped regulatory behaviour to a remarkable degree and reduced the differences between the two countries' policy decisions on major issues to a very low level. Even the choice of rhetoric employed by those responsible for monetary and financial affairs was strikingly similar, as will be evident from the analysis that follows. The collective culture did not depend on the so-called 'special relationship' between

American and British political leaders or shared political and strategic interests. A common frame of reference emerged despite considerable differences between the two countries' political and institutional arrangements for overseeing monetary and financial affairs.[32] Their common outlook withstood occasional sharp conflicts of opinion.[33] It persisted regardless of changes in national leadership or ruling party. The year after the 2008 presidential election in the United States, mutual commitment to the consensus was reaffirmed publicly in the context of the 'SEC-FSA Strategic Dialogue' and what the American side described as an important role of 'the regulators of two of the world's major market centres'.[34]

The culture begins with a firm belief in the virtues of free market forces. This assumption gained increasing international credibility as governments even of socialist countries started to dismantle state controls and liberalise both domestic markets and their foreign trade and investment sectors. Neither 'hegemonic pressure' nor the 'Washington consensus' was its driving force, and 'the United States — the avatar of economic liberalism' did not need to induce governments 'to announce policies that they would not have embraced otherwise'.[35] Political leaders around the world could see the evidence of the sustained growth at extremely high levels that were achieved especially in Asia once governments reduced state direction of their economies.[36] From the 1980s on, the case for liberalisation was strengthened by the changing global environment. This period saw the transformation of advanced economies into post-industrial societies, relying on their services sectors to generate their own wealth and on emerging and transition economies for manufactured products.

Cultural comfort zone

A key element in the shared Anglo-American culture was the market reality: their enormously successful financial services industries. The United States and the United Kingdom led the international trend towards deregulation, and their financial sectors boomed. The two countries dominated world financial and securities markets, and they were the largest exporters of financial services. Worldwide economic growth over the three decades up to 2007 offered them exceptional profit opportunities. But business culture also played a substantial part in the success of their financial services. New York and London have the biggest concentration of regulatory expertise, and they became the arbiters of world best practice, with which other countries had to conform. Thus American and British firms had the additional and market-enhancing advantage that internationally they operated increasingly within a cultural zone originally designed for their convenience. Market dominance meant that the American and British financial authorities were able to impose a large measure of harmonisation of regulatory goals and behaviour — if not the specific political and legal rules and practices — on the day-to-day oversight of international financial business.[37]

Until 2007 this discipline seemed to be a natural consequence of how global markets led to 'financial integration and capital mobility'.[38] The assumption was that Anglo-American regulatory practices would work equally well anywhere regardless of cultural and institutional differences.[39] The danger seemed small that imitation of Anglo-American models would open global capital markets to malignant as well as to benign features of American and British financial behaviour. On the contrary, the message from Washington and London was that their standards of excellence would ensure global stability.

American and British regulators claimed to have assessed the impact of the increasingly esoteric and exotic products launched on their financial markets and to have found the risks involved to be limited and acceptable.[40] For example, the 2001 Enron scandal in the United States offered abundant evidence of how blind the market and its supporting institutions (accounting firms, in particular) could be to the real worth of a major corporation. In response American regulators pledged a commitment to greater watchfulness on the part of the banking industry.[41] Subsequent events showed that, in practice, the underlying weaknesses had not been eliminated (as this chapter discusses later). But for the foreign clients of the world's largest financial markets in New York and London, the Federal Reserve Board's commitment to better corporate performance seemed close to a regulatory guarantee that Anglo-American financial institutions would operate at the highest standards of prudential management.

The Anglo-American advantage was reinforced by the absence of serious rivals to its cultural as well as its market dominance. The European Union in theory could offer an alternative system, but European countries have split the management of monetary affairs. Monetary stability goals are set centrally, while fiscal policies and financial stability remain the responsibility of member governments whose priorities are national rather than European or global.[42] During the global crisis, harmonisation of policy relating to rescue measures and future reforms was a complex and contested process,[43] and differences between Eurozone members in their financial and fiscal policies produced very different outcomes for individual national economies within the European Union.[44] The European Central Bank's performance was impressive given the political and institutional obstacles it faced. But the constraints on the Eurozone's ability to provide a competitive alternative to the Anglo-American consensus were well illustrated by the bitter criticism the Bank aroused for its initiatives to save the more vulnerable nation members from financial collapse.

> ... [it] saved the euro but lost part of [its] reputation for probity ... willingness to bend or break the rules and buy government bonds — aimed at halting a potentially catastrophic sell-off — served as final confirmation that the central bank had stepped once and for all beyond its narrow founding mission solely as a bulwark against inflation. The European Central Bank now seems to have been pushed into the much larger role of guardian of financial stability in the 16 countries that belong to the euro area.[45]

Virtuous markets

Chapter 2 will analyse the main areas in which American and British central bankers and financial regulators identified potential threats to stability but decided not to act on the grounds that markets should be trusted to find the appropriate remedies. This behaviour reflected a deeply entrenched belief in the sound judgment of markets and their ability to impose whatever discipline was necessary to achieve efficiency and integrity. The belief in the superiority of this collective good sense was, and remains, a defining principle in the Anglo-American regulatory approach. This conviction had worrying origins. After his retirement, Alan Greenspan, the doyen of British as well as American financial officials,[46] revealed that his reluctance to regulate was inspired not so much by a perception of markets as innately wise or virtuous but, rather, by what sounds like a counsel of despair. He was convinced that markets were beyond human control, which made financial regulation an empty pretence.

'Markets have become too huge, complex, and fast-moving to be subject to twentieth-century supervision and regulation', Greenspan declared. 'This globalized behemoth stretches beyond the full comprehension of even the most sophisticated market participants'. He also believed that markets recovered best from crises when left alone by governments to 'rebalance'.

> Today, oversight of these [financial market] transactions is essentially by means of individual-market-participant counterparty surveillance. Each lender, to protect its shareholders, keeps a tab on its customers' investment positions. Regulators can still pretend to provide oversight, but their capabilities are much diminished and declining ... Since markets have become too complex for effective human intervention, the most promising anticrisis policies are those that maintain maximum market flexibility — freedom of action for

key market participants such as hedge funds, private equity funds, and investment banks ... Regulation by its nature inhibits freedom of market action, and that freedom to act expeditiously is what rebalances markets.[47]

As a result of this sort of thinking, regulation itself was depicted as a serious source of financial instability which should be opposed. For example, in a 2006 discussion of the risks that followed the rapid growth of hedge funds, the Federal Reserve Board described the capacity of financial markets to erase the pain of previous crises and to seek to evade market discipline once more, aided and abetted by over-generous credit from banks and other sources. American officials decided, nevertheless, to oppose any form of 'prescriptive regulatory regime' on the grounds that, 'by creating moral hazard in the marketplace, it leaves the system less rather than more stable'.[48]

The reluctance of financial officials to learn from experience was a related feature of the Anglo-American regulatory culture. Past crises were regarded as dangerous guides to the future. 'It is not uncommon to see legislators and regulators rush to promulgate new laws and rules in response to market breakdowns', Greenspan insisted, 'and the mistakes that result often take decades to correct',[49] The British view as expressed by the Governor of the Bank of England matched the American outlook.

After another twenty years or so, memories of the Panic of 2008 will have faded, and the regulations put in place in its wake will no doubt be seen as old-fashioned, inhibiting the potential of the City, and as ripe to be swept away as was the Glass-Steagall separation of commercial and investment banking in the United States a few years ago.[50]

Official mistrust of reforming responses to financial crises had serious scholarly support and was presented almost as an historical imperative. 'The aftermath of crises are moments of high risk in public policy', declared Charles Solaris, the distinguished American financial economist, in a 2010 essay. They provoke banking reforms that are 'quick, comprehensive, and unusually responsive to popular opinion', he stated, 'Each of these three aspects increases the risk that regulation will have adverse consequences'. He concluded with a warning that current reform proposals exhibited the similarly dangerous features of 'little deliberation, a comprehensive agenda, and an engaged public'.[51]

Thus, little was to be learnt from past crises and scandals, and they had a limited impact on regulatory arrangements. For example, during 1998 the United States had faced a serious emergency with the collapse of LTCM. This firm 'received generous terms from the banks and broker-dealers that provided credit and served as counterparties, even though LTCM took exceptional risks', Ben Bernanke, Chairman of the Federal

Reserve Board later observed. Investors, 'awed by the reputations of LTCM's principals', he said, 'did not ask sufficiently tough questions about the risks that were being taken to generate the high returns'.[52] When he highlighted this lesson from the past in 2006, this mindset was still prevalent, and the dire consequences of the continuing regulatory tolerance of such imprudence were about to cause an even bigger shock. The Enron collapse was another American scandal whose lessons were largely ignored. Publicly, officials declared that the incident offered a serious warning to the markets. But few practical measures were taken to strengthen the investor's protection against malpractices, according to the chairman of the Federal Deposit Insurance Corporation in 2009. 'The same off-balance sheet-vehicles were permitted beyond the reach of prudential regulation, including holding company capital requirements', she alleged, and there had been little effort to block financial products that in the Enron case had threatened the safety and soundness of financial institutions.[53]

Policies in practice

This chapter has already shown how financial officials in Washington and London first developed a shared culture as they struggled to restore stability to financial markets in the currency collapses and corporate failures of the 1970s. Although their consensus began as a response to market turbulence, the potential for future crises was being built unwittingly into the new financial world order they were fashioning. London's 'big bang' in 1986 accelerated the dismantling of controls and regulations designed to protect national economies that dated back to World War II but the full dimensions of the financial revolution taking place were not perceived immediately. It was still possible in 1987 to assert that although deposits worldwide were being switched to 'Eurobank or offshore banks' which were unconstrained by government controls on interest rates and official reserve requirements, 'most bank transactions — and indeed most financial services produced in each country — are consumed in that country'.[54] Thus, crises continued to be viewed very much as national rather than international events, and the global market crash of that year did little to moderate the growing confidence in the merits of free markets.

    Deregulation dominated national policies in the following decade, rendering political frontiers largely irrelevant to financial services. As the global system became a new 'single market', its activities became 'real time' because technology now permitted funds and information to be transmitted instantly around the world and paperless transactions meant trading was almost instantaneous. Still unrecognised, though, was the extent to which management of the risks involved had become far more difficult. Increased competition squeezed profit margins and intensified the search for additional revenue sources, while deregulation facilitated innovation and the supply of novel products whose complex risks were difficult to calculate.[55] American and British financial officials were convinced that the markets and the growth they generated were self-correcting and that regulators themselves were a source of inefficiency and instability. These preconceptions were widely embraced by policymakers almost everywhere as liberalisation became the dominant feature of the world economy during the last two decades of the 20th century, thanks to a 'growing willingness of governments to open up the national economy to global market forces' and to embrace 'the rollback of policies that block the free movement of goods and capital'. There were some warning voices, nevertheless. There was no reason to assume that this benign process would continue indefinitely, some academics pointed out. In particular, there was no certainty 'about the conditions that underlie the ebb and flow of liberalization worldwide', and 'the risk is high that political economy models of economic liberalization have been under- or even misspecified'.[56]

There were also grounds for doubting how universal would be the record growth rates promised by liberal reformers. The former Soviet bloc countries failed to catch up with their 1990 levels of output during the rest of that decade; GDP growth per capita in Latin America was slower than between 1950 and 1980; while emerging economies generally suffered 'frequent and painful financial crises'. But scepticism seemed out of place when confronted with the evidence from Asia. Here, liberalisation and globalisation propelled a take-off to prosperity on such a scale as to achieve the miracle of a bigger reduction in world poverty than in any previous decade.[57]

The challenge for policy-makers was how to strike an appropriate balance between regulation as a safeguard for financial stability and increased competition as a key driver not only of financial market development but also of global economic growth.[58] The Anglo-American culture and its supporting consensus emphasised the concept of moral hazard: financial institutions ought to accept the full risks of competitive markets and go into liquidation like any other type of enterprise when they failed. But the political arithmetic was far from clear. In practice, there was the reality that the losses from the failure of a commercial bank were not confined to the shareholders. Even larger were the losses suffered by depositors, who were not its owners and who had no involvement in its management. The failed bank's borrowers, too, would be hit as they tried to replace their loan facilities under very adverse conditions.[59]

American and British policy-makers could argue that such losses were acceptable given the additional economic growth that market freedom encouraged. A financial crisis dictates its own agenda, however, as they were to learn in 2007–09. No matter how sustained the previous momentum of growth may have been, financial crises and bank collapses are traumatic events for which society as a whole is asked to pay a price that is both immediate and severe as businesses fail, jobs are lost, family assets slump in value and public services are slashed.[60] The outcome of an individual crisis is decided in the last resort by whether the public shows a willingness to accept the disruption caused by bank closures and the credit squeezes that follow or prefers to endure the pressure on public finances that rescue operations and reflation may require.

End of an era?

'The autumn of 2008 marks the end of an era', it has been said.

> After a generation of standing ever further back from the business of finance, governments have been forced to step in to rescue banking systems and the markets. In America, the bulwark of free enterprise, and in Britain, the pioneer of privatisation, financial firms have had to accept rescue and part-ownership by the state.[61]

For this unhappy close to decades of liberalisation, the laissez-faire mentality of central bankers and financial regulators had much to answer. Investor and depositor confidence had been shaken to a degree not matched in any previous American crisis, a Federal Reserve Governor reported. It was dramatised by 'the inability of Bear Stearns to borrow even against U.S. government securities [which] led to its collapse'.[62] Decades of optimism about the financial markets' ability to generate prosperity were replaced by distrust. Long-standing assumptions about the market's collective good sense were being discarded, and disillusion-ment, if not despair, was the dominant sentiment at every level by 2009.

> Investors of all stripes — sovereign wealth funds, large long-only institutional investors, private equity sponsors, hedge funds, and retail investors — are searching for new rules of asset allocation and appropriate risk premiums in an uncertain and unusual economic environment.[63]

In the United Kingdom, there was similar disarray within the financial services industry.

> The business models of the first years of this century have already been consigned to the dustbin. The acquire-to-arbitrage model employed by leading investment banks is dead. The stand alone investment bank is dead; they are now bank holding companies. Also dead is the retail banking model that depended practically exclusively on securitisation to fund a growth in mortgages and

other consumer credit far in excess of the institution's retail deposits. And, the so-called "free banking" model is under attack — at least in the UK — under pressure from the courts and from zero interest rates.[64]

In retrospect, the markets can be seen to have been an unreliable guide to the soundness of firms, their business models and their managements. The banks that performed best on the world's stock exchanges after the crisis got underway were 'more traditional', a large-scale study discovered. They had reported a much higher ratio of deposits to assets at the end of 2006, lower leverage and more equity. Regulation was also crucial. The best performers were found in jurisdictions with 'more powerful supervisors, more restrictions on what counts as capital, more restrictions on banking activities, and more private monitoring'.[65] On this analysis, the markets only came round to the view that prudent management and hands-on regulation mattered after the crisis got underway and far too late to curb self-destructive behaviour among financial corporations.

The global crisis had undermined the credibility of claims that markets would spontaneously correct their excesses and discipline wayward participants. The case against the 'invisible hand' and the free operation of market forces was made very powerfully in an official British report.

> In the past, an important school of thought has argued that market discipline can play a key role in incentivising banks to constrain capital and liquidity risks ... But a strong case can be made that the events of the last five years have illustrated the inadequacy of market discipline: indeed, they suggest that in some ways market prices and market pressures may have played positively harmful roles ... A reasonable conclusion is that market discipline expressed via market prices cannot be expected to play a major role in constraining bank risk taking, and that the primary constraint needs to come from regulation and supervision.[66]

Even before 2007, ample evidence had accumulated that markets were neither self-correcting nor self-regulating. But the principle that the market must be left free to decide the fate of banks and other financial institution remained an article of faith at the heart of Anglo-American culture. This resilience in the face of a calamitous gap between policy and performance was put in context by Kevin Warsh, a Federal Reserve Board Governor. Financial liberalisation won its credibility during a long period of prosperity, he noted, in which 'articles of faith accumulate'. 'Some of these understandings are strong and enduring and well grounded', he observed, 'others, more problematic or misplaced; others still, properly and promptly discarded'.[67] In this case, the 'misplaced' articles of faith were protected by officials who, this chapter has already shown, chose not to take action against threats to market integrity and financial stability out of a confidence in the operation of free markets which the global crisis has shown to be unjustified.

Conclusions

The analysis presented in this chapter suggests that probably the greatest damage was done by regulators who regarded themselves as almost redundant once free markets prevailed — even in the face of clear evidence that markets were malfunctioning. Central bankers and regulators did not agree that prudential supervision to minimise unsound and unlawful business practices could contribute significantly to financial stability or would have made any significant difference to the events of 2007–09.[68] Confronted with the accusation that 'too many banks had made too many rotten individual-loan underwriting decisions', the Bank of England would concede no more than 'there was some of that'.[69]

Preconceptions about self-regulating market and the perils of moral hazard had not been overthrown, although there was a protracted debate about whether or not the largest banks could be allowed to fail. 'I don't preach the infallibility of market discipline in policing risks', Warsh declared in 2010, 'Market discipline, like regulatory discipline, is imperfect'. Nevertheless, he argued, it was the only defence against moral hazard.

> ... the too-big-to-fail problem — exacerbated by recent events — could undermine our financial system and do long-term harm to the real economy. The growing specter of government support threatens to weaken market discipline, confuse price signals, and create a class of institutions that operate under different rules of the game. This state is not acceptable. We need a system in which insolvent firms fail.[70]

In addition, conventional wisdom continued to claim that increased regulation would handicap innovation and would do more economic damage than the collapse of a mismanaged financial institution. Calls to expand regulation were misguided and misconceived, declared the Governor of the Bank of England, who insisted that 'regulators will never be able to keep up with the pace and scale of financial innovation'.[71] Thus, the promise of improved regulatory performance did not imply the downfall of the Anglo-American culture and the intellectual consensus which had defined the regulators' role in the past. On the contrary, its basic economic assumptions, outlined earlier in this chapter, retained their credibility and their influence.[72]

2

Fatal Decisions — Washington and London's Deliberate Mistakes

The most serious accusation against the officials who presided over monetary affairs but failed to prevent the global crash is that they repeatedly ignored evidence of impending disaster.

> The financial crisis … [was] rooted in the refusal of regulators, lawmakers and executive-branch officials to heed warnings about risks in the system and to use their powers to head them off. It is the result of antiregulatory bias and deregulatory zeal — ascendant over the last three decades, but especially prevalent in the last 10 years — that eclipsed not only rules and regulations, but the very will to regulate.[1]

Under indictment here is the Anglo-American regulatory culture, which reflected a wider political consensus that extended well beyond the officials themselves.

This chapter presents four case studies of regulatory negligence in response to: the 1997–98 Asian financial crisis; property bubbles; the role of the credit rating agencies; and the insurance industry's links with banking. These were all areas in which major malfunctions of the financial markets could be identified. Officials have tried to claim that before 2007, their hands had been tied. 'The problem with the old style of regulation was that it was retrospective', it has been argued, 'We rarely intervened until there was clear evidence that something had gone wrong. And intervention needed to be evidence-based; based on observable facts'.[2] In the official 2011 American post-mortem into the global crisis, considerable stress was laid on the evidence showing that central bankers and financial officials ought to have recognised the clear signs of mounting instability during the previous decade.[3] The analysis that follows will show how very aware they were of potential dangers and will explain the rationale they offered well before the onset of the global crisis in 2007 for not taking remedial action. It will also review the debate over consumer protection.

Washington and London's deliberate mistakes

Financial officials have publicly conceded that the global crisis was fore-seeable. 'Most of the underlying causes of the crisis [had] attracted attention from economists, central banks, international financial insti-tutions and regulators', the Governor of the Bank of England, Mervyn King, has since confessed. However, 'regulators could never prove that the risks they identified would crystallize', he asserted, while 'central banks and the IMF discussed the imbalances for so long that some came to believe that they were crying wolf'.[4] American officials claimed that the international regulatory community as a whole was at fault for believ-ing that financial institutions operating in global markets could operate safely despite significant reductions in capital requirements thanks to 'diversification and advanced risk management practices'.[5]

A major contributing cause of the catastrophe was more humdrum: a reluctance to enforce the law. American officials admit in retrospect that they had considerable legal powers to halt the malpractices and mis-management which destabilised financial markets (notably in relation to mortgages): 'For various reasons, these powers were not used effec-tively and, as a consequence, supervision was not sufficiently proactive'.[6] Before 2007, the United Kingdom focussed on 'financial services not financial stability', it is now officially admitted. But even so, malpractices were widespread, with 'a series of waves of major customer detriment' through financial products mis-sold to the public for decades because the regulators responsible stuck to 'the predominant free market ideol-ogy of the day'.[7]

Domestic politics also played a part, officials claim in their own defence. The central bankers and financial regulators have argued that their reluctance to regulate represented political realities. They have con-tended that their minimalist approach reflected the majority view in most countries. British public opinion would have opposed efforts to improve the regulation of the banks as 'constraints on the growth and profitabil-ity' of the industry and 'a tax on the success of the investment banking community', King has claimed, while a more liberal regulatory régime was identified in 2007 as an important asset in London's rivalry with New York.[8] On this view, politicians and the public would have opposed any regulatory innovations that reduced this competitive advantage.

In the current discussions over what changes should be made to regulatory policies and practices to take account of the global crisis, financial officials insist that their intervention in business affairs should continue to be as minimalist as possible. They claim that regulation increases moral hazard: investors and executives will act less prudently and efficiently if they can assume that the government will rescue firms from the consequences of their own mismanagement. The case studies presented below will suggest that the regulators' excessive respect for moral hazard before 2007 facilitated the self-destructive business practices which led to the extensive market scandals and corporate collapses of the global crisis.

In their response to the lessons of the global crisis, American and British officials have been unable to reject entirely the case for improved oversight of individual financial institutions. But they insist that the regulatory priority must be 'the financial system as a whole ... not just its individual components' and that the aim should be to control 'systemic' risk.[9] In fact, a more important distinction to make is 'between the regulation of *structure* and the regulation of *conduct*'. That is: 'Regulators may be concerned with the way the market is organized (structural regulation), or with behaviour within the market (conduct regulation)'.[10] In the events that led up to the global crisis, this chapter will show, the major damage was caused by 'behaviour within the market' — the imprudence of mortgage institutions in the sub-prime market, for example, and the incompetence of ratings agencies.

Rules of the game

A strong case can be made that all regulatory activities have an effect on business behaviour because they act as signals to investors and executives as to what sort of conduct the political and legal authorities will condone and what they will penalise. This process goes beyond the threat of criminal penalties or civil liabilities. The eminent American economist, William J. Baumol, has argued that it is 'the rules of the game that determine the relative payoffs to different entrepreneurial activities' and that 'at times the entrepreneur may even lead a parasitical existence that is actually damaging the economy'. These 'rules' are set by a variety of pressures including government policy, statutory and regulatory requirements and their enforcement.[11] When regulators are reluctant to use their legal powers to prevent abuses or they disregard business innovations that create products harmful to their purchasers, investors and executives have a clear indication of how nominal the penalties for misconduct will be in practice.

Differences in regulatory policies offer an excellent contemporary example of Baumol's hypothesis at work in today's financial markets. Here, supervision of the average employee's day-to-day operations, whether by senior management or by official regulators, often seems remote. Corporate structures have become 'flatter, rely more on teamwork and less on hard rules and narrow job descriptions'. Currency traders working for international banks in Switzerland, for example, have been depicted in a prize-winning academic study as operating 'in a domain that is not subject to national or international legal regulation' and having a 'part-employee/part-entrepreneur pay structure'. The result is that 'traders keep track of their profit and loss balance with practically every trade', the authors report, and 'their worth is explicit not only to themselves but also to their supervisors, at every moment in time'. Except for the individual's profitability, however, oversight of employees' conduct is random rather than regular. The clear impression left by this research is that they are free to develop patterns of behaviour which are in breach of such rules of conduct as have been prescribed for them.[12]

This mismatch between the way business is conducted and the rules laid down by the firm itself and its regulators is neither universal nor unavoidable. In a 2010 IMF exercise to examine why by comparison with other economies, the financial systems of Hong Kong and Singapore had proved so robust in the global crisis, their regulators' much more interventionist approach was shown to have a considerable impact on business attitudes and behaviour. Officials 'took an active role in monitoring banks' internal management, limiting leverage in specific markets (such as property loans), while questioning and guiding bank behavior'. This 'stronger regulation appears to have been supported by more prudent behavior by the rest of the private sector', the report noted. Foreign banks (HSBC and Standard Chartered) were more cautious lenders in Hong Kong than in London — home of their head offices — where they were 'subject to "light touch" U.K. home regulation' (though they were less conservative than banks headquartered in Hong Kong).[13] Plainly, the local regulatory culture was significant in its effects on bank executives and had an indirect influence on business attitudes generally. The regulators' cultural leverage was also strong enough to offset — though not entirely — the influence of a more liberal headquarters' environment.

The Anglo-American culture finds such 'judgmental' regulatory intervention difficult to come to terms with. In a rare official comment on how 'behavioural issues' contributed to the global crash, Hector Sants, Chief Executive of the British Financial Services Authority, declared that 'regulators have an obligation to consider the question of whether they should have a role to play in relation to the ethics and culture of the firms they regulate'. But he proved no readier to go into specifics than American and British officials had been before 2007. 'Determining an ethical framework is for society as a whole', Sants asserted, 'not an unelected regulatory agency'. The one concrete example he cited of the 'positive culture' he had in mind was that 'one of the good behaviours that regulators should be considering and are required to consider is that of the promotion of equality and diversity'.[14] This politically correct sentiment had no obvious relevance to financial regulation and its reform. Baumol's hypothesis is of special relevance in this context. As Sants frankly admitted, officials feel inhibited about discussing values and behaviour even when highlighting the financial instability caused by the failure of firms to behave with probity and integrity. His message to the markets was plain: regulators remained confused about their own role and the basis for judging the rights and wrongs of business behaviour.

Asia's revenge

Before 2007, the American and British regulators' preference for non-interventionism seemed to be vindicated by the robustness of the global financial system and the sustained momentum of overall world economic growth in the wake of the Asian financial crisis of 1997–98. This event had been truly catastrophic for the region, and Asian economies suffered 'far more dramatic falls in output and employment than the major developed countries have faced' since 2007.[15] But its causes and consequences seemed strictly regional, with only limited global fallout. This crisis was, in fact, the first unambiguous signal that financial markets could not be trusted to generate global prosperity indefinitely with minimal financial volatility.[16] The lessons of that painful episode were to be largely ignored, however, in Washington and London.[17]

Several sources of instability that contributed to the downturn in Asia's fortunes at the end of the previous century were to reappear as prominent features of the global crisis in 2007. In the 1990s, financial institutions took a highly optimistic view of the new Asian opportunities, and the region was hailed as an 'economic miracle'.[18] Its glittering performance seemed to promise large profits, which attracted substantial inflows of foreign investment.[19] International banks showed a considerable appetite for assets throughout Southeast and East Asia with little regard for the risks involved. The profits proved fragile and often illusory, as the World Bank was to demonstrate in a survey of 5,550 publicly-listed corporations in nine East Asian economies covering the period 1988–96.

> Ex-post, it has become clear that the operational performance of East Asian corporates was indeed not as stellar as many had thought and in fact involved investment with high risks ... poor performance and risky financing structures of East Asian corporates were, however, not notably featured among observers writing on East Asia prior to the financial crisis. Quite the opposite, East Asian corporates were considered an important contributing part of the East Asian miracle and were generally looked upon as very competitive

and adept at exploiting new market opportunities, and consequently attracted considerable amounts of foreign capital.[20]

Reckless disregard for Asian business realities was intractable. 'Even the most sophisticated operators in global financial markets' were prepared to go on lending 'well after the increased risks in the region were generally apparent', a prominent economist warned. He identified the increasing use of structured derivatives by global banks as contributing to this perverse behaviour. In the aftermath of the Asian financial crisis, he described these products as a serious threat to financial stability in terms that foreshadowed their subsequent contribution to the making of the 2007–09 crisis.

> It is the role of most derivative packages to mask the actual risk involved in an investment, and to increase the difficulty in assessing the final return on funds provided for the primary lenders and for market regulators. The incentives motivating such [products] provide little support for the common belief in the self-regulating nature of private capital markets in terms of risk assessment or of their ability to allocate capital efficiently.[21]

The disregard for reality was especially evident in the case of China. Here, an economic liberalisation programme was making the country the Third World's most attractive location for foreign direct investment even though state controls and national and local five-year plans remained prominent features of the business landscape.[22] Foreign bankers felt able to dispense with the costs and complexities of undertaking rigorous due diligence. The temptation to cut corners was particularly strong when investing via 'international trust and investment corporations' (ITICs) and similar bodies. These state-owned vehicles had been established with special exemptions from normal government controls so that they could help to accelerate economic development.[23] Foreign financial institutions assumed that since the ITICs were entities established and owned directly by the central and local governments, they would have the status of government borrowers, which would relieve their foreign partners from the burdensome regulations usually imposed on foreign investments. In the Asian crisis, this assumption was to prove painfully misconceived.[24] The Chinese government resisted vigorous foreign lobbying to come to the aid of ailing ITICs in 1998, and they were left to default at the expense of their foreign partners. Chapter 4 discusses this affair in more detail and explains how this secondary banking crisis led to a regulatory revolution in China.

These financial scandals did not hinder China's breakneck growth. The continued expansion of the global economy led to massive trade surpluses for China and other emerging economies in the new century.

The flow of capital was now reversed, with Asian funds flooding into Western assets. Ironically, Asia's economic success later came to be viewed as an important factor in the financial woes of the United States and Europe. American and British officials claimed that the 'growth of significant global imbalances over the last decade' — particularly from 'newly emerging countries, like China' — was a major cause of financial instability.[25] This allegation was tantamount to self-incrimination as it was an acknowledgment that the much-vaunted American and British financial markets could not absorb these inflows efficiently.

Officials from both countries attributed the breakdown in the good sense expected of the markets to 'the ex-ante excess supply of global savings over investment, which pushed real interest rates on safe assets to historically low levels, reinforced by loose monetary policy', as the Bank of England later explained.

> This 'savings glut', as Chairman Ben Bernanke christened it, was in part the result of high national savings rates in some Asian emerging economies, especially China, which despite high investment rates, chose to export capital rather than import it, as standard theory would lead one to expect ... One factor behind the high level of savings by the emerging market economies was their experience during the 1997–8 Asia crisis, when several countries were forced to tighten policy sharply in the face of a 'sudden stop' of capital inflows from abroad. Thereafter, a strategy of relying on domestic savings to finance investment and the accumulation of a substantial war chest of foreign reserves looked more appealing.[26]

But this shared American and British version of Asia's contribution to the making of the global crisis will not do. Unexplained is the most striking market failure in the prelude to the global crisis: the inability of the American financial system in particular to accommodate free flows of capital from overseas. The net volume of foreign savings received by the United States quadrupled as a share of GDP from 1995 to reach around 6 per cent of GDP in 2006. Properly invested, these inflows would have been highly beneficial to the American economy, the Federal Reserve Board Chairman, Ben Bernanke, has admitted.

> Unfortunately, that was not always the case in the United States ... Financial institutions reacted to the surplus of available funds by competing aggressively for borrowers, and, in the years leading up to the crisis, credit to both households and businesses became relatively cheap and easy to obtain. One important consequence was a housing boom in the United States, a boom that was fueled in large part by a rapid expansion of mortgage lending. Unfortunately, much of this lending was poorly done, involving, for example, little or no down payment by the borrower or insufficient consideration by the lender of the borrower's ability to make the monthly payments.[27]

Regulatory intervention could have corrected this mismanagement, Bernanke added in conclusion, but the American regulatory system was not up to the task. The market, left to its own devices, was unwilling to halt the imprudent lending.

On the Federal Reserve Board's own analysis, incompetent bank lending and defective regulation in the United States combined to transform a benign inflow from overseas into toxic assets through which contagion was subsequently exported to world markets. But there was another regulatory failure. 'The global imbalances were the joint responsibility of the United States and our trading partners', Bernanke has stated, but not enough effort was made to resolve the situation 'although the topic was a perennial one at international conferences'.[28] His British counterpart has made an almost identical confession. A serious threat had been identified well in advance of the global crisis, he admitted, but the world's central bankers and financial regulators had failed to give it the priority which it deserved.[29]

Property bubbles

The immediate shock that started the worldwide collapse in market sentiment and the financial crisis that followed in 2007 came from the United States property market and its sub-prime mortgage products. The Securities and Exchange Commission has described the origins of the sub-prime debacle as excessive enthusiasm for 'the noble goal of broader home ownership' that led 'to a range of bad policies and dangerous lending practices'. The most notorious were 'the "no-doc" loans in which borrowers not only didn't have to disclose income or assets, but even employment wasn't verified'.[30]

Initially, it seemed that the downturn in the American property sector would be manageable. In 2006 total mortgage-backed assets had accounted for only 7.4 per cent of the aggregate value of assets issued on the world's securities markets, while non-agency, sub-prime mortgages accounted for less than 1 per cent of the total.[31] A British regulatory official felt able to issue what amounted to an unconditional assurance in July 2007 that the economic and financial indicators were robust not only for the American and British economies but for global markets as well, with no danger of financial instability.[32] This optimism was shattered when American mortgage defaults became an international issue on 9 August 2007 after the French bank, BNP Paribas, revealed that 'three of its investment funds were no longer able to value a series of complex financial instruments backed by so called "sub–prime" residential mortgages in the United States'.[33] Overnight, the collapse of institutional as well as depositor confidence had been transformed from a regional American disaster into a worldwide calamity.

A British regulatory agency's post-mortem on the global crisis has provided what is perhaps the best summary of how the collapse of sub-prime mortgages and other securitised products came to wreak such global havoc.

> ... the new model of securitised credit intermediation was not one of 'originate and distribute' ... [but] 'acquire and arbitrage' [which] resulted in the majority of incurred losses falling not on investors outside the banking system, but on banks and investment banks themselves ... with financial sector assets and liabilities in the UK and the US growing far more rapidly as a proportion of gross domestic product than those of corporates and households.[34]

As with so much of the global crisis, this market downturn had been a disaster waiting to happen. The United States sub-prime mortgage crisis began as a typical property bubble in which bank loans financed increased competition for real estate. The new (higher) property prices allowed the banks to expand their lending on the security of these property assets in line with their new valuations, which fuelled yet another round of price increases. As with most bubble markets, the nation's monetary policies were facilitating lower real interest rates, which further stimulated bank lending, while loan quality deteriorated as the property market boomed.[35]

Signs were already accumulating at the turn of the century that American real estate had 'taken on some of the characteristics of a commodity market'. An important factor was a change in investment management fashions that dated back to the 1980s. Portfolio theory had begun to advocate a higher weighting for real estate because of the opportunities it provided for pension funds and investment companies to diversify their asset allocations. By 2000 the mortgage market was described in a careful academic study as 'much more sophisticated in managing and pricing interest rate risk, prepayment risk, and credit risk'. Nevertheless, the high-growth sub-prime sector stood out as an obvious source of instability, leading the academics to forecast that 'default rates will rise sharply' if house prices were to drop. Yet, optimism remained the dominant sentiment, and the study's overall finding was that 'the industry is better positioned than it was a decade ago to withstand a substantial national downturn'.[36]

The regulators were about to adopt a similar optimism about the robustness of the housing market. American officials, in their inquest into how the good intentions behind the drive to finance an expansion of home ownership could go so disastrously wrong, have been candid about their own culpability. In 2002, the regulators now point out, the capital weighting for triple and double-A rated asset and mortgage-backed securities was substantially reduced. As a result, 'the same dollar of capital could now support as much as five times the volume of these triple-A securities'. 'In retrospect', the Federal Deposit Insurance Corporation has admitted, 'regulators may have unintentionally, encouraged banks to bet heavily on a new class of non-transparent securities'.[37]

The American sub-prime market was expanding at a spectacular rate, and the comprehensive data continuously available on its current performance gave the market's professionals and its regulators ample warning of the rising risks from mortgage-based securities well before 2007. In 1995 these had totalled US$65 billion, of which 30 per cent was securitised. In 2005 market volume reached US$500 billion, with a securitisation rate of over 80 per cent. Business growth now depended on lending to new cohorts of retail customers despite their diminishing credit-worthiness. In the next two years, delinquencies in this market increased by 50 per cent, ruining many mortgage institutions and finally triggering global panic in 2007.[38] Much of the rise in delinquencies can be attributed to a decline in the standards of screening for loan applicants that, in turn, was linked to the increasing ease with which mortgages could be sold down to third parties. In short, a deterioration in due diligence among purchasers of securitised sub-prime mortgages encouraged a rise in the volume of lending to higher-risk customers for mortgages.[39]

The dangers created by property bubbles had been reviewed by British officials well ahead of the sub-prime disaster. The Bank of England had claimed in 2002 that the United Kingdom's real estate collapses in the 1970s and 1990s had made it particularly alert to property markets as 'barometers of economic conditions and potentially also the source of financial risks; and even, in extreme cases, financial crises'. This analysis, however, took a benign view of the American trend towards greater securitisation of mortgages. Its general conclusion was that 'new instruments and structures have the potential to deliver a better match between borrowers' and lenders' preferences'. The Bank acknowledged, nevertheless, that 'new financing techniques give rise to new risks — for borrowers, lenders and policy makers'. Its response to this uncertain situation was to do little more than 'seek to identify potential problems'.[40]

As things turned out, there was a heavy price to pay for the confidence of British regulators in the property market's ability to correct its own excesses. The United Kingdom's banking system suffered its own property meltdown in 2007 after the collapse of Northern Rock. This bank's unsustainable business model had relied on short-term market funding to finance mortgages which went increasingly to unqualified and undocumented applicants in much the same way as American sub-prime mortgages did. A 2008 parliamentary inquiry reported that while the directors of Northern Rock 'pursued a reckless business model which was excessively reliant on wholesale funding', 'the regulatory authority systematically failed in its regulatory duty'.

> The FSA [Financial Services Authority] did not supervise Northern Rock properly. It did not allocate sufficient resources or time to monitoring a bank whose business model was so clearly an outlier ... the FSA appears to have systematically failed in its duty as a regulator to ensure Northern Rock would not pose such a systemic risk, and this failure contributed significantly to the difficulties, and risks to the public purse, that have followed.[41]

Misleading ratings

The Securities and Exchange Commission has declared that the credit rating agencies and their misconduct were particularly culpable for the disaster that overtook the sub-prime mortgage market and triggered the global crisis. Christopher Cox, the Commission's Chairman, described agency attitudes ahead of the looming crisis.

> ... the CEO of Moody's, told a meeting of the firm's managing directors that the sub-prime market "was a slippery slope." He said that what happened in 2004 and 2005 with respect to subordinated tranches was that firms in the credit rating industry "went nuts" and that "[e]verything was investment grade. It didn't really matter."[42]

The charges against the rating agencies are not confined to the property sector. Central bankers and financial regulators have tried to place a large share of the overall blame for the global crisis and its market disasters on the agencies (which became subject to United States regulation only in 2006). 'The Big Three credit rating agencies have failed investors', declared Kathleen L. Casey, Securities and Exchange Commissioner, 'The largest rating agencies awarded their highest ratings to complex debt instruments that were undeserving of investment grade status'. But the misinformation, which played such a calamitous role in the prelude to the global crisis, was not a new phenomenon. This senior American regulator described the rating errors that came to light during the 2007–09 crisis as one more instalment in a long line of flawed assessments that could be traced back to California's Orange County scandal in the 1990s. Her indictment included the investment grade status which 'Enron, WorldCom, Parmalat, and many other companies earlier this decade' retained right up to their bankruptcies.[43]

The rating agencies' shortcomings had been dissected well before the start of the global crash. They were dominated by American firms and governed by American legislation. But the United Kingdom and other nations had also conferred on them a legal status that made them the arbiters of a company's public reputation and its worth to its shareholders and creditors. Firms had to meet the agencies' expectations in order to qualify for respectable ratings, which had a powerful influence on 'the "ground rules" of international capital markets, thereby reshaping the internal organization and behavior of those institutions seeking funds'. The agencies thus set the standards for what the market would regard as 'acceptable' behaviour and helped to mould both attitudes and conduct. An important consequence was to allow 'these private institutions [to] shape the basic norms that produce action in governments and business organizations' (exactly in line with the Baumol hypothesis discussed earlier in this chapter). They were given this privileged status even though their rating techniques tended to ignore the cyclical factors which affected the banking industry. They were largely protected from financial liability for negligent or unprofessional conduct and, unlike lawyers and accountants, were not subject to professional or regulatory oversight until the eve of the global crisis.[44] Furthermore, the rating agencies' own behaviour was not free from self-interest, almost unavoidably, since they were commercial enterprises.[45]

Nevertheless, the rating agencies' role in the financial markets had been seen as a bulwark against potential instability. In 1999 the Basel Committee had endorsed the use of the agencies as a way of standardising the treatment of risk and an effective strategy for dealing with the proliferation of the 'special purpose vehicle (SPV) issuing paper secured on a pool of assets' earlier in that decade. At the same time, the Committee drew attention to 'concerns about the incentive and consequential effects of a more extensive use of external assessments ... on the agencies themselves'. It emphasised that both the regulators and the individual banks should accept responsibility for 'the quality of the assessment source and methodology'.[46] But this caution was ignored in practice. The rating agencies were widely assumed to be fully qualified to set the standards with which financial institutions would have to conform in order to defend their market reputations; and the regulators were expected to undertake their own rating exercises.[47] It quickly became apparent that, in practice, the growing reliance on rating agencies would aggravate rather than reduce the bond markets' difficulties in assessing risk.[48]

Officials had long been aware of the growing threat posed by reliance on unregulated ratings agencies. In 2004, for example, the Deputy Governor of the Bank of England, had discussed how the growing dependence on the agencies' assessments could increase instability, especially 'in the case of collateralised debt obligations [where] whole categories of assets are dependent on their rating'. He stated that 'the increasingly public significance' of the rating agencies 'raises calls for them to be regulated'. Once again, however, the official preference was not to intervene out of fear that 'attempts to do so could actually create additional moral hazard, particularly in today's compensation orientated society'. 'If rating agencies were regulated', he asked, 'who would you blame if mistakes are made: the rating agency, the regulator, or both?'[49]

The obvious question is why this state of affairs was tolerated for so long. Plainly, the markets themselves were at fault. They were not performing with the wisdom that the Anglo-American regulatory culture took for granted. In addition, as regulatory officials later pointed out, whatever the shortcomings of the agencies and their analytical techniques, their assessments were never intended to replace the investor's own due diligence.[50] Financial institutions holding derivatives and similar products ought to have carried out their own credit reviews. However, in a world of increasingly esoteric products, officials have since admitted, financial institutions were tempted by the apparent efficiency of contracting out this responsibility to specialists employed by professional rating agencies, especially as in-house expertise to investigate financial engineering was expensive to hire. In the event, the agencies proved no more successful than the individual corporation in overcoming 'the highly complex information problems underlying some securities'. Their ill-conceived recommendations had disastrous consequences for investors in the global crisis.[51]

The professional misjudgements were compounded by mismanagement and misconduct within the agencies. The Securities and Exchange Commission reviewed the past record of the three largest agencies, which issued 98 per cent of all ratings and received 90 per cent of the industry's revenue. This investigation uncovered extensive evidence of serious malpractice and gross conflicts of interest.[52]

Mismatched insurance

In 2008 the United States intervened to save Allied International Group (AIG), the world's largest insurance corporation. Its 'disorderly failure', the Chairman of the Federal Reserve Board explained, 'would have put at risk not only the company's own customers and creditors but the entire global financial system'. The arithmetic in support of AIG's rescue was formidable.

> AIG had insured many billions of dollars of loans and securities held by banks around the world ... banks had extended more than $50 billion in credit to the company ... state and local governments had lent more than $10 billion to AIG; workers' 401(k) plans had purchased $40 billion of insurance from AIG against the risk of loss ...

substantial quantities of commercial paper would have also borne serious losses.[53]

The vulnerability of the insurance sector had been recognised by American and British financial officials since the start of the century.[54] They had also openly identified the reasons for alarm. Financial engineering had allowed banks to convert loans to their customers — mortgages, credit cards, auto finance, for example — into collateralised debt obligations (CDOs), that is, into an investment product backed by a package of fixed income assets, which could then be sold on to investors.

With the appropriate financial engineering, products were tailored to meet the risk appetite of different classes of investors. In theory, the banks themselves benefitted from these securitisation exercises. They could achieve better management of their risks by buying and selling packages of loans to achieve an optimal balance among their assets, diversifying risk across the entire financial market and thus improving overall stability. The securitisation process also enabled the banks to escape from regulatory restrictions on their lending and to earn handsome fees which became a major source of profit growth. This financial engineering involved more than creating new products which could be packaged and marketed according to the investors' specifications. Credit ratings were also 'engineered', a practice that was to prove dangerously illusory, as the insurance industry was to find out. The result was to create 'thousands of structured finance products with a triple A rating', a British parliamentary inquiry was told. This figure was in astonishing contrast to the miniscule total of 'perhaps 30 or 40 triple A rated sovereign credits, whilst globally only a "handful" of banks and corporates enjoyed a triple A rating'. Nevertheless, in 2007 American and British officials, as well as the IMF, hailed the proliferation of triple A rated structured products.[55]

The insurance industry's woes began with its involvement in the process of transforming credit derivatives into products which, in reality, were close to insurance contracts. In a discussion of this development in 2000, the Bank of England's Deputy Governor had warned that the apparent contribution to greater financial stability from diversifying a bank's risks was illusory.

> The most recent area of growth, however, is not so much in these sales of assets to remove them from the balance sheet. Rather it is in the use of unfunded credit derivatives that leave the underlying asset on the balance sheet but transfer some or all of the credit risk. The most common credit derivatives are credit default swaps, although they are not swaps in the normal sense but are more akin to guarantee or insurance arrangements.

The market suffered from a lack of transparency, he continued, and from considerable uncertainty about what the fate of these products might be in a crisis. More serious still was the growing inter-dependence of the banking and insurance industries, whose basic businesses were radically different and whose funding and risk profiles were very dissimilar.[56]

Another Bank of England official warned in 2003 that this mismatch between the two industries' models for managing risk 'can give rise to cash flow and liquidity implications which, for bankers and others in the financial markets, are potentially highly disruptive'. There was also a divergence in regulatory régimes which allowed banks to evade official supervision through 'using credit risk transfers to insurance subsidiaries, or asset securitisation sales to third party insurers, or credit insurance and derivatives sold by insurers'. The case for the regulators to become involved was strong. But the Bank of England resisted intervention. Its officials were more worried about the damage that could be inflicted on market growth by 'a call for harmonisation of regulation or a blind assertion of the need for a completely level playing field'. Instead of urging preventive action, the official recommendation was confined to a call for re-examination of the issue.[57]

American central bankers were even more complacent about allowing banking institutions to become dependent on the insurance industry through its role in the development of the derivatives market and credit default swaps. An official review in 2002 identified 'the increasingly active portfolio management of credit risk, by both banks and insurance companies' as the driving force behind the credit derivatives market, but it played down fears about the influence of 'regulatory capital arbitrage'. These officials were convinced that credit derivatives were acting as a force for stability. The evidence in support of this reassuring conclusion came from market perceptions about major corporate collapses earlier in the new century. These products appeared to have successfully 'spread the credit risk associated with these large borrowers' who had defaulted.

American officials' verdict was that this was now a mature market whose participants 'understood the risks and [were] willing and able to bear them'. The official recommendation was that 'the regulators should continue to insist that banks manage their counterparty credit risk prudently, [which] includes paying attention to potential concentrations of counterparty credit risk'. But this reassurance was not meant to lead to any concrete measures because, it was claimed, the regulatory process itself was more a peril to progress than a protection for the public.

> ... just as important is ensuring that regulators keep enough distance from the markets to give financial innovations such as credit derivatives a chance to succeed. The new market for credit

derivatives has grown largely outside of traditional regulatory oversight, and as I have described, evidence to date suggests that it has made an important contribution to financial stability in the most recent credit cycle.[58]

Ironically, the banks did not need such forbearance from the Federal Reserve Board. Through these products, the insurance industry was already at work assisting banks to avoid inconvenient regulation and to participate in activities which promised greater profits but at a potentially higher risk.[59]

The results of the American and British regulators' decision not to get involved were disastrous both for the insurance industry and for global financial stability. The American insurance giant, AIG, was second only to Citigroup in its losses and write-offs during 2007–09, the OECD has calculated. But it was not alone in its industry. Out of the 12 biggest loss-makers among insurance industry companies worldwide, six were American, and they accounted for 52 per cent of the sector's US$264 billion in global losses.[60]

Was this outcome avoidable? When the Securities and Exchange Commission's former Chief Accountant testified at a Congressional hearing on the failure of AIG, he declared that 'if honest lending practices had been followed, much of this crisis quite simply would not have occurred'.[61] The range and volume of the illegal and improper practices that had flourished with the rapid expansion of the derivatives market was remarkable. Involved were many of the most respected names in the international financial community. For example, after the failure of the US$330 billion Auction Rate Securities (ARS) market in 2008, UBS, Citigroup, Merrill Lynch and Bank of America, among others, were forced to reach settlements with their investors worth US$67 billion — 'the largest settlement sums levied in the Commission's history'.[62]

Protecting the public

In their response to the global crisis, a persistent theme of the policy-makers was a warning that this crisis could lead to campaigns for more stringent regulation which would cripple the future growth of the vital financial services sector.[63] The regulators' rearguard action was made necessary by what may prove a lasting legacy of the global crisis: the community's disillusionment with the market's ethics and the public's mistrust of invocations of the dangers of moral hazard. The financial markets' collapse slashed personal wealth drastically in 2008. In the United States, household net worth dropped by some 18 per cent, the largest annual fall ever recorded. Household net worth relative to disposable income fell from a ratio of some 6:1 to less than 5:1, 'erasing about a full year's worth of income in wealth'. The public no longer felt able to entrust its financial fortunes to the markets, and the prevailing mood of helplessness was movingly summed up by Federal Reserve Governor Kevin Warsh.

> Traditional rules of income and asset diversification appear to offer scarcer protection than generally advertised. As a result, households are questioning the route to financial security. Homeownership is no longer perceived to ensure low-risk capital appreciation. And assurances by investment managers to invest in "stocks for the long haul" are being subjected to intense scrutiny.[64]

The impoverishment of American families through the catastrophic decline in the value of their homes and personal savings highlighted 'the link between protecting consumers from abusive products and practices and the safety and soundness of the financial system'. A leading regulator called for 'a new independent financial product safety commission' on the ground that 'products and practices that strip individual and family wealth undermine the foundation of the economy'.[65]

The Anglo-American regulatory culture and its commitment to unfettered market freedom made it inevitable that this proposal would encounter considerable opposition, and protection for consumers of financial services became probably the most bitterly contested reform proposal in the wake of the global crash.[66] Sheila Bair, Chairman of the Federal Deposit Insurance Corporation, was one of the most outspoken advocates of consumer protection among American regulators. But even she had to promise the banking industry that the new Consumer Financial Protection Bureau would not 'impose an additional level of regulation on banks and thrifts and interfere with their ability to earn a fair rate of return in consumer and mortgage lending'.[67] The Federal Reserve Board initially presented its consumer protection proposals as a postscript to its larger plans for regulatory initiatives dealing with the systemic weaknesses that contemporary banking was said to create.[68] In the United Kingdom, regulatory officials who did not want to be distracted from the task of controlling systemic risk felt free to openly mock consumers' concerns.[69] In addition, the British government felt justified in taking a cautious approach to reforms because of the perceived loss of business opportunities for financial services that would follow increased regulation.[70]

The Chairman of the Federal Reserve Board defined the battle lines. He noted the public's mistrust of financial innovation, and he acknowledged that regulators ought 'to strive for the highest standards of consumer protection'. But he expressed alarm that 'innovation, once held up as the solution, is now more often than not perceived as the problem'. Regulators, in his opinion, must find a balance that protects the freedom of 'responsible innovation' despite public resentment at the havoc wreaked by 'sub-prime mortgage loans, credit default swaps, structured investment vehicles, which have become emblematic of our present financial crisis'.[71] It was also argued that the public did not need more protection because the current programme to defend the consumer was already very extensive.[72] In reality, the Federal Reserve Board's record was poor, particularly in the sub-prime mortgage market. A government report in 2000 had warned that 'certain terms of sub-prime loans appear to be harmful or abusive in practically all cases'. In response to public lobbying and Congressional hearings in 2000–01, the Board introduced only minimalist measures 'to prohibit certain unfair, deceptive and abusive practices by lenders and third parties' in this market whose excesses were the trigger for the international financial crisis. Not until 2008 did the Board agree to close the worst loopholes.[73]

A similar battle was fought by British officials who insisted that banking regulators should not be responsible for 'consumer protection and market conduct'.[74] The political pressures in London for better protection of the public were hard to resist, however. As a leading regulator admitted, 'we cannot leave retail financial markets entirely to themselves and continue to accept the waves of mis-selling which have been such a feature of UK financial services for the last 20 years — personal pensions, endowment mortgages, split capital trusts'. But the measures taken in 2010 to put an end to such scandals were not impressive. For a start, the regulatory body responsible for their implementation warned publicly — and patronisingly — against a 'swing to the other extreme and [an] attempt to ensure that nobody ever exercises free choice to make decisions they subsequently regret'. It also argued that freedom of the market must remain a high priority, with reform initiatives seeking 'continually [to] balance alternative desirable objectives: product innovation versus product safety; and intervention to protect consumers versus customer freedom to choose'.[75]

Calls for consumer protection created a potentially large political challenge to the consensus that had dominated the American and British regulatory environment for the previous three decades. Public indignation has compelled other industries to accept regulatory intervention, most notably pharmaceuticals whose case against government oversight is at least as strong as that of financial services. The bulk of the pharmaceutical products that could cause concern are subject to strict testing before being marketed. They are prescribed and administered by trained professionals so that at every stage of their use, the purchaser of the product has access to expert advice and monitoring. Firms in this industry face severe reputational costs if their products prove unsafe, and the penalties for adverse results from their use can be punitive, especially at the hands of American courts. There is, in addition, the risk that over-cautious regulators could inhibit the development of new or improved products. Yet the United States Food and Drug Administration cannot be abolished as long as successful litigation involving even the largest and most reputable manufacturers continues to reveal how they suppress unfavourable test results, suborn expert opinion and deliberately mis-sell products in order to maximise their profits.[76] Consumer protection for financial services is a cause that is likely to gather momentum if regulatory reforms fail to convince the public that the lessons of 2007–09 have been learnt.

Conclusions

The analysis presented above indicates that not only were the potential financial shocks foreseeable but that they could have been prevented though appropriate intervention. Indeed, central bankers and financial regulators themselves have identified the major areas in which they had the powers needed to halt what, in retrospect, can be labelled a process of self-destruction by financial markets and their participants. King has pledged to preserve 'an institutional memory ... so that the lessons from the crisis are not forgotten and those impediments to excessive risk-taking are not swept away once memories of the crisis recede'.[77] There were few signs, however, that officials — or their political masters — would be more proactive when faced with similarly perilous situations in the future. 'The essence of our financial system is to let people take chances with their money', a Securities and Exchange Commission Director declared in 2009, 'and to enjoy most of the benefits and to endure most of the pain associated with taking those risks'. 'From a policy perspective', she went on, the goal must be 'to let financial entities fail if they make bad decisions'.[78] Not surprisingly perhaps, reform initiatives proceeded at a leisurely pace even where the evidence of past abuses was overwhelming. Not until August 2010, for example, did American officials start a public consultation on 'alternatives to the use of credit ratings within the various U.S. bank regulations and capital standards' despite the unacceptable performance of the credit ratings industry discussed earlier in this chapter.[79]

Reluctance to intervene prior to the global crisis owed a great deal to cultural preconceptions which convinced regulators that markets were best left to remedy their own deficiencies and that regulation would do more harm than good. That culture continued to command political credibility in Washington and London after 2007, as well as to enjoy widespread business support. The Federal Reserve Board worried openly about possible reforms by which our 'financial firms are micro-managed as quasi-public utilities ... immunized from real competition',[80] while the Bank of England expressed alarm at the prospect of 'an overly legalistic culture with its associated compliance-driven style of regulation'.[81] There was little likelihood of dramatic regulatory initiatives to match, for example, the radical change in the mindset of central bankers that had followed the crisis caused by the Herstatt Bank collapse in 1974 and which first inspired the collaboration between Washington and London in search of international commitment to effective regulation.[82] In the wake of the worst international crisis in modern financial history, the best that could be said about prospects for 'an overhaul of international standards of bank regulation' was that it 'remains a clear but highly uncertain goal'.[83]

3

China — Reforms vs Regulation

China was not supposed to fall victim to the international financial crisis. On the contrary, there was a widespread expectation that 'it would be an indispensable partner — just conceivably a leader — in hauling the world out of trouble'.[1] Although the Chinese government generally discouraged suggestions that the nation could expect to emerge completely unscathed, Prime Minister Wen Jiabao declared himself confident that the financial sector would not be seriously affected because 'after more than 10 years of reform, [it] is relatively stable and healthy and capable of withstanding the crisis'.[2] The biggest boost to confidence was the government's announcement in November 2008 of a US$586 billion economic stimulus package, an impressive demonstration of the spending power created by 30 years of breakneck growth since Deng Xiaoping first proposed his 'open door' policies. Its boldness, as much as its scale, was convincing proof that China could buy its way out of trouble.

This confidence persisted even after officials had realised that the economy was being hit by a sharp decline in its manufacturers' ability to maintain export growth.[3] After all, China's underlying strength still seemed beyond challenge. Its foreign reserves continued to accumulate, and none of its banks had collapsed. Within China there was a belief that its financial markets and institutions would be largely insulated from contagion because of their lack of sophistication and because of exchange controls and other restrictions on the freedom to invest overseas.[4] Where difficulties did arise, state supervision of the media ensured that there was no sensational coverage that might create panic. The central bank was discretion itself in reporting adverse incidents in 2008 where it had been forced to come to the rescue of institutions in trouble:

> ... liquidity stress experienced by some foreign-funded financial institutions in China, and ... the temporary liquidity risks of certain insurance companies that were insolvent for a while and certain domestic institutions that got into trouble because of derivatives trading.[5]

But banking was still vulnerable,[6] and policy-making was handicapped by the size and complexity of the nation's financial system whose capacity to adjust to changing business conditions remained limited. (See Table 1) Although the market was no longer virtually monopolised by the four state commercial banks, competition was effectively controlled not only for the industry as a whole but also between the different types of institution because the state continued to decide deposit rates and the growth of lending. The role of the foreign banks was limited by restrictions on their entry to the Mainland market. Not surprisingly, 'there are wide inefficiencies in the banking system', an IMF study reported in 2009, 'Moreover, less efficient banks are not necessarily less profitable'.[7]

Table 1
China's Financial System 2008, by type of institution and percentage shares in national totals[8]

	No. of institutions	Assets	Loans	Deposits
State commercial banks	4	48.4	43.2	53.3
Joint stock commercial banks	12	18.4	19.4	17.5
Policy banks	3	9.0	15.6	0.9
Postal savings bank	1	3.4	1.4	4.9
Foreign banks	29	2.1	2.5	0.9
Urban credit cooperatives	42	0.1	0.1	0.2
Rural credit cooperatives	4,965	7.8	6.0	9.7
Finance companies	84	1.5	1.9	1.7

Ironically, the economic stimulus package itself was to create a new threat to the stability of the banking industry. It placed in jeopardy improvements that had been hard won since the 1997–98 Asian financial crisis, which had first convinced China's leaders of the urgent need for reforms. This chapter will explain how the nation's credit culture had been distorted by systemic problems that recurred from one decade to the next from the 1950s and why the reform initiatives which had been promulgated with similar regularity had so often been frustrated.

Political realities

As the 'Introduction' explained, a special factor that affects every aspect of Chinese life is the continuing control of the economy by the state. An added complication is that ultimate political power is in the hands of the Chinese Communist Party. Its dominant position is enshrined in law and is beyond challenge.[9] This separate and higher authority has had to be lobbied and convinced at each step of China's financial modernisation.[10] Thus, introduction of corporate governance reforms could not begin until the Party had endorsed the principle. Only after six years' hesitation, the People's Bank has recounted, did a 1999 Party Plenary Session formally accept the concept of corporate governance in which 'shareholders, Board of Directors, management and employees' should be involved. Left unresolved, the central bank went on, was how to deal with the fact that 'in China, the Communist Party Committee, in addition to investors, Board of Directors, management and stakeholders, also plays a role in corporate governance'.[11] The People's Bank itself put the Chinese Communist Party ahead of the government when it came to developing the policies which the nation needed.[12] There is, in practice, no formula by which Party influence can be ignored in any state agency or sizeable private sector firm.[13]

The Party's authority is supposed to be exercised within a bureaucratic structure. After the Asian financial crisis, banking reforms were introduced whose implementation seemed assured under a new People's Bank Governor, Zhou Xiaochuan. Observers described him as 'a Communist Party heavyweight' because of his politically impeccable family background and the personal patronage of four premiers.[14] But it will become apparent in this chapter that he did not rank high enough in the Party hierarchy to overcome his institutional and administrative handicaps. In a process that has obvious parallels with the United States' confirmation procedures for the Chairman of the Federal Reserve Board, the Governor of the People's Bank is formally appointed by China's President after nomination by the Prime Minister and endorsement by the legislature (National People's Congress). The People's Bank itself is by law supposed to have a significant degree of freedom to decide policy issues, manage their implementation and direct the enforcement of legal and regulatory requirements. The autonomy of the Governor of the People's Bank, however, is far more constrained than his American and British counterparts since he is subject to the overall direction of the State Council chaired by the Prime Minister.

The China Banking Regulatory Commission is supposed to enjoy a similar legal autonomy but in practice, its chairman is even more constrained by the tightly regimented hierarchy within the Party and state bureaucracies. For example, senior executives in the four largest state-owned banks are not just professional bankers. They are also 'quasi-governmental officials, and may even rank equally with the Chairman of the China Banking Regulatory Commission in the hierarchy of China's administrative system'.[15]

The consequences of these political and administrative arrangements can be illustrated from what occurred after a decision in 2007 to curb investment and shrink production capacity in selected industries. In July that year, the government publicised the concept of the 'environmentally-friendly loan' and instructed banks to stop lending to 'high-energy consuming and polluting industries'.[16] The People's Bank dutifully 'guided commercial banks to optimize the credit structure, rigorously limit lending to low efficiency enterprises in industries with high energy consumption, heavy pollution' and also — it was to prove important — where there was 'excess production capacity'. The central bank's explanatory comment revealed that the laudable 'green credit policy' had already been expanded into an exercise in state direction of capital spending across a wide range of industries, with the banks required to help police their customers' investment behaviour.[17]

A 2009 State Council meeting issued a formal document setting out a list of businesses which were to be denied equal access to bank funds and development opportunities and, by implication, to suffer administrative harassment in order to eliminate 'overcapacity and redundant projects'. 'Guidance would be particularly enhanced', it directed, 'on the development of steel, cement, plate glass, coal chemical, poly silicon, and wind power sectors'.[18] A later official document included the use of 'market forces' in this campaign, but direct state action was the main weapon, Prime Minister Wen Jiabao had already made plain.[19] Yet, the People's Bank had for several years been intent on promoting a business culture in which the state's role would be minimised and companies would make their own decisions about what was in the best interests of their shareholders in much the same way as in any OECD country.[20] Despite the impressive political connections of Zhou personally, he was unable as Governor of the People's Bank to block the change in policy, and China's political arrangements did not permit the central bank to offer public opposition to this development.

Companies themselves were not happy with the campaign to control their expansion plans, and industrialists now showed that the government's policy-makers had to take the manufacturing sector more seriously than they did the banking industry (a recurring theme in this chapter). In 2009 an official account of the government's anti-recession measures included 'a support package for the [automobile industry] which also highlighted eliminating outdated capacity'. By now, China had become the world's largest market for cars; demand was still growing; and the industry ignored the call to cut capacity.[21] The following year, the powerful National Development and Reform Commission stated publicly that this industry's 'excess capacity would bring vicious competition, and hurt corporate profitability ... threatened sustainable economic development and must be "resolutely" stopped'. An array of statistics was published to support this charge. But the industry's lobby was politically powerful enough to ensure that the official media reported both its rejection of this allegation and its own counter-claim that there was actually a shortage of production capacity. Car manufacturers were able to rally support from the National Development and Reform Commission's own affiliate, the State Information Centre, which denied any danger of 'excessive capacity' and declared that the industry was 'manufacturing at 120 per cent of its capacity, and most manufacturers were operating more than 20 hours a day'.[22] Unlike the manufacturing sector, the People's Bank was not able to engage in a similar public debate over policy directives affecting its industry.

The lowest priority

Despite the emergence of such open clashes over development priorities in recent years, the relentless pace of China's economic take-off since liberalisation got underway in 1979 has made the process seem nearly effortless, almost inevitable and virtually irresistible.[23] This image of three decades of uncontested growth is natural enough because modernisation was faster and more far-reaching than had ever been envisaged in its early years. Banking was the great exception, however, a fact that the country's regulators are not always ready to admit. The Chairman of the China Banking Regulatory Commission, for example, has claimed that in the 30 years since the nation embarked on economic reforms, 'China's banking sector has made remarkable improvements, evolving from a monopolistic, highly risky and under-developed system to one that is competitive and prudent'.[24] This and the following chapter will show that such accounts gloss over the repeated setbacks and frustrations that have occurred in the campaigns to modernise the banking industry.

The need for banking reforms was widely ignored in the earlier debates among China's economists about modernisation. This omission was of considerable importance because in a state under the rule of a Marxist party, 'market-oriented changes have to be theoretically justified'.[25] Financial institutions were the lowest priority on China's reform programme, and they were the last sector of the economy to be 'subjected to market forces'. As a result, the banks had been obliged to provide state-owned enterprises and capital projects with whatever credit facilities officials directed, the People's Bank complained in 2000, because the government took it for granted that 'the economic risks of the whole society' could be transferred to this sector.[26]

After the first two decades of economic reform, the banking industry seemed to have made less progress in modernising itself than any other sector of the economy. Whereas manufacturing had taken world markets by storm, China's financial institutions were intimidated by the increased risks perceived in lending to hi-tech and small enterprises which had become the driving force of economic growth, the central bank reported. Manufacturers were producing goods that met the demands of the world's most sophisticated markets. The banks, however, still lacked a range of modern products to offer their customers. Many bank branches were incapable of making loans as a routine part of their business, the People's Bank added in 2005. Their loan default records were so dreadful that head offices ought to withdraw their freedom to do more than 'one or two loan businesses per year'. For the system as a whole, the People's Bank went on, non-performing loans continued to be such a scandal even after generous government bail-outs that the banking industry enjoyed little public support and the government was left reluctant 'to remove unwarranted controls and encourage financial innovation'.[27]

Unfortunately, the situation was to deteriorate during the global financial crisis as an unintended consequence of the government's ambitious stimulus package to minimise deflation after world demand for Chinese exports shrank. This rescue programme created a real risk of reversing a decade of banking reforms, it will be argued later in this and the next chapter, because of the central government's decision not to pay for the package from its own resources. Beijing instead announced that 70 per cent of the US$586 billion required would be financed by local governments and the private sector. However, funds from these sources were simply not available at such short notice. To cover the shortfall, banks were ordered in 2009 to resume the former practice of automatically funding the government's investment projects even if their financial viability was doubtful. In addition, the desperate urge to expand public sector investment as rapidly as possible led to the decision to ignore the legal prohibition on local governments raising loans or extending guarantees on their own authority. The ban on such borrowings was well justified by the poor credit standing of local governments in general, which the next chapter will recount.[28] In consequence, China's central bankers and financial regulators found themselves operating in an environment which owed much to the 'command economy mentality' of the pre-1978 era. Policy once again was being made on the assumption that, instead of modern open and competitive markets, the Chinese Communist Party and the government were the best judges of what prices, output and investment ought to be. This attitude went hand in hand with a preference for central directives rather than legislation or consultation with industry and made it almost impossible to insist on due regard for moral hazard.

Twin evils

In late 2007, Zhou Xiaochuan, Governor of the People's Bank, presented an analysis of the mounting international crisis in which he predicted quite accurately what was in store for China's banking industry. He highlighted the need to protect what had been achieved in the past by describing the 'long and painful process [of] rectifying China's unsound credit culture'. Zhou evidently foresaw that financial officials' views would carry little weight in the future if the government needed to take special measures, and he seemed to accept that his personal standing within the Chinese Communist Party and the state bureaucracy was not high enough to change the situation. Thus, the Governor argued the case for Beijing to accept the advice of external experts. He endorsed 'the IMF's annual surveillance mechanism' with its 'Article IV Consultation' as 'an effective tool for regular health check-ups' of the economy.[29] As things turned out, Beijing declined to authorise the public release of the IMF's yearly assessment until 2010, when the document showed that regulatory problems had worsened in the wake of the government's measures to prevent an economic downturn.[30]

The Governor had also foreseen what would cause this deterioration. There were two lending practices that were long-standing threats to the integrity and stability of the financial system, he said, 'policy' and 'relationship-based' lending.

Policy lending

The phenomenon dated back to the pre-1978 central planning régime when such lending had been dictated by the state plan or 'administrative interventions'. This practice evolved and expanded after the post-1978 economics reforms because of the transfer to local governments of considerable control over assets and economic administration. This process unintentionally gave local officials a powerful incentive to ensure that banks gave priority to the local economy and also provided an inducement for bank branches to cooperate with the local power-holders in defiance of national policies and directives.[31] Henceforward, the most damaging state intervention in bank lending would come from local governments.[32] Not until November 1997 were 'both the central and local governments … prohibited from interfering with loan decisions'. At this point, by 'international accounting standards', the Governor of the People's Bank warned, the rate of non-performing loans had reached 'more than 40 percent' and 'many banks were technically insolvent'.[33] This alarming figure was not an indicator of the inability of Mainland bankers to manage credit effectively, according to a 2003 People's Bank survey.

- 60 per cent of non-performing loans were attributable to government directives: 'intervention by the central and local governments [and] ... mandatory credit support to state-owned enterprises'.
- 10 per cent were caused by the state's economic reform initiatives and its 'industrial restructuring' which led to 'closing down, suspending operations, merging [enterprises] with others or shifting to different lines of production'.
- 10 per cent of loans could not be recovered because of the 'poor legal environment and weak law enforcement'.
- Only 20 per cent of non-performing loans could be attributed to 'business operation and management of the state-owned banks themselves'.[34]

Relationship lending

This practice was rampant, and 'enterprises' access to credit was largely based on their management's personal relationship to the banks', Zhou said. The problem was hard to eradicate because of 'large deficiencies in the standards of accounting, information disclosure and financial statements'. Efforts had been made from 2002 onwards to strengthen corporate standards for the commercial banks and other deposit-taking institutions, and there were hopes that stock market listings would change the commercial banks' credit culture through greater transparency and accountability.[35] However, much of this 'relationship' lending had nothing to do with the poor quality of corporate governance. In many cases, it was outright corruption.[36] Significantly, when the 2008 stimulus package was announced, a senior Chinese Communist Party official warned publicly that the 'massive investments in infrastructure and social projects' would make fraud and corruption a 'major, pressing and serious issue'.[37]

Political legacy was also involved. The influence over bank branches exercised by local Party officials had long allowed them and their work units to obtain bank credits on privileged terms. In such an environment, financial officials had been particularly prone to malpractice and corruption even before the reform era.[38] Once the economic liberalisation movement got underway after 1978, government agencies went into business on their own account, and 'bureaucratic commerce' mushroomed. This trend marked the beginning of the transfer of profitable state assets into the personal control of the officials who had previously been in charge of state-owned enterprises and of the state agencies involved in commercial, financial and industrial administration. (Unprofitable operations were left largely under state ownership.) As these bureaucrats developed businesses on their own account, they retained their Party status and their political connections. As a result, they profited handsomely from access to loans from state-owned banks which could be rolled over indefinitely and to public land which they occupied with impunity.[39] The state's assets were the foundations of the future fortunes of these officials, who were to make up the bulk of the most successful, new entrepreneurs.

The Asian financial crisis

In 2007 it was still possible for central bankers and regulators to hope that these grim statistics belonged to another age which had been brought to an end by the 1997–98 Asian financial crisis. As with the global crisis, this earlier disaster had seemed to leave China virtually unscathed although in reality its impact had been so traumatic that Beijing had been converted virtually overnight into offering vigorous support for radical regulatory reforms. Almost all China's own accounts of banking reforms date them to the Asian crisis and its sharp reminder of the vulnerability of the banking industry to sudden changes in market conditions. The government had then found it could no longer ignore the case for urgent action to deal with non-performing loans and injected US$33 billion into the four largest banks in 1998. The following year it provided four special asset management companies with a further US$170 billion to take over these banks' non-performing assets.[40]

It was easy to argue — especially on the basis of the 2003 survey quoted above — that, left to themselves, market forces would exert a powerful pressure for reform and efficiency. After all, as was pointed out earlier, bankers could be held directly responsible for only 20 per cent of their bad loans. But moral hazard was also an issue, the People's Bank Governor noted, and this risk had been largely ignored in the aftermath of the Asian crisis. A recent study of the results of the gigantic rescue operation in 1998–99 claims that the subsequent performance of the bailout's beneficiaries — i.e., the four largest banks — was, if anything, worse than previously. Other banking institutions were left to find their own salvation from 1999, and although not all had survived, this group as a whole improved its lending record, according to the study's authors.[41] As a result, the renunciation of 'policy lending' in 1997 had not been enough to ensure quality management.

Disregard for moral hazard helps to explain why a decade later, an IMF study discovered that the profits of a bank were not necessarily linked to its efficiency. There was no fear of failure among the largest players, and banking competition remained limited (although it improved somewhat in this century). Banks recorded high earnings, according to this 2009 IMF research, but had small incentive to improve their efficiency because of official policies which allocated specific market sectors to the major banks, controlled interest rates and restricted the activities of foreign institutions.[42] Little seemed to have changed since a 2002 study, when the state-owned banks were found to enjoy 'monopolistic profits' and the pressures to 'force them to improve their efficiency and skills of financial management' were said to be inadequate.[43]

Moral hazard was made all the more serious by the peculiar obstacles to recovering bad debts in China. The People's Bank has drawn attention to the pathetically low recovery rate of less than 20 per cent for the non-performing loans transferred in 1999 to the special asset management companies set up to handle them. The initial projections made by the World Bank and other foreign experts had been for a recovery level of 40 per cent or more. In some cases, reported loan defaults were fraudulent but beyond the reach of Chinese criminal law at the time. But another factor was political: 'the administration is more powerful than the market', the People's Bank Governor noted. Thus, one bank 'sold its non-performing loans in a package to the local government', whose officials achieved a recovery rate of 'an encouraging 30 percent' thanks to their 'power in reinforcing judicial, enforcement and restructuring processes'. These officials were also able to slash the payroll of troubled enterprises on a scale that a bank could not hope to match. The moral hazard here, according to Zhou Xiaochuan, was that financial discipline was weakened because a business could choose to default in the expectation that local officials would take over the debt and then 'help to restructure the loan'.[44]

Reforming instincts

Chinese economists who strove to provide an intellectual framework for the original 1978 reforms had been well aware of the damage done to the financial system by the 'state command mentality' of the past.[45] Soon after coming to power in 1949, the Chinese Communist Party had copied the Soviet approach to banking, which neglected sound credit policies. The political pressures to expand lending were, in any case, intense, and funds were poured into agricultural expansion and the takeover of the privately-owned manufacturing and commercial sectors. The start of the 1958 Great Leap Forward 'led to aimless extension of loans', most of which had to be written off as they had been made 'without considering economic limits'. The 1950s provided clear warning of the losses to be incurred from 'policy lending' and its inevitable non-performing loans. The three years of famine that followed the failure of then 1958 'Great Leap Forward' led to a revival of pragmatic policy-making. Lending based exclusively on ideologically correct policies went out of favour, and a decision was taken at the highest levels in 1962 to strengthen the banks' autonomy. Enterprises which 'depended on bank credit ... for keeping things going' were shut down, while others were forced 'to strengthen business accounting and improve management'. By 1964 lending problems, reportedly, had been eliminated.

The 1966–76 Cultural Revolution was reported to have undone these reforms and 'delivered a crushing blow to banking'. Loans were not repaid, 'and all the necessary rules and regulations were branded as shackles and discarded' by Maoist extremists. The biggest losses were attributed to the funds wasted on state investment projects, which were granted free of interest and repayment obligations and 'only a fraction of which yielded economic returns'. Even before the end of the Cultural Revolution, however, professional banking standards were reappearing. Financial units were given regular encouragement to act as catalysts for improvements in every aspect of the borrowing enterprise's operations. In addition to monitoring accounting, inventory control, investment, revenue growth and cost control, banking personnel were expected to prevent fraud and expose malpractices.[46]

Thus, the banking sector was already bent on reform well before Deng Xiaoping unveiled his modernisation programme in 1978. The Construction Bank was a striking example. The Chinese Communist Party's newspaper, *People's Daily*, reported how the bank's staff had resisted a particularly pernicious combination of 'policy' and 'relationship' lending:

> ... leading cadres [who] issue open "notices" instructing that without their "consent" and "approval", activities and problems must not be made known to the bank's upper echelons.

The bank is described as having had the authority in 1977 to save the state several billion renminbi by 'cutting down or postponing unnecessary projects', 'disposing of stockpiled materials', speeding up completion and retrenching extravagant local projects. While still described as 'book keepers', the bank's staff were also presented as gatekeepers, the professional experts able to judge a project's merits and ensure its progress. Given an opportunity, China's bankers were already very keen to impose proper lending practices, to police spending and to combat 'policy' and 'relationship' lending.[47]

Banking renaissance

The momentum for financial modernisation had already gathered considerable pace when, in February 1979, a national conference of People's Bank managers was convened. It was attended by five deputy premiers who had extensive personal experience of the damage done by past attempts to replace professional financial management with either the Soviet system or Maoist populism. This high-powered group was led by the nation's financial guru, Li Xiannian. Between them, these men were now responsible for China's entire state planning and control apparatus.[48] Their power and prestige made them ideal sponsors of a new deal for the nation's banking industry, and the official report of the proceedings demonstrated that participants were fully aware of the crucial role that banking ought to play in the economic reforms that were just being launched.

The conference approved specific solutions for the two abiding threats to good banking in China.

- *Policy lending:* No longer should all enterprises within a specific sector of a state plan qualify for bank finance regardless of their efficiency or the market outlets for their output. Bank credit should be granted on the basis of an individual enterprise's past borrowing, repayment and production records. Lending to producers unable to respond to market demand should be restricted. Interest rates were to be variable, and short-term borrowers with faster turnover should get the lowest rates.
- *Relationship lending:* In theory, all lending had always been subject to banking regulations. But, in the past, 'if leading comrades expressed support for a loan, banks normally felt powerless to refuse'. In future, the conference laid down, 'if a leading comrade recommends a loan contrary to credit regulations, the bank should not hesitate to resolutely exercise its authority and reject it'.[49]

The conference had good reason to emphasise the economic gains that would come from granting the banking system the freedom to increase the range of its services and to manage its business on the basis of commercial criteria instead of political pressures. Economic liberalisation had created demands for financial facilities that had been abolished on ideological grounds in the 1950s, and the nation's banking system was being rebuilt from scratch. Previously, the bulk of the nation's industrial output had been distributed through state agencies and did not involve commercial transactions. Now as state-owned enterprises were being forced to seek their own markets, there was no banking infrastructure to finance consignments to the purchasers and to transfer sales proceeds to the producers. Thus, in 1980, the People's Bank authorised an experiment organised by Shanghai to provide the equivalent of letters of credit to cover shipments within Jiangsu, Zhejiang and Anhui provinces.[50] Shanghai played a leading part in creating payments systems that were to extend up the Yangtze River as far as Sichuan province after a system of economic agreements between provinces, regions and cities had mushroomed in response to the increased local autonomy that followed the retreat from central planning.[51] These deals shared many of the characteristics of the China's new foreign trade relationships that were emerging, including barter, compensation trade, investment project finance and joint ventures.[52] In 1984, the revival of traditional banking was symbolised dramatically by Shanghai's reintroduction on an experimental basis of personal cheque facilities which had been eliminated during the anti-capitalist drives of the mid-1950s.[53]

In the meantime, the financial system's leadership were 'tacitly or even explicitly supportive of the private sector' in the rural areas, and liberalisation of rural lending funded an impressive development surge outside the cities during the 1980s. While these trends demonstrated the reformist convictions of the nation's senior bankers, overall banking reforms stalled. 'Financial controls remained tight in the form of lending quotas and interest-rate caps', a major study of this issue has explained, 'and the urban areas were immune to these financial reforms'. During this period, the demand for commercial credit intensified as the economy took off. The banking industry's own constraints allowed informal financing to become a major feature of business life.[54] Enterprises themselves were providing credit facilities for their customers in very large quantities. Significantly, an official study showed that at this level, neither 'policy' nor 'relationship' was involved. 'Whether or not one enterprise would extend commercial credit to another enterprise depended on the latter's reputation, and hence, unlike bank loans, such loans had to be repaid on time', it was observed.[55]

Thus, within China, financial entrepreneurs had been reborn. The basic rules of banking were well known. The institutional and cultural innovations required for the creation of a modern banking system were daunting, but this chapter has provided ample examples of what the transition to the market could accomplish if given sufficient scope.[56] The private sector could have become a substantial feature of the banking landscape, just as it had done in manufacturing for example. Instead, 'informal' and private financial institutions were subject to a crackdown in the 1990s that was 'both determined and ferocious'.[57]

Reversing the revolution

So, why was the role of the private and the foreign sectors so much smaller in banking than elsewhere in the banking system? After all, despite the Maoist era's comprehensive denunciation of capitalism, the Chinese Communist Party had long recognised the importance of a sound and efficient banking system.[58] Furthermore, Maoism and Marxism were not the obstacle once the Chinese Communist Party had adopted the simple slogan 'practice is the sole criterion for testing truth' in 1978 to replace the ideological rhetoric that had prevailed since 1949.[59] The explanation lies in the Party's general failure to envisage the consequences of the economic liberalisation launched in 1978.

Contrary to popular belief, as the 'Introduction' pointed out, the reforms were not intended to replace the state's direction of the economy with free market forces. The Chinese Communist Party had not envisaged that free enterprise would come to dominate economic life.[60] Deng Xiaoping did not expect private ownership of business to overtake the state sector. As late as 1985, he confidently predicted that even 'after 20 to 30 years' of economic reform, the state sector would still control 90 per cent of the national economy. That year, the private sector accounted for a mere 3 per cent of industrial output; by 1994, it had raised its share to 61 per cent.[61] Even after nearly three decades of reform, mistrust of the private sector remained a powerful instinct among the nation's leaders, and private property was only given formal political acceptance and full legal protection in 2007.[62] Not until 2008 were farmers given the right to lease or 'transfer their land use rights', telling evidence of the Party's continuing anxiety to set limits to the private sector's expansion.[63]

In the banking sector, this conflict between market reform and state control had been apparent from the start. Following the 1979 conference discussed earlier in this chapter, the banks were officially described as 'the economy's nerve centre', and a flourishing banking industry was said to be crucial to the fortunes of both individual businesses and the economy as a whole.[64] However, the five deputy premiers who had lent their prestige to the conference's proceedings belonged to the Party's 'senior' generation. They were communist revolutionaries by conviction. They were opposed to the weaknesses of the Soviet-style planning but were not in favour of a capitalist restoration. They had engaged since 1976 in a losing battle 'to "reform" the legacy of the chaotic Cultural Revolution and return to the "golden age" of the 1950s'". They launched a new attack on pro-market reforms in the early 1980s.[65] Against this background, the suggestion that banking regulation worked best through encouraging competitive markets remained a challenging concept for the Party leadership. As a result, the banking sector's need for a legal and regulatory structure to oversee the integrity and stability of the emerging free markets and private sector activities was not adequately recognised.[66]

To be fair to the Chinese Communist Party, political unrest was a more immediate danger than the poor banking performance that would result from a failure to establish an adequate regulatory system. The 1978 reforms had been the Party's response to widespread discontent. For example, the evidence is overwhelming that Deng Xiaoping and the Party struggled hard — although in vain — to prevent the end of collective farming. It is only in retrospect that the abolition of the rural communes has come to be seen as the symbol of a new and liberalising mindset within the Chinese Communist Party of the new era.[67] The threat of social unrest had very disturbing implications when it came to the banking industry. An immediate attempt by the government to eliminate 'policy' lending by the banks could have caused a public backlash because the decision to reject or recall bank loans in the case of the larger, unprofitable state-owned enterprises would have led to factory closures. Workers would have become unemployed in large numbers, and existing and retired employees and their families would have lost the pension and welfare rights that the state-owned enterprises provided.

As for 'relationship lending', the involvement of the Chinese Communist Party and the state in every aspect of national life remains a defining feature of China's political system, as this chapter earlier discussed, even though formal controls and central planning have been drastically reduced since 1978.[68] Until 1994, even the People's Bank had to consult provincial and municipal governments before appointing local representatives. Bank managers generally had to rely on the goodwill of local Party and state officials for a range of authorisations and public services essential to their daily operations. Political relationships continued to matter, regardless of the autonomy which reform measures had promised to bank loan officers.[69]

Foreign catalysts

The strategy of using exports to accelerate modernisation could have been the real catalyst for banking reforms. With the breakneck growth of China's foreign trade, the nation's banks faced demands for an escalating volume of financial transactions that interfaced with an increasingly sophisticated, creative and competitive global banking system. At the very least, exposure to foreign techniques and technology, to international management systems and audit processes encouraged by the 'open door' policies should have altered corporate attitudes and businesses procedures in banking just as much as in the rest of the economy. The role of foreign entrepreneurs and investors reached astonishing levels. By July 2010, '698,000 foreign-invested enterprises' with a total paid-up capital of US$1.05 trillion had been set up on the Mainland, and they generated:

- 22 per cent of total tax revenues
- 28 per cent of the nation's industrial value added
- 55 per cent of total foreign trade
- 50 per cent of technology imports
- 45 million jobs[70]

The official Chinese view is that the nation's banking industry was a major beneficiary of this internationalisation and that foreign banks had been essential to the transformation of the nation's banking industry. They had introduced modern banking practices, products and services, the People's Bank has claimed, and they created competition which provided 'incentives for their Chinese counterparts to improve and transform business strategies and management'. Even as minority shareholders, overseas partners were powerful agents for change, offering 'business concepts and management skills so as to further improve the corporate governance of domestic banks'.[71] National banking statistics give a very different impression, however, of the contribution to banking modernisation attributable to foreign banks' activities on the Mainland. At the end of 2009, they accounted for only 1.71 per cent of total assets held by financial institutions in China and an almost identically slim share of their total lending.[72] The truth was that export-driven, foreign-financed growth did not imply that China wished to integrate its banking industry into the international financial system. Nor did it mean that the government proposed to modernise the financial sector through a transformation as rapid and radical as the industrial sector.

The reluctance to adopt the same level of 'open door' treatment for banking as for manufacturing had begun with ideology. Before 1978, China was a bitter critic of the international financial system and a vigorous advocate of fiscal conservatism of the strictest sort. The government boasted of achieving 'a balanced budget with a small surplus' from one year to another which generated 'huge sums for large-scale construction'. This 'self-reliance', Beijing insisted, was 'diametrically opposed' to the dangers of dependence on foreign loans and inflationary deficit finance which prevailed elsewhere.[73] In the mid-1970s, Taiwan's rulers were denounced for 'the economic policy of subservience to foreign capital and national betrayal'. Their offence was to offer foreign investors cheap labour, tax concessions and other investment incentives, together with a dominant role in the island's export industries.[74] The former Soviet Union was castigated for 'its voracity for Western credits' and its large borrowings from United States and West European banks.[75] China then seemed very unlikely to embrace globalisation.

But rhetoric could be forced into second place by economic realities, although until 1978, ideology always carried the greater weight. Prime

Minister Zhou Enlai and his supporters within the Chinese Communist Party leadership had long concluded that growth and modernisation could not be self-financed. In the 1950 and 1960s, they had argued with mixed success in favour of foreign trade and finance to accelerate the rate of technological progress to a level that could not be achieved with the current Party preference for import substitution. In the 1970s, they became even more ingenious in financing imports required for modernisation with foreign credits despite the Party's continuing ideological insistence on self-reliance.[76] Thus, when Deputy Premier Li Xiannian — Prime Minister Zhou's appointee as Finance Minister — announced publicly in 1978 that China would raise foreign loans, 'this may not be quite as dramatic a turnabout in policy as at face value it would seem', the *Financial Times* commented at the time, 'The Chinese have been borrowing abroad through a number of covert means'.[77] As early as 1973, for example, Tianjin officials, in cooperation with the local banking system, had been authorised to introduce compensation trade which relied on funds borrowed from overseas to finance the import of machinery and raw materials needed to boost exports and repay the foreign loan.[78]

With hindsight, it is plain that, by 1978, ideological opposition to moves to liberalise and globalise the economy was doomed. Among the political heresies for which Deng Xiaoping had been dismissed in disgrace by the Maoist radicals in 1976 was his campaign to finance the importation of advanced technology through an export drive, suppliers' credits and foreign borrowings.[79] His recall to office after Mao Zedong's death that year meant that his strategy would prevail.[80] In 1979 Deng personally endorsed the establishment of the China International Trust and Investment Corporation (CITIC). This initiative, according to the official history, brought to an end 'the rigid doctrine that confined the country to the smug fallacy of "a nation of no domestic and external debt"'.[81] At this point, international banks seemed better placed to profit from the economic reforms than foreign industrialists. By 1981 overseas borrowings had been relabelled as another feature of 'economic cooperation'. The government proclaimed that 'the world market and economic and technical cooperation with other countries' — i.e., foreign-financed export industries — would help drive the nation's rush to riches.[82]

But the Chinese bankers' head-start in reviving direct links with international business did not ensure an early solution to the obstacles that blocked the rapid development of foreign participation in Mainland banking. Foreign manufacturers were offered all the forbidden fruits of the pre-1978 era — generous tax and tariff concessions and cheap land and low-cost labour — to induce them to locate their production facilities in China. Foreign bankers, by contrast, were beset with obstacles that changed only slowly in the first 30 years of economic reform. The

Chinese side often sought credits with structures so complex as to be deterrents in themselves, and the overseas lender encountered endless difficulties in trying to verify the credentials of would-be Mainland borrowers and the legal powers of the state agencies authorising the loans and offering guarantees.[83] Confusion and competing interests were common within the various Chinese bureaucracies with whom the foreign bankers had to deal. As the reform era got underway, even physical access to the Mainland was a challenge for bankers, and the approval of a multi-entry visa for an American executive attracted considerable publicity.[84]

Thus, for the foreign banker, the pursuit of China profits was a long and painful process. In early 1986 an official commentary highlighted the gulf between Mainland and overseas business cultures.

> During the past few years, our country has enacted a large quantity of legislation dealing with foreign economic relations. Some of their provisions are vague and open to conflicting interpretations. Others vary according to the locality, the project, the type of investment and other factors which makes them difficult to enforce and difficult for foreigners to understand. Some provisions are baffling because they can be applied at the discretion of the Chinese side but are mandatory for the foreign party. In addition, we are accustomed to being bound by official documents and leading officials' speeches, and for us what counts are policies rather than legislation. This can create the impression for foreigners that even when laws exist, they will be difficult to comply with.[85]

This clash between Mainland practices and overseas expectations continued to cause misunderstanding. During the 1997–98 Asian financial crisis, for example, foreign banks were to discover how misguided were their assumptions about the commitment of the Chinese government to underwrite the overseas borrowings of state-controlled financial institutions, as chapter 4 will explain.

Generation gaps

The persistently low priority given to banking reform is very evident, and its adverse consequences are equally apparent. What is not clear is why banking proved so much less capable of jettisoning the legacy of the past than other sectors of the economy. 'Policy' and 'relationship' lending proved crippling but such practices were not unique to banking.[86] This banking behaviour amounted to discrimination against the private sector generally and independent entrepreneurs in particular but did not prevent them from prospering.[87] The manufacturing sector was subject to arbitrary state directives and the pressures of personal connections.[88]

The rise of world-class export industries is proof that these constraints did not have to become permanent handicaps. Furthermore, in the past, China's bankers had proved themselves extremely resilient in dealing with political challenges. The banks had continued to operate with surprising efficiency throughout the civil wars, Japanese invasion and the constant economic and political turmoil before 1949. Only from that date had the normal services provided by a commercial banking system started to disappear. After 1978, they had to be rebuilt from scratch, it has already been noted, and the banks responded with considerable speed and resourcefulness to the new market environment once the government began to leave enterprises to negotiate their own investment, procurement and marketing deals. The improvisation and ingenuity shown by the banking profession, described earlier in this chapter, made it possible to devise the financial techniques that the transition to a market economy would require.

The bankers involved were survivors of a generation which got its professional training and experience before 1949, especially in Shanghai. The mass campaigns of the Maoist era were designed to eradicate this capitalist heritage, but memories of the past plainly survived.[89] And so did entrepreneurial instincts. The quality of that legacy was demonstrated dramatically in Hong Kong, where senior managers of the state-owned banks had mostly started their careers in pre-1949 Shanghai. In 1979 the Bank of China committed itself to a new business culture. Henceforward, its managers in Hong Kong and abroad were informed, they were to comply with 'international banking practice'. This new-found freedom for its Hong Kong and other offshore branches from past restrictions on undertaking 'capitalist' or 'speculative' activities was credited with enabling a leap in deposits the following year of almost 40 per cent and the highest profits achieved since the Chinese Communist Party came to power.[90] The older generation had forgotten little of their original business skills.

While in the 1980s China's banking industry was able to rely on a useful number of pre-1949 personnel, age and retirement made them a diminishing asset, and they were not numerous enough to perpetuate their professional banking culture, it seems. In the case of Hong Kong, the succession issue was a very visible challenge. Although the average age of the 8,000 staff of the Bank of China group in Hong Kong and Macao was said to be '30 or so' in the mid-1980s, the organisation admitted that 'the problem of aging is rather serious at the leading levels'. The replacements for elderly executives would be chosen, it was officially reported, on 'the principle' of appointing the 'younger in average age, better educated and professionally competent'.[91] The difficulty was that even in Hong Kong, there was no ready pool of such youthful talent that could match the generation which was retiring. On the Mainland the situation was even more serious, and it handicapped the development of a modern banking culture.[92] The best business talent of the next generation had more attractive opportunities with foreign financial institutions, in the securities and export industries or in the 'informal' and often illegal banking sector. Hence, the People's Bank's despair in 1999 that even after 20 years of reforms, the transformation of banking was obstructed by a lack of competent and reliable senior managers capable of reaching the standards demanded by modern banking.[93]

There is another dimension to the generational change. Well before the economic reforms began, the banking profession took very high political risks in managing China's international financial affairs because condemnation of capitalism and imperialism was unrelenting. Bankers managed to ensure, nevertheless, that relations with leading foreign financial institutions survived.[94] This international expertise was visible most conspicuously in Hong Kong, naturally enough because its British status offered some protection against the Mainland's mass campaigns. The introduction of a basket of currencies in the 1970s to manage the Renminbi's parity with major currencies via the Hong Kong dollar was impressive technically but involved ideological as well as commercial risks. The Mainland's bankers in Hong Kong were also dealing with political sensitivities in Beijing when they developed financial procedures to protect Mainland export consignments and their proceeds from court seizure in the United States until outstanding American legal claims against the Chinese government were resolved in 1984.[95] At the same time, senior officials in Beijing required considerable personal courage, as well as political backing, in authorising these involvements in capitalist activities under colonial auspices.

Before 1978, the personnel running the banking system regularly sought to 'normalise' an industry which was always open to disruption for ideological reasons. When economic reforms became national policy, the banking environment was already prepared for a market-driven modernisation. Bankers continued this 'normalisation'. But the enthusiasm for 'modernisation' in terms of institutional change and regulatory reform seemed to shrink, perhaps because the necessary political skills had not been passed on to their successors. This break with the past can be viewed as part of a larger cultural change in bankers' attitudes. Deng Xiaoping's reforms led to a 'transformation of state functionaries' and Party cadres' behavior', an important study of changes in China's banking culture has observed. 'The rigid Maoist ethic of the past with its ban on any form of self-interest and on material incentives' was abandoned, and personal priorities shifted from 'advancing the national interest toward one of self-advancement'.[96]

Conclusion

The issues raised in this chapter point to an important aspect of China's approach to the reform and regulation of banking: rapid improvement has simply not been so essential as the creation of an industrial export base, for example. The nation's overall economic performance has been so outstanding that the non-performing loans and others costs of its banking deficiencies were absorbed without slowing growth. It is true that the banks' poor lending performance could bring even the largest of them to the verge of insolvency. These were essentially domestic problems, however, with the government free to choose its own solutions and the timing of their implementation. China's international financial relations were also buoyant although here losses could not be written off so conveniently or discreetly because global markets are competitive and beyond the reach of Chinese government directives. China's leaders seemed to regard the external situation as also manageable. The next chapter will explain that thanks to Hong Kong, Beijing has always possessed an offshore financial centre that matches global standards and can act as a secure and profitable interface between China's financial system and the rest of the world.[97] The next chapter will also discuss why Hong Kong's role in Mainland banking reforms has been so limited.

4

China's Painful Decisions — Politics in Command

The global financial crisis began with misguided decisions in Washington and London that had catastrophic consequences worldwide. The policy makers stand accused of failing disastrously to recognise there were limits to the virtues of lightly regulated markets and to the efficacy of moral hazard. China's experience of financial modernisation, by contrast, represents the case for the defence in assessing the merits of the intellectual consensus which shaped the Anglo-American regulatory culture. The persistence of state interference with banking business, a disregard for moral hazard and the continued constraints on both domestic and foreign competition imposed serious burdens on China's financial institutions and public finances. These worsened during the international financial crisis, and past banking reforms were put at risk during the struggle to protect the nation from recession in 2008–09. This chapter presents four case studies which review the causes and consequences of this state of affairs.

The first deals with the shock created in Beijing by the 1997–98 Asian financial crisis and which led to radical reforms. Henceforth, it was decided, banks would no longer be forced to provide whatever funds the central or local governments requested as long as the project was part of the state plan. Nor would bank staff be under pressure to approve loans requested by senior Chinese Communist Party or state officials. The tradition of 'policy' and 'relationship' lending was repudiated, and its damage to the banking industry's solvency was audited, publicised and roundly denounced. Similar reform directives in the past had failed (as the previous chapter recounted). Now prospects seemed more promising. Nevertheless, it will be shown, the principles of sound financial regulation were still subject to restrictions which undermined market competition and corporate governance.

The second and third case studies trace the impact of the global financial crisis on the banking industry. Chapter 3 noted how banking modernisation consistently failed to command the sort of priority enjoyed by the industrial sector. As China's exports slowed in 2008, manufacturing had to come first on the national agenda. This sector was generating the prosperity still desperately needed when annual urban disposable income in 2007 was only US$2,000 per head, and a mere US$600 per head for the rural population.[1] The benefits of promoting competitive financial markets and of avoiding moral hazard seemed far less urgent than escaping recession. 'Policy' and 'relationship' lending returned. One case study analyses what happened when financial regulators were obliged to condone the expansion of bank lending to local government vehicles which the state had long condemned as uncreditworthy. The second examines the impact of this inflated lending on the property sector, where a bubble could not be halted without causing loan defaults which the banks would have to absorb.

The final case study deals with the relationship between China's banking reforms and Hong Kong, whose financial markets were free and competitive by the best world standards and which was among the few international financial centres to emerge from the global financial crisis with credit. The study explores why Beijing has made only limited use of the Hong Kong model in driving Mainland banking reforms. This hesitancy does not arise out of any misgivings among China's leadership about Hong Kong's commitment to the nation's best interests.[2] Even under the British colonial administration, this chapter will show, overwhelming priority was given to meeting the requirements of the Chinese authorities.[3] The analysis will describe how Hong Kong's usefulness to China has lain in meeting the Mainland's relatively limited needs for world-class financial institutions and services at this stage of its development.

As the case studies from the United States and the United Kingdom in chapter 2 demonstrated, the threat to financial stability began with official decisions to suspend strict enforcement of the law and regulatory policies. A similar phenomenon had been prominent in the run-up to the Asian financial crisis, and World Bank research had reported that comparable threats to financial stability were common not only throughout Asia but also in such regions as Latin America. A surprisingly large number of bank failures could be traced to political interference, whose consequences were aggravated because 'freedom of the press and an open democratic process are not well established'. Personal and family relationships also tended to play an inordinate role in banking decisions in such countries, this research noted. 'A final dysfunctional sort of government interference' occurred when governments failed to enforce their own regulatory policies designed to promote financial stability.[4] There was an important difference between China and other countries, however. Elsewhere, political interference was generally exercised by relatively weak governments protecting their personal or family fortunes.

In China, the return to 'policy' lending in 2008 was a decision made by a strong administration in pursuit of what its leaders judged to be the best national interests, which made it more difficult for Chinese financial officials to resist.

In China the obstacles to full and free implementation of proper banking behaviour and its regulation were supposed to have been abolished in 1998. 'Policy' lending would end because banks would no longer be compelled 'to allocate credits to support the operations of loss-making state-owned enterprises' and would be free to lend according to commercial considerations. At the same time, 'relationship' lending would be halted by a reorganisation of the People's Bank that would 'strengthen and depoliticise the banking supervision and examination process' and 'deter/prevent local governments from encouraging banks to finance their favoured projects, many of which are over-ambitious and not profitable'.[5] These initiatives failed to achieve their promised goals, and ten years later the IMF was to discover that these two defects had mushroomed in importance, as this chapter later discusses.

Crisis responses

The 1997–98 Asian financial crisis had been a blessing in disguise for China's regulators, and they regularly refer to this event as the real starting point for the modernisation of the nation's financial system and the creation of an impartial and professional regulatory system with an effective measure of autonomy. Official reports of its direct impact on China were carefully understated. Serious casualties seemed confined to ITICs (the international trust and investment corporations). These special investment vehicles established by state agencies and local governments to raise overseas capital had proved attractive to foreign banks. Their drawbacks only emerged after the government refused to bail out illiquid ITICs, as chapter 2 recounted. The People's Bank's published a brief account in 1999 of how eight out of the 238 ITICs had been 'singled out to exit the market'. This exercise was presented as beneficial and intended to 'deter non-compliance and poor management',[6] and the scale and scandal of the defaults seemed to shrink into insignificance. Behind the bland generalisations, however, China had suffered a serious secondary banking crisis.

From the start of the reform era in 1978, Chinese officials frequently resisted foreign bankers' insistence on contractual and similar formalities instead of putting their trust in Chinese goodwill, and foreigners were usually left convinced that legalities did not count.[7] Yet, very early on, China had demonstrated how seriously foreigners ought to take Chinese law. In 1979 exchange rate fluctuations had made a US$2.6

billion contract with Japan more expensive than the state importer in Shanghai had expected. A contractual technicality was invoked that allowed the deal to be cancelled pending renegotiation.[8] Japanese bankers forgot this lesson and were among the victims of ITIC defaults 20 years later. In the case of the ITICs, foreign bankers assumed that since the borrowers were state-owned and controlled, they would not be subject to exchange-control procedures even after this exemption had been withdrawn in 1995.[9] When ITICs ran into trouble during the Asian crisis, officials disclaimed any obligation to intervene and insisted that foreigners were unable to recover their funds because their loans were not in compliance with China's legal requirements (especially its exchange controls). The reality was that the defaulting ITICs were insolvent, and the foreigners could not have been repaid by the ITICs concerned even if the loans had complied with all the legal requirements.

The ITIC crisis surfaced in late 1998 when the Guangdong International Trust and Investment Corporation (GITIC) was discovered to be virtually insolvent with liabilities estimated at over US$4 billion. The Chinese government declined to authorise its rescue.[10] Foreign bankers now learnt that legalities mattered. The insolvent ITICs were not regarded as state entities under Chinese law, and loans which did not comply with state exchange control regulations were at risk of being categorised as unlawful and, therefore, unrecoverable.[11] Chinese officials insisted on strict regard for the law, a message underlined in the then Prime Minister's response to overseas lobbying on behalf of the foreign investors.[12] GITIC's insolvency was followed by a collapse of similar vehicles in other parts of the country and by defaults on samurai and other foreign bonds issued by a dozen or so ITICs. The government decided on a radical overhaul of these institutions, purging firms engaged in unauthorised activities and arresting corrupt officials. By 2004, only 25 per cent of the ITICs originally established were still in business.[13] Foreign lenders had either failed to uncover these unsavoury backgrounds through poor due diligence or had chosen to ignore illicit or imprudent activities on the assumption that as state vehicles, ITICs were above the law. This affair set an important precedent in China's development of the concept of moral hazard: there was no blank cheque for gullible foreigners.

Domestic joint-stock commercial banks were also in trouble, but they were given a temporary reprieve when the government underwrote their liabilities for a year (effectively, until the regional crisis had ended).[14] Here, too, moral hazard was at work. After a bank and 20 small deposit-taking companies in southern China were allowed to fail in 1997–98, the public was on notice that depositors could not take for granted that the state would automatically come to their rescue.[15]

These tremors in the secondary banking sector were minor compared with the plight of other financial institutions in the region. But
the Asian crisis itself proved enough to shock Beijing into a comprehensive review of the financial system. There was now compelling evidence
that a 'fragile financial regulatory system was the main reason behind
the financial crisis', Zhou Xiaochuan, Governor of the People's Bank,
later declared. China could no longer ignore the 'enormous financial
risks' inherited from the era of the 'command economy' in the form
of non-performing loans. On some estimates, according to Zhou, these
were equivalent to half the total assets of the state-owned commercial
banks.[16] The nation's financial system was too vulnerable for comfort,
and the search for stability became urgent.

The objective of the new reform initiatives was the creation of a
system of 'comprehensive, enterprise-like, commercial banks without
direct administrative controls', Zhou stated.[17] The banks were recapi-
talised, as the previous chapter noted, and their non-performing assets
transferred to special-purpose asset management companies. The
largest banks were to be prepared for international listings, which would
introduce 'corporate transparency ... and supervision based on international accounting standards and external audit requirements'. New
regulatory commissions were set up for banking and insurance, in addition to the securities industry.[18] By 2007 'a full-fledged regulatory framework ... has taken shape', the People's Bank confidently asserted, based
on modern legislation and supported by 'effective coordination and risk
monitoring'.[19]

Local, illegal and in default

But old habits proved easy to revive. The global financial crisis gave a
new lease of life to both 'policy' and 'relationship' lending. The US$586
billion economic stimulus package unveiled in 2008 led unavoidably to
an expansion of the state's direct involvement in the economy. Its potential impact on financial stability was largely ignored amidst widespread
endorsement of the anti-recession programme at home and abroad. The
applause was premature since its scale was 'unprecedented', according
to the IMF which warned that 'international history' provided 'compelling' evidence that it would lead to a decline in the quality of bank loans
and an increase in nonperforming assets.[20] A crucial weakness in the
plan was that only 30 per cent of the funds needed were to come from
the central authorities. Local governments were made responsible for
financing a substantial part of the balance, the National Development
and Reform Commission revealed at a press conference. These bodies
were banned from borrowing, either directly or through providing debt

guarantees, but the Commission's Vice Director refused to take this legal obstacle seriously.

> Though Chinese law prohibited local governments from raising capital through bond issues, the central government was considering allowing 'local governments raise funds by loan transfers or through appropriate channels or measures with central approval'.[21]

There was a certain pragmatism about this approach. The 'common practice for a number of years', the IMF report later observed, had been 'for local governments to establish corporate vehicles (capitalized by transfers of money, land, equity, or other government assets), which are then used to borrow' substantial sums, with 'implicit or explicit guarantees from the local government'.[22] Furthermore, the Chinese government believed that local governments could make a larger contribution to the stimulus package than their official accounts indicated.[23] A hunt started in 2009 for 'small coffers', the hidden reserves accumulated by Chinese Communist Party and government agencies.[24]

In addition, the plan to mobilise local government funds had already been tried and tested as a practical response to the global recession. The strategy had been pioneered by Dongguan county, an industrial export base in Guangdong province with a population of 10 million and a 2007 GDP of US$44 billion. One of the first districts to be hit by falling exports in 2008, its local officials put together a package of unemployment benefits, tax concessions, business incentives and investment finance, to be funded with US$570 million from the county's own funds. The county's senior Chinese Communist Party official drew special attention to the package's provisions to prevent a local credit squeeze.

> Since banks are usually cautious about lending during uncertain times, the Dongguan government is helping companies borrow by providing guarantees. "And if loans go bad, the government will help banks by bearing 50 percent of the loans," said [Party Secretary] Liu.[25]

The merits of Dongguan's initiative won national recognition. Its most striking features were the financial reserves at the free disposal of the county and the speed with which county officials were able to announce such financial commitments, including a deal with the local banks. The lack of any legal authority for guaranteeing business borrowers appears to have troubled no one. There was a similar but larger programme announced by another Guangdong entity that pledged to spend over US$4 billion in the next three years on bailing out enterprises hit by the global crisis. It expected this initiative to trigger additional investment by the private sector of more than US$10 billion over the same period.[26] Guangdong appeared to prove that there were ample funds available to local governments, especially in the manufacturing regions, and that local officials could be left to make the best use of available resources to solve local problems, including the creation of partnerships with local banks.

Previously, however, the Chinese authorities had condemned local government borrowings as a threat to financial stability. A national campaign to halt the practice had been launched in 1999 but had little effect. By 2005, the situation had become alarming. Even though the available data were far from comprehensive, local government loans were known to represent a 'menace to the country's fiscal system', and to be well beyond 'repayment capabilities', according to the Party newspaper, *People's Daily*.[27] (The IMF was to repeat this gloomy verdict in its 2010 report.[28]) The practice proved hard to suppress because this financing was the basis of local governments' fiscal autonomy and their ability to adapt or avoid national policies in response to local political and economic realities, an IMF study had discovered in 2005.[29] In addition, despite the problems of servicing local government debt, banks were attracted to this business by the potential profits they could obtain especially from providing credit to the lowest levels of local government. 'Lending rates for township governments and village committees are excessively high', the official media reported in 2006, 'generally above 15 percent, and even up to 30 percent'. The Ministry of Finance was directed that year to begin a new assault on the mounting debt which one local official was reported to have described as 'so huge that no one except the central government can clear it'. The priorities for liquidation included loans raised for 'infrastructure construction and public welfare undertakings'.[30]

Such projects were to be the core of the economic stimulus package announced in 2008 when Beijing's immediate concern was to stave off recession. The Ministry of Finance had hoped that local governments would be able to finance their share of the package through issuing bonds which would be subject to 'very strict regulatory requirements' including full disclosure of their finances. Apparently, only provincial-level governments were able to follow this route, and they raised a mere US$29 billion through bonds floated in 2009 and 2010 and issued on their behalf by the Ministry of Finance.[31] For the rest, an insuperable obstacle soon emerged: 'If they reveal their books, no one would agree to lend', the state media commented. According to this reporting, officials appeared to have no choice but to allow the law to be flouted and let local governments arrange their own borrowings in order to achieve the spending goals set for them by the stimulus package.[32] Even so, these targets could not be met because local governments had run out of both cash and credit before the end of 2009.[33]

Under considerable pressure from Beijing to increase their expenditure, the IMF observed, 'the use of local government invest-ment platforms to finance infrastructure and other projects has been extraordinary'. In defence of the local officials' unlawful behaviour, the IMF accepted that 'many of the investments ... were needed and would ultimately improve the livelihoods of the Chinese people'. In the mean-time, however, Beijing was warned, these illegal practices had increased the threat of financial instability.

> Some part of the expansion in this quasi-fiscal lending will end up as nonperforming loans with negative implications for both local government finances, bank balance sheets, or, potentially, central government finances.[34]

The IMF, nevertheless, did not see instability as an immediate danger: 'The banking system looks well-placed to withstand a significant deterioration in credit quality. Profitability is solid, most banks meet the regulatory requirements of being well capitalized'. Unfortunately, the IMF team was unable to quantify the risks from the illegal borrow-ing. 'Information on the activities of these [local government vehicles] (and their underlying financial condition) is sparse', it discovered, and Beijing was 'only now putting in place systems' to uncover how much they had borrowed.[35] In plain terms, the dangers threatened by local government borrowings which Chinese officials had warned of in 2005 and 2006 could no longer be ignored.

The decision had been taken at high levels in 2008 to encourage financial behaviour that was illegal from the start and potentially impru-dent on an enormous scale. As in the past, the risks involved and the volume of potential defaults were deemed to be affordable. However, in an economy which had spent three decades dismantling the former command and control system, 'policy' lending had become a recipe for mismanagement and misappropriation. China's Auditor General, Liu Jiayi, revealed that a mere 9 per cent of local government borrowing in 2009 was spent on projects related to Beijing's stimulus package. Instead, loans were used to finance 'transport and other infrastructure facili-ties that were started before 2008', his published report declared, and local governments had 'constantly violated state law' to fuel the prop-erty boom.[36] In July 2010, the China Banking Regulatory Commission admitted that 'nearly one-fifth of the bank loans disbursed to local gov-ernments are questionable' but insisted that they would not cause 'any systemic risks to the banking sector'.[37] Despite this reassurance, doubts continued about their impact on the solvency of individual financial institutions.[38]

Perils of property

Prudent management of property exposure was crucial to the health of the banking industry since the People's Bank estimated in 2010 that 'approximately 70 percent of the credit collateral received by commercial banks in China is real estate'.[39] Like many other nations in the first decade of this century, China faced a serious dilemma in managing its property market. 'In an increasing number of the larger cities ... a property bubble is beginning to inflate', the IMF pointed out, which, if left unchecked, risks 'leading to an acceleration of property price inflation followed by a crash in the real estate market', a fate experienced 'repeatedly in other countries'. In the IMF's opinion, the Chinese property market suffered from a deeper, structural problem than a price bubble. Thus, Beijing ought to resist the temptation to leave the market to its own devices even though official intervention could destroy investor confidence unless skilfully managed.[40]

The threat from the property bubble was not just the possibility of 'a misstep in the government's response to rising property prices'. More serious still was the novelty of the housing mortgage business which was barely two decades old. 'Real estate lending in China is relatively a new business that has not been tested in economic cycle changes', Xiang Junbo, Deputy Governor of the People's Bank, had pointed out in 2005, 'there is no available data on the medium and long-term default ratio' to shape lending models. It was also a business especially vulnerable to fraud in China, he warned.[41] The false accounting and outright illegality involved in the business vehicles set up by local governments inevitably fostered crony relations between business and the powerful bureaucracy. Not surprisingly perhaps, the property sector was officially described as among the worst sources of corruption and misconduct within both the Party and state bureaucracies.[42]

For many local governments, financial survival depended on keeping the real estate boom going. Beijing had tacitly recognised this reality from the start, and among the first emergency measures taken in 2008 to counter the global financial crisis were tax concessions and easier mortgage terms to remove any danger of 'a falling property sector'.[43] Reliance on a property bubble had always been a likely outcome of the economic stimulus package and its pressures on local governments. Their borrowings 'had risen beyond their repayment capacity', according to Xiao Gang, Chairman of the Bank of China in late 2009, which threatened the financial system with 'systemic risks'.[44] But local governments still had not raised enough to pay their allotted share of the stimulus package. In October that year, the Ministry of Finance was making desperate efforts to raise an immediate US$173 billion to support the stimulus package. The Ministry, for the first time, authorised local governments to sell more publicly-owned land to finance stimulus projects. This concession reversed efforts made in previous years to reduce their financial dependence on land sales. By now, however, these land receipts were the only hope of repaying their swollen borrowings.[45]

'Land sale revenues for China's local governments rose more than 60 percent in 2009 as the country's property market surged', the Ministry of Land Resources revealed, with housing prices up by almost 8 per cent. Out of total sales receipts of US$233 billion, 84 per cent came from sites bought by property developers.[46] There was a serious moral hazard factor here. China's political system and the limited autonomy of the nation's central bankers and regulators meant that the financial institutions and government agencies hit by losses could take for granted that they would be rescued, for example, by administrative and other measures to avoid forced property sales that could cause prices to collapse.[47]

This chapter explained earlier that financial officials did not have the freedom to resist the government's policy proposals. Thus, even after public alarm had surfaced about the property bubble, Liu Mingkang, Chairman of the China Banking Regulatory Commission, who prided himself on his caution, rejected suggestions in early 2010 that China's fiscal stability was in danger.[48] In mid-2010, Beijing sought to restore both law and orderly markets. The promise of exemption of local governments from the law had proved invaluable in raising bank loans to boost public expenditure and counter an economic downturn. But this 'amnesty' proved illusory, and local governments were left to find their own solution. 'Outstanding loans to local government financing units' had increased by 70 per cent in 2009, according to the Commission, with the help of guarantees which the law forbade. Local governments were now ordered to halt this unlawful practice, clear existing debts and wind up vehicles that were being funded illegally.[49]

Once Beijing had confirmed the risk of a crisis, Liu was free to take action. He announced 'reinforced regulatory requirements' to counter the threat to 'sustainable and sound development' from lending to local government and property. By now 20 per cent of all local government debt to the banks was classified as 'questionable' according to the Commission, which warned that 'surging bad loans could hamper efforts to overhaul the banking sector'.[50] The sense of crisis grew, and a Ministry of Finance research institute estimated that local governments had borrowed the equivalent of 20 per cent of GDP.[51] The banks themselves became targets for criticism as willing accomplices in this improper lending. They had been tempted to disregard the risks involved by 'excessive profits' offered by 'a widening gap between lending and deposit rates', the Commission's Deputy Chairman, Wang Zhaoxing, declared. He indicated very plainly that this imprudent behaviour could have been prevented by effective regulation and promised a tougher regulatory environment and market reforms to eliminate 'unscrupulous and unhealthy financial institutions' in the future.[52] Banking reform and regulation were returning to the agenda once more. In late 2010, the Commission's Chairman was offering an indirect rebuke to his political masters for the 2008-09 measures imposed on the banking industry and calling for a new assertiveness from China's financial regulators. 'Supervisory authorities must have and should have the mandates and independence to do their jobs and to resist any relaxation of supervisory and regulatory standards over time', he boldly insisted, and 'supervisory practices should be invasive and interactive'.[53] At the same time, financial reform and banking regulation were now being hailed by both Party and state as crucial in 'the long-haul, complicated and arduous... undertaking of combating corruption and building a clean government'.[54] In addition, the global crisis had strengthened the case for further market liberalisation, claimed the Bank of China's Chairman, Xiao Gang. China's banking system had proved its resilience, he argued in early 2011, and the time had come to free bankers from state controls on their interest rate decisions and allow them to compete directly for business.[55]

The Hong Kong dimension

As chapter 3 described in detail, China has transformed its economy through mobilising foreign capital and relying on overseas markets on a much vaster and continuing scale than most transition economies and Third World nations. Foreign banks were among the less significant beneficiaries of the 'open door', however, and China has stringently rationed their entry. Beijing has been able to defer international access to its financial markets not only through controls on foreign banks' involvement in onshore business but also through administrative measures, exchange controls and resistance to international pressures for less direct management of its currency. Thus, the expertise needed for financial modernisation has been imported at a minimum cost in terms of competitive threats to Mainland banks and their profits.[56] This situation has been made possible by Hong Kong whose economy throughout its entire modern history — and not just since the end of British rule in 1997 — adjusted to whatever were the prevailing requirements of Beijing, regardless of the United Kingdom's interests, United States' threats or such traditional policy commitments as laissez faire. The following are the key incidents in the development of this relationship.

Guomindang threats

In 1929, China recovered control over its foreign trade and introduced tariffs to protect Mainland industries from foreign competition, including goods shipped via Hong Kong (which accounted for a quarter of the nation's total imports). The ruling Guomindang forced a reluctant Hong Kong to negotiate an agreement to allow Mainland officials to police trade within the colony.[57] After World War II, the Guomindang denounced Hong Kong as a haven for the smugglers and black marketeers blamed for the collapse of the national currency and hyper-inflation. Hong Kong was threatened with a blockade unless it cooperated in outlawing all commercial and currency transactions with the Mainland that violated Chinese law.[58]

In dealing with the Guomindang, not even the colonial tradition of laissez faire was sacrosanct. In the mid-1930s a Hong Kong government report recommended that Hong Kong should be prepared to respond to Mainland protectionism by modifying its opposition to state promotion of local trade and manufacturing.[59] In 1948, the first Banking Ordinance was enacted after arduous negotiations with Guomindang officials determined to see Hong Kong's banks brought under government regulation. (The colonial administration had firmly resisted similar legislation when proposed by London both before and after World War II.)[60]

Cold War embargoes

In 1949 the original foundations of Hong Kong's prosperity disappeared as it lost, almost overnight, all its Mainland business. For a start, the Chinese Communist Party took charge of the nation's foreign trade and its banking. Then the United States imposed a total ban on all commercial and financial transactions with China. Originally a similar embargo was also enforced by the United Nations in response to Korean hostilities, which ended in 1953. But Washington maintained its blockade until 1971.

Even before 1949 Hong Kong had laid the foundations for its survival as Asia's freest business centre in a world of state regulation and licensing. The colonial administration had convinced London that Hong Kong's economic relationship with the Mainland justified exemption from the stringent trade and foreign exchange controls imposed on other Sterling Area members since the start of World War II.[61] This autonomy allowed Hong Kong to operate its international financial centre with considerable political neutrality during the Cold War, when it became the leading source of China's foreign exchange requirements. 'From 1952 to 1979, the Mainland consistently enjoyed a favourable balance of trade with Hong Kong', totalling some US$20 billion, almost 20 per cent of China's total export earnings in this period, a Mainland official later acknowledged.[62] Beijing obtained from Hong Kong enough convertible currency to cover 29 per cent of total Mainland imports during the worst period of China's diplomatic isolation between the start of the Sino-Soviet rupture in 1957 and the onset of normal commercial relations with United States in 1972.[63] That year, China started to use short-term foreign loans to upgrade industry and financed a substantial portion of this new development initiative from deposits garnered by the Bank of China in Hong Kong.[64]

Return to the past

In 1978 recent history was reversed after the 'open door' policies began the restoration of the world's access to Mainland markets. China's economic reform programme allocated to Hong Kong a substantial role in upgrading production capacity especially in Guangdong province.[65] Not that the process was trouble-free. For a start, the province seemed an unlikely candidate for an industrial revolution. Its record of economic development since 1949 was dismal. Its per capita economic growth was amongst the least impressive of China's provinces and major cities from 1952; was actually negative in some years; and in the 1980s was still not top of the national league as it was later to become.[66] Another obstacle was a legacy from the intense Maoist political indoctrination of the past with state personnel posted to the early joint ventures treating their Hong Kong partners with the same hostility as had been shown to businessmen when the state was taking control of China's capitalist activities in the 1950s.[67] Nevertheless, from 1978 Hong Kong transferred the bulk of its manufacturing capacity to southern China, and its historical entrepôt relationship was restored. Its financial institutions were to provide almost half the Mainland's total foreign direct investment, and services became the dominant sector of Hong Kong's economy.

So important did financial services become for Hong Kong that uniquely among advanced economies, its government had a statutory — and after 1997 a constitutional — commitment to maintain Hong Kong's status as an international financial centre.[68] This responsibility has been viewed in a broad sense to include a duty to ensure that that Hong Kong is ranked high among the best international financial centres.[69]

Market power

Hong Kong has also offered foreign investors considerable comfort. A stock market flotation could take place here, offshore from China,

completely free from exchange controls, managed by legal and accounting professionals from American and British firms if preferred, to standards of corporate governance that matched New York and London. The
Hong Kong package included a respected judiciary, independent news
media and an absence of official discrimination against foreign firms
regardless of the political climate. Furthermore, London before 1997
and Beijing thereafter left the Hong Kong monetary and regulatory
authorities with a degree of autonomy that allowed the banking system
and the currency to achieve an unbroken record of stability and integrity from 1986.

Hong Kong acted as the external extension of the Mainland's financial system, an interface with global financial markets which Beijing
could use with complete safety whatever the economic and political circumstances.[70] After China launched its economic reforms in 1978, Hong
Kong's facilities and expertise as an international financial centre put
Beijing in a position to deal with multinational banks on a basis of equality. Beijing was able to adopt an unusual 'transactional model' for modernising the banking system.

> China's approach to banking reform stands out as unique among
> emerging markets with a recent history of financial sector reform.
> Rather than privatizing banks and transferring control to foreign
> investors — the dominant strategy in Eastern Europe and most of
> Latin America — China sold minority stakes in its largest banks
> to a group of selected foreign strategic investors ... Foreign finan-
> cial intermediaries were sought as strategic partners for helping
> to transform China's banks and making them competitive both at
> home and abroad.[71]

This model was not designed originally for the banking industry. Instead, it was part of Beijing's broader strategy to compel major
Mainland corporations to transform their managements and corporate
governance. They would be forced to submit themselves to the discipline of obtaining a quotation on a modern, competitive stock market.
Between 1993 and the start of the exercise in 2005 to list China's four
largest banks, 316 Mainland enterprises had already been floated in
Hong Kong, raising over US$120 billion.[72] In terms of improved cor-
porate performance, the results of these flotations were impressive.
Research evidence indicated that overall, Mainland firms which listed
in Hong Kong achieved better standards of corporate governance
than firms with Mainland listings only, and were rewarded with higher
market valuations.[73] The model smoothly delivered a similar success in
bringing China Construction Bank, Bank of China and Industrial and
Commercial Bank to the market. The state retained control, but formal

ownership — and accountability — was transferred to a variety of investors including a handful of foreign banks.

The fourth candidate for flotation was the Agricultural Bank, which proved a far more difficult operation and could not be launched until 2010. This bank's prospectus revealed the strains suffered by China during the global crisis. In 2008 the government had spent US$117 billion on a new bailout of this bank, equivalent to almost a quarter of its loan book. But the following year it had to participate in the general expansion of bank lending in response to official directives to support the economic stimulus programme, which created the danger of substantial quantities of new non-performing loans. [74] To achieve what turned out to be the world's largest ever IPO, heroic efforts were made by the Chinese authorities to mobilise the maximum possible support for the flotation from institutional investors, both Mainland and offshore.[75] Beijing could make it look profitable enough to launch, but there were misgivings about the Agricultural Bank's business prospects thereafter.[76]

Investor scepticism had increased with the realisation that in 2010 the 'transactional model' did not match the market mood. Foreign bankers were no longer attracted by a role as catalysts for the modernisation of China's banking industry once global markets had plunged and their own capital adequacy was under pressure. Of the six overseas financial institutions which had become minority shareholders in the original bank offerings, two (RBS and UBS) were glad to sell their stakes and take the profits, while the other four liquidated part of their holdings.[77] The euphoria was over.[78] The concept of a flotation that would create a reform dynamism in giant state banks had lost its persuasiveness, and the 'transactional model's' limitations were now more obvious. When the model was first unveiled, the perception had been that 'overseas investors provided a "one-stop" shop for enterprise reforms' with 'a professional investor base intent on scrutinizing accounts and management decisions [and creating] in most cases … better-managed, more profitable and transparent companies'.[79] If there was an improvement in banking performance, it was barely perceptible to business executives if the reports in the World Bank's *Doing Business* surveys were anything to go by.[80]

Had it ever been reasonable to expect that a handful of non-executive directors from abroad and some scores of expatriate professionals on secondment could have much impact on the culture of the 1.5 million employees of the four state-owned commercial banks that were floated? Worse still, although the listing exercise exerted considerable pressure for 'corporate transparency enhancement, and supervision based on international accounting standards and external audit requirements', according to the People's Bank,[81] these improvements did nothing to overcome 'policy' and 'relationship' lending. The new shareholders were not consulted over the forced expansion of lending in support of the government's economic stimulus package (whose adverse implications were discussed earlier in this chapter).

There was one important but unanticipated reform that these bank flotations achieved. They compelled financial officials to account for their policies and performance to the general public. Beijing claimed that the flotations were all about modernisation and reform. China did not need the money which the banks raised, it was argued, since its burgeoning foreign reserves were already a source of serious international embarrassment. The Chinese public took a totally different view, however, and officials were forced to deny publicly that foreigners were getting assets on the cheap.[82] The truth was that the national programme to list state enterprises led, almost always, to assets being sold cheap to anyone lucky enough to get a share allocation.[83] Under-pricing of share flotations in China was described as the world's worst by the World Bank. Unlike other countries, the loser was the public because all the shares sold were state-owned. The World Bank calculated that on the flotations in the first quarter of 2007 alone, the equivalent of US$9.5 billion was lost in potential government revenue, which was 'US$1.5 billion more than the total sum the central government spends on the free rural education program'. To the credit of China's financial officials, they had made a public pledge to match bank flotations to market conditions, which they honoured. There was no significant mispricing.[84]

Cultural exchanges

A final issue is the impact of the special relationship with Hong Kong on the Mainland's regulatory culture. By the mid-1980s, the potential contribution of Hong Kong's banks to China's rapid economic development was well understood. The colonial administration's decision to liberalise bank licences in that decade was followed by a surge in applications from foreign banks. These regarded Hong Kong as 'an ideal base' from which to develop their China business, one detailed Mainland analysis reported. As an international financial centre, Hong Kong had access to 'abundant capital' and earned 'high fees for high quality services and made big profits from the large-scale trade in commodities'. It could mobilise investment capital on a 'huge scale', and detailed cases were cited of how its international bankers were funding the transformation of the nation's industrial capacity. And this report also recognised the broader range of financial services which Hong Kong offered in support of business.[85] There was considerable official encouragement to use Hong Kong as a 'reference' and for learning from its success in eradicating corruption, preventing state-business cronyism and establishing the legal framework for financial markets.[86] Nevertheless, in practice, there was no rush by the Mainland to import the drastic measures that had reformed Hong Kong banking so radically from 1986 onwards.

The China Banking Regulatory Commission established a substantial working relationship with the Hong Kong Monetary Authority with regular meetings between their officials. But Hong Kong's input appears to have been related mainly to enforcement and supervision and contributed through staff secondments and training of professional personnel.[87] There were some similarities in approach, all the same. The Commission's Chairman advocated keeping regulation 'simple and basic', which meant 'prudential rules, ratios, limits and targets'. His Commission adopted as its best defence against imprudence quantitative restrictions on bank lending which were very similar to Hong Kong's own practice.[88] On the whole, however, China's financial officials preferred to take as their template 'the international financial standards developed by the Basel Committee on Banking Supervision and other informal networks of financial supervisors'.[89] China needed time to develop its capacity to make full use of what Hong Kong had to offer. The Mainland and Hong Kong had made some 'notable cooperative efforts', Joseph Yam, the Hong Kong Monetary Authority's Chief Executive stated, but for two such very different financial systems, 'the process has not always been a smooth one [and] neither has the outcome been as productive as it could be'. Obstacles were inevitable in the transition from state controls, Yam pointed out, and 'the Mainland authorities have to weigh carefully the benefits of financial liberalisation with the over-riding need to avoid doing anything that will destabilise such a large and complex economy'.[90]

To the extent that Mainland banks needed to match international standards in conducting their business, they could use Hong Kong for the purpose, and Beijing could be confident that there they would be compelled by its financial regulators and market competition to conform to world best practice. As an international financial centre, Hong Kong has enjoyed the approval of China's leaders since the start of the Cold War. In 1957 Prime Minister Zhou Enlai publicly emphasised Hong Kong's crucial role in China's financial relations with the rest of the world and consistently defended it against ideological extremists thereafter, even from the grave.[91] Its performance has ensured its pre-eminence ever since. Regulatory standards were an essential ingredient in Hong Kong's success, Prime Minister Wen Jiabao pointed out in 2009. However, 'the status of an international financial center is established not by a government decision but through market competition', he declared.

I have said years ago that Hong Kong's status as an international financial center is irreplaceable due to its unique geographical advantage, a long history of financial management, extensive channels of financial operation, a full-fledged legal system and a rich pool of financial expertise.[92]

5

Hong Kong — From Scandals to Stability

As a remote and indefensible British colony perched on the edge of China which did not recognise London's right to rule, Hong Kong was a political anachronism whose survival was always at risk. Its economic strategy was also a relic from the 19th century: free trade and no import or currency restrictions; low taxes and small government; negligible state borrowing and regular budget surpluses; minimal interference with market forces and no state planning; no development subsidies and no investment incentives. The city, nevertheless, boasts an exceptional record of economic success against even more extraordinary odds.

World War II had left it 'the most looted city in the world'.[1] Its pre-war population of some 2 million had been reduced to 600,000 during the Japanese occupation. By 1949 Hong Kong had been overwhelmed by a million immigrants seeking refuge from civil war and the Chinese Communist Party's revolution on the Mainland, yet it was to receive almost nothing in foreign aid and no international development assistance. Although Western governments were to seek to shut their markets to Asian exports of light industrial goods, Hong Kong managed to become 'the de facto control centre of the world's textile and garment trade', a status that lasted until the end of the century.[2] Its GDP increased every single year in real terms from at least 1961 until 1998, and its 6.5 million people had achieved prosperity faster than any other society in history, it has been claimed.[3] At the same time Hong Kong stood out by Asian standards for its political and social stability even though the British declined to introduce parliamentary democracy.[4]

Remarkable, too, was Hong Kong's ability to function as an autonomous international financial centre with its own currency despite its lack of political sovereignty. It maintained a free currency market when the rest of Asia and most Western nations imposed severe exchange controls, and its banking system was the most open and international in the region. Hong Kong became the largest source of the external investments that financed China's breakneck growth from 1978. Until the final

years of the British era, its financial affairs were controlled by expatriate colonial officials remote from the community and whose judgments
were deeply flawed, as will be discussed in the analysis that follows. All
the same, China's leaders regarded its contribution to the nation's economic wellbeing as so important that they took extraordinary measures
to preserve its capitalist system and its economic, financial and commercial autonomy after the end of colonial rule in 1997. As this chapter
will explain, however, its achievements as the nation's principal interface
with the international financial system were accompanied by a history of
regulatory misjudgments and financial crises that had much in common
with the defective performance of American and British central bankers
and financial regulators in recent decades.

This chapter will recount how Hong Kong learnt the lessons of its
scandalous banking history. Financial stability became a goal for which
laissez-faire doctrines had to be sacrificed. Financial markets were the
special case, the one sector of the economy in which traditional non-
interventionist policies were discarded because they had proved unacceptable to the business community and the general public alike. In
the process, Hong Kong discovered that strict regulation of financial
markets and their players did not stifle either growth or innovation nor
did it diminish its attractions as an international financial centre. The
discussion will also recount how disturbing observers have found this
disparity between Hong Kong's staunch free-market reputation and its
increasingly strict financial regulation.

The Hong Kong challenge

The contrast between Hong Kong's apparent vulnerability and its ability
to prosper in an unpromising environment was very evident during the
2007–09 international financial crisis. Why were some economies so
much less affected by the global disaster than countries with much the
same financial systems and regulatory arrangements, an International
Monetary Fund (IMF) team has asked. The explanation, it suggested,
was 'simply "better supervision"'.[5] Hong Kong's record supports the
IMF's verdict. 'As one of the most open economies in the world and with
its focus on financial and trade services', Hong Kong could have been
especially vulnerable 'to the unfolding crisis in international financial
markets and to the slowdown in the global economy', the IMF observed.[6]
New York and London were its closest trading and corporate partners in
the financial services sector (which accounted for 20 per cent of Hong
Kong's GDP). In contrast to light-touch American and British policies,
Hong Kong had adopted 'more hands-on supervision and regulation to
limit risk ... [and] subjected banks to strict liquidity requirements', the

IMF noted, 'This left financial institutions in a better position to cope with deposit runs ... produced safer financial systems'.[7] Exactly a decade earlier, it will be noted later, the IMF had joined a chorus of disapproval of Hong Kong's interventionist approach to market stability. Thanks to what the IMF now lauded as 'steady strengthening of financial sector regulation and supervision in recent years', Hong Kong suffered far less damage in terms of market disruption, institutional stability and public confidence than did New York and London.[8]

Hong Kong's performance presents a serious challenge to the Anglo-American prescription of deregulation which has been widely accepted elsewhere in the world as the best strategy for financial development. An increasingly strict regulatory régime since 1986 did nothing to hinder Hong Kong's success as a major location for financial institutions active in Asia, and its financial markets flourished, as its 2009–10 international rankings indicated.[9]

- International banking: 71 of the world's 100 largest banks had offices in Hong Kong
- FDI: the world's fourth largest recipient and Asia's second largest
- Foreign exchange market: the world's seventh largest
- Stock market capitalisation: seventh highest in the world and third in Asia
- IPOs: the world's largest total of funds raised

These impressive volumes of transactions were generated overwhelmingly by demand from the Chinese Mainland. Nevertheless, Hong Kong's financial markets continued to be influenced more by developments in United States markets than by Mainland trends.[10]

Heroes or heretics?

In a 2009 review of the global crisis by the Bank of England, its Deputy Governor drew attention to the contribution made by regulatory intervention to Hong Kong's financial stability and its relevance to policy-making elsewhere.

> Loan to income and loan to value ratios tend to rise in any credit boom as lending standards become lax and asset prices inflate. In theory, a ceiling on these ratios could have provided an effective brake on the excesses of the last boom [in the United Kingdom] ... the Hong Kong Monetary Authority showed how such an approach could work in practice in the 1990s: tightening the constraint on loan-to-value ratios as their property market threatened to overheat.[11]

This endorsement was all the more impressive given the general opposition from leading officials and academics to quantitative restraints on bank lending and mortgages as a protection against the emergence of property bubbles.[12]

Such commendations for Hong Kong's regulatory endeavours were a very recent development. An almost universal assumption was that this was the one economy which imposed virtually no restrictions on market behaviour. A post-1998 survey of governments in the East Asian region showed that Hong Kong remained the conspicuous exception to almost every form of state involvement in management of the economy and state interference with business.[13] Its non-interventionism was of special importance to proponents of economic liberalism, for whom Hong Kong had taken on an iconic status.

> The United States has not enjoyed fully-fledged laissez-faire capital-ism since the First World War. Indeed, the only country that has enjoyed such status in living memory was the small British colony of Hong Kong before it became the Hong Kong Special Administrative Region of the People's Republic of China in 1997. For laissez- faire implies the existence only of a minimal state that serves primarily as a free market referee.[14]

Custodians of the Anglo-American regulatory culture claimed that the most heroic advocates of their principles were to be found in Hong Kong. For Milton Friedman, the paragon of economic rectitude in rejecting Keynesian heresies was Sir John Cowperthwaite. He had first become involved in Hong Kong affairs when he joined a team in London planning the colony's future during World War II. He quickly won the confidence of his senior colleagues after he arrived in Hong Kong in 1946 and had a powerful influence on economic policy even while still relatively junior. As Hong Kong's Financial Secretary in the 1960s, Friedman declared, Cowperthwaite pursued 'a laissez-faire capi-talist policy', and his legacy was 'a striking demonstration of the pro-ductivity of freedom, of what people can do when they are left free to pursue their own interests'.[15] His principal achievement in fact had been political rather than economic: the successful campaign to win financial autonomy from the United Kingdom and establish the local currency's independence after the sterling crisis of 1967. Friedman also mentioned approvingly Cowperthwaite's successor Sir Philip Haddon-Cave. He had started his colonial career in Africa and came to fame in Hong Kong as a tough textile negotiator. Less intelligent than Cowperthwaite, he took over as Financial Secretary in 1971. The world's adoption of float-ing exchange rates in the 1970s and Hong Kong's mounting inflation in the same decade left him baffled but he kept his job until 1981.

The historical record demonstrates that neither official adhered to non-intervention as an article of faith. Cowperthwaite had frequently advocated departures from laissez faire: cheap land and subsidised finance to promote manufacturing in the 1940s and anti-monopoly measures against public utilities in the 1950s.[16] He introduced rent controls in 1962 and contemplated assistance for 'infant industries' and the introduction of building licences to control the over-heated property sector.[17] Haddon-Cave was more interventionist still. He reversed his predecessor's rejection of demands for subsidised industrial loans and government measures to promote Hong Kong as a financial centre.[18] He endorsed proposals in 1979 for government incentives to take advantage of the expected oil boom in the South China Sea (which did not materialise), and he actively sought to facilitate the shift from manufacturing to services.[19]

Stability first

All the same, Hong Kong's activist approach to financial regulation was in sharp contrast to its general commitment to laissez-faire as a basic principle for social as well as economic policy. This apparent ideological contradiction had a long history. Stability of the financial system had been the great exception to the non-interventionism preached by the classical British advocates of laissez faire. They had warned that threats to the stability and integrity of the financial system could not be ignored with impunity.[20] Hong Kong's government had long since learnt this lesson, as the Hong Kong Monetary Authority explained:

> The fact of the matter is that free markets can sometimes fail. Free markets can sometimes behave in a manner very much against the long term interests of society. When this occurs, if those of us in the Administration hide conveniently behind the banner of free markets and do nothing, we are failing in our duties.[21]

In modern Hong Kong, regulation is expected to be a continuous and predictable feature of its financial markets, and statutory oversight of financial markets and institutions has come to be regarded as a normal function of government rather than as an assault on economic freedom. Under Hong Kong's monetary arrangements, intervention includes using public funds to defend the stability of the financial system (together with the linked exchange rate to the United States currency). This is a remedy of last resort but is regarded as the unavoidable price to be paid if depositor confidence starts to crumble after the regulators fail to ensure the solvency and integrity of the banks. Such government intervention is also accepted as the cost of stabilising financial markets when threatened by external shocks which are outside Hong Kong's control.[22]

The insistence on its own regulatory model was especially striking because Hong Kong had not resisted any other aspect of the globalisation process. The United States and the United Kingdom were its largest trading partners in financial services.[23] This continuing Anglo-American connection was the natural outcome of Hong Kong's status as a leading — and often the largest — Asian international financial centre since early in the 20th century.[24] The legal standards, corporate governance and business practices adopted by New York and London had been imported wholesale. Yet, when it came to its financial affairs, Hong Kong rejected the consensus in favour of deregulation which the United States and United Kingdom had made the guiding principle for financial markets worldwide. Significantly, rejection of the key concepts espoused by the Anglo-American regulatory culture — virtuous markets and moral hazard in particular — came only after they had been discredited in Hong Kong during six decades of recurrent financial crises from the 1920s.

Overseas reaction to this approach offers an important illustration of the powerful emotions associated with the 'conviction economics' that have underlain the Anglo-American regulatory culture. Hong Kong would not be budged from its belief that its special circumstances required the development of its 'own mechanism for a macro-prudential approach to financial regulation and supervision' regardless of the dominant Anglo-American regulatory culture and despite its long-standing integration into global markets to a very high degree.[25] This refusal to follow the prevailing intellectual consensus in its regulatory measures and monetary arrangements provoked intense and potentially damaging denunciation from foreign financial officials and opinion-makers, as this chapter will recount.

Conflicting images

Hong Kong may have been more interventionist in practice than the purists would like, but it had also been rated as the world's 'freest economy' by such institutions as the American Heritage Foundation and the Canadian Fraser Institute every year since the mid-1990s. It remained as laissez-faire as was compatible with financial stability and the community's expectations of accountable government. Nevertheless, to the indignation of those who lauded Hong Kong as a model of uncompromising laissez-faire, its officials were ready to intervene dramatically during a crisis. Critics rarely understood that laissez-faire had never been unlimited in Hong Kong but primarily a matter of political convenience.[26] The rare but dramatic examples of direct government intervention in financial markets over the last three decades led to shocked outrage among advocates of Hong Kong as the ultimate free economy. Few commentators realised that although deregulation had been widely accepted elsewhere in the world as the best strategy for financial services since the 1980s, Hong Kong's own financial markets had grown rapidly despite the tougher regulatory standards imposed since 1986.[27]

The contrast between Hong Kong's laissez-faire reputation and its regulatory realities first provoked overseas criticism in the year following these radical reforms. After world stock markets collapsed on 'Black Monday' in October 1987, the Hong Kong government felt compelled to bail out the futures market. But a bigger offence still for many critics was that Hong Kong became 'the only major stock exchange to close its doors during the crash', an emergency measure made necessary because its two stock and futures exchanges were 'particularly vulnerable to abuse'.

> The decision provoked enormous criticism from around the world. Hong Kong was denigrated as a "Mickey Mouse" market and was accused of reneging on its financial responsibilities. It was widely suggested that it had destroyed its credibility as an international financial center.[28]

Hong Kong was to face almost identical criticism during the Asian financial crisis that began in 1997. During the summer of 1998, its financial system came under severe pressure. The government believed that the economy's survival could not be left to the mercy of the markets, as Donald Tsang, the Financial Secretary, later explained.

> Our econometric models told us that had we not done anything, the Hang Seng Index, which was then trading at about 6,000, would go down to about 4,000 in a couple of days and then keep on falling. Interest rates would rise to 50% for weeks and stay there ... We asked ourselves, what's wrong with Hong Kong. What's happened to us. We balance our budget. We regulate our banks well. We have a reasonable balance of payments. We do not deserve this.[29]

In defiance of the Anglo-American culture which dominated regulatory policies elsewhere, the government embarked on an intervention exercise that was 'almost unique' not only in 'size, scope and intensity', according to the distinguished banking economist, Charles Goodhart, but also 'a rare example of waging a successful battle against speculators'.[30] Bitter attacks on Hong Kong followed, nevertheless, with the most damaging comments coming from Alan Greenspan, then Chairman of the Federal Reserve Board.

> I think that the effort on the part of the Hong Kong authorities

to try to jack up their stock market was an unwise effort. One, I don't think it can succeed. And, two, I think that the consequences of doing that erode some of the extraordinary credibility that the Hong Kong monetary authorities have achieved over the years.[31]

This gloomy prediction proved no more accurate than the ominous forebodings that had followed the 1987 market intervention. The linked exchange rate did not buckle in 1998, and share prices quickly stabilised. The government was showing a profit of over US$11 billion a year later on the US$15 billion initially allocated to this rescue operation.[32]

Greenspan had been speaking on behalf of a very wide constituency well beyond the United States. The IMF expressed misgivings, albeit in measured terms. It had no hesitation in declaring in 1998 that 'the financial position of Hong Kong's banks, and the quality of the regulatory and supervisory system, are very strong by international standards'. But it warned that 'the [intervention] strategy has also had costs'.

> ... in particular, it has raised concern about the role of the government in the securities market, potential conflicts of interest, a reduction in the free float for many shares; greater difficulties in hedging, which has affected trading in certain derivatives markets; and a loss of competitiveness of certain financial products compared with offshore markets.[33]

The financial press was much less restrained, both editorially and in reporting the views of business executives and economists.

> ... the government casually tossed aside the carefully cultivated free-market ethics that have distinguished Hong Kong from other Asian markets ... The ultimate ignominy now seems to lurk on the horizon — a forced end of the 14-year-old link to the U.S. dollar. (*Far Eastern Economic Review*)[34]

> Donald Tsang, Hong Kong's financial secretary ... is left with an estimated US$13bn to US$14bn hole in the US$96bn reserves, strained investor confidence and plenty of speculators betting on a falling market into September. (*Financial Times*)[35]

> A poisonous air of mistrust pervades Hong Kong following the government's stock market intervention of 1998 ... [Some bankers] say the rhetoric employed by Hong Kong civil servants during the intervention period was the sort of thing they're used to hearing from Beijing's propaganda machine. (*FinanceAsia*)[36]

Prejudice persists

This long-running controversy was less about practical issues than 'ideological' principles.

Hong Kong was seen by academics as an exemplar of the relationship between economic growth and liberal, non-interventionist, but properly regulated, institutional environments. Milton Friedman even went so far as to suggest that to understand "how the free market really works, Hong Kong is the place to go". However, by 1999, Friedman was bemoaning a Hong Kong government that was "disposed to more frequent regulation" … a series of government actions [in the following years] seemed conspicuously to have eroded the free-market, non-interventionist, impartial image with which the city had, correctly or otherwise, become synonymous.[37]

In criticising Hong Kong, Friedman and Greenspan were acting in defence of what a leading British regulator has described as the intellectual consensus embraced by bankers, officials and economists almost everywhere prior to the global crisis.

… there was a philosophy of regulation which emerged, not just in this country but in other countries, which was based upon too extreme a form of confidence in markets and confidence in the ideas that markets were self-correcting, which therefore believed that the fundamental role of the supervision of financial institutions, in particular banks, was to make sure that processes and procedures and systems were in place, while leaving it to the judgment of individual management to make fundamentally sensible decisions. As Alan Greenspan said, that is the intellectual framework which has received an extraordinary challenge.[38]

As Chairman of the Federal Reserve of the United States from 1987 to 2006, Greenspan had been the leading proponent of this international regulatory culture. His opposition to state involvement in the markets was uncompromising and justified by an insistence on 'how much better situated and staffed banks were to understand what other banks and hedge funds were doing as compared with the "by-the-book" regulation done by government financial regulatory agencies'.[39]

Even after it became clear that Hong Kong had done much more than merely survive the Asian financial crisis, former critics found it hard to abandon their 'conviction economics'. The IMF could not bring itself to withdraw its original misgivings about the 1998 market stabilisation. Despite conceding that by every criterion of prudent banking, sound regulation and effective monetary decisions, Hong Kong's record in 1997–98 was outstanding, a 2001 IMF report could not resist citing 'good luck' as an explanatory variable.[40] In 2007–09, policy postures altered, and market intervention had become the first line of defence for American and European governments as they struggled to stabilise their crumbling financial systems. Hong Kong's 1998 stock market foray now looked respectable. Greenspan was a good indicator of changing views, and in 2009 he belatedly complimented Hong Kong on the success of its 1998 strategy.[41] The Bank of England was prepared to go further back in history, and in 2010 it acknowledged that the emergency measures taken by Hong Kong in response to the 1987 global crash had been justified.[42] But there were limits to this 'rehabilitation'. The IMF was generally complimentary about the contribution made to Hong Kong's outstanding record in 2007–09 by its interventionist policies. But its achievements were depicted very much as a special case and of limited global relevance.[43]

An ideal partner

Hong Kong looked like a natural Asian outpost for the Anglo-American regulatory culture which paralleled a similar phenomenon in an earlier age. In the 19th century, there had developed a 'global civil society', it has been argued, modelled on British values, most notably in 'business transactions across continents and cultures', from which emerged 'a "like-mindedness" … created, managed and financed by Britain'.[44] Hong Kong was a British colony until 1997, and its legal and administrative arrangements were an imperial importation. How could it avoid acting as an extension of the United Kingdom economy and a branch of the London markets?[45] Furthermore, the commitment to laissez faire seemed to have become even stronger after 1997 because the Chinese government had entrenched the non-interventionist traditions of the British era in the Basic Law, the constitutional blueprint for the post-colonial administration, including the free port, free movement of capital and currency, balanced budgets and minimal taxation.

Hong Kong also seemed very close to the United States and the United Kingdom in its economic 'ideology'. Its professional economists, almost without exception, belonged to the Chicago School[46] and believed that Hong Kong's 'economic miracle' was best explained by its 'minimal government intervention in the market' and 'an unusual degree of economic and civic freedoms'.[47] They vigorously opposed government involvement in economic and social affairs, even during the Asian financial crisis.[48] The colonial administration itself was rarely doctrinaire. But when it came to economic theories, officials were implacably opposed to Keynesianism.[49] This hostility had once been a feature of British colonial territories in general, which preferred balanced budgets to deficit financing and foreign loans.[50] But after World War II, colonial attitudes altered rapidly except in Hong Kong where officials argued that Keynesianism was particularly unsuited to the small open economy; would lead to financial irresponsibility; and would 'create an immediate balance of payments crisis'.[51]

By the 1970s the Financial Secretary, Haddon-Cave, was so fearful of raising expectations of a Keynesian approach to public finance that he avoided using the words 'monetary policy' in public.[52] This outlook survived the end of British rule. After 1997, Tung Chee Hwa, the first Chief Executive, declared himself unable to adopt reflationary policies despite the first recession in some four decades.

> It would have been easier for all of us, in the short run, to ease back into another bubble economy built on asset price inflation, and supplementing them with heavy doses of Keynesian fiscal and monetary stimulus. But let me tell you, we are definitely not taking that route.[53]

With this anti-Keynesianism went a conviction that the Hong Kong economy was self-correcting.[54] The economy was believed to adjust automatically so that markets were best left to find their own solutions to monetary shocks and to the ups and downs of the business cycle.[55] During a financial crisis at the start of the 1980s, the exchange rate collapsed, and the need for more activist monetary policies seemed overwhelming. The currency was only stabilised by linking it to the United States dollar in 1983. But the 'ideological' bias against market involvement was so strong that officials could not bring themselves to reveal how much intervention was required to make a success of the newly-established linked exchange rate.[56]

Legacy of mistrust

An important factor in forming Hong Kong's economic and financial policies was a struggle for autonomy which created very powerful disincentives against adopting the Anglo-American culture. Hong Kong had a long history of political and economic disputes first with London and later also with Washington. Hong Kong had developed its own political culture in which an absence of 'patriotism' and a preference for 'political neutrality' were defining features of its external policies.[57] As early as 1935, an official Hong Kong report had stated bluntly that the colony's interests were generally ignored or even sacrificed by London when it came to foreign trade and recommended that Hong Kong ought to be free to ignore Colonial Office economic directives and manage its own external commercial relations.[58] By 1961 London had realised that 'crudely stated', Hong Kong's policy was that if the United Kingdom's textile industry 'was going to be ruined, it might as well be at the hands of Hong Kong as those of third countries'.[59]

The most telling example of Hong Kong's determination to protect its financial interests regardless of London's instructions was its reluctance to help defend the British pound in the years when this was the overwhelming concern of the British government. Hong Kong resisted enforcing the Sterling Area's exchange controls. This policy of insubordination was initiated discreetly by the Governor himself,[60] and it was reinforced by starving London of information it needed to monitor foreign exchange flows and banking activities in the colony.[61] As sterling's crisis worsened in the 1960s, Hong Kong intensified its efforts to manage its monetary affairs independently of London.[62] By the 1970s, London had been compelled to accept Hong Kong's financial autonomy — despite its colonial status — but warned that this freedom came at a price: Hong Kong could not depend on the United Kingdom to come to its rescue in any future crisis.[63]

Relations with Washington were always going to be strained because of American protectionist policies. The United States, like other developed countries, tended 'to discriminate against finished products from simple, labour-intensive industries and in favour of trade in raw materials and semi-processed natural resources', with Hong Kong as a major target.[64] Washington's demands for the right to police export controls on the ground in Hong Kong also created friction, as did disputes over intellectual property rights.[65] After Hong Kong had become a major international financial centre, American officials accused Hong Kong of tolerating dubious business practices in the financial sector, a row which did not end until the late 1990s.[66]

But the biggest cause of resentment in Hong Kong was Washington's campaign during the Cold War to block all China's commercial and financial transactions with the outside world. Hong Kong's survival depended on its economic relations with the Mainland, and it was identified as the largest potential loophole in the blockade and made a prime target for American surveillance and sanctions.[67] When North Vietnam also became subject to a United States embargo, Washington used investment pressure in an unsuccessful bid to force Hong Kong to close the port to ships bound for Hanoi.[68]

Even without these political tensions, Hong Kong had persuasive grounds for reservations about the gains to be obtained from falling in with the Anglo-American regulatory culture. Hong Kong's financial officials believed that they did not need Anglo-American guidance on professional oversight of financial markets.[69] Its 1964 Banking Ordinance had established a modern regulatory system with statutory authority, one of its senior financial officials boasted, '15 years before Britain took much milder supervisory powers'.[70] In the 1970s, the arrival of the new, American, money-centre banking model was accompanied by an increase in self-destructive behaviour among international financial institutions in Hong Kong which, as will be explained below, created an irresistible case for more regulation.[71] In the 1980s, Hong Kong's financial independence became all the more important as the transition to the resumption of Chinese sovereignty began and the process of defining the 'high degree of autonomy' to be incorporated into the Basic Law got under way.[72] Hong Kong could not hope to win Beijing's endorsement of its role as a financial centre if it were perceived as a satellite of New York or London.

Concepts in common

Hong Kong, nevertheless, had begun the development of its regulatory arrangements with very much the same preconceptions that the Anglo-American culture was to incorporate in a later period. The colonial administration's earliest discussions of monetary affairs frequently foreshadowed the Chicago School, and the presentations of contemporary American and British regulators are very similar in outlook to their Hong Kong counterparts in earlier decades especially in addressing the concepts of virtuous markets and moral hazard.

Virtuous markets

The Anglo-American consensus asserts that the regulatory process does more harm than good. American officials argued in 2002, for example, that interference in the market did little to protect the public while hampering the market's freedom to innovate and expand, citing specifically the development of credit derivatives.[73] In 2009, Ben Bernanke, Chairman of the Federal Reserve Board, expressed alarm that post-crisis reform proposals would stifle innovation and constrain future market growth.[74] The British government expressed much the same fears about the danger of stricter regulation reducing business opportunities for financial services.[75]

Four decades earlier, the concept of the virtuous market had also been widespread in Hong Kong. The government was convinced that the economy had an in-built and automatic self-adjustment mechanism, which made state involvement unnecessary.[76] 'In the long run, the aggregate of the decisions of individual businessmen, exercising individual judgment in a free economy, even if often mistaken, is likely to do less harm', Cowperthwaite, the then Financial Secretary, had proclaimed, 'than the centralized decisions of a Government; and certainly the harm is likely to be counteracted faster'.[77]

This self-confident, laissez-faire rhetoric concealed the extent to which the government had lost faith in the theory that in the case of financial markets, free and fair competition automatically led to optimal outcomes.[78] In the 1950s the government's belief was that freedom to enter the banking market was a beneficial and important principle. When Cowperthwaite became Financial Secretary in 1961, he reversed this policy. He declared that Hong Kong was dangerously over-banked (despite a lack of evidence to support this assertion).[79] He insisted that the banking industry's interest rate cartel, together with a moratorium on new bank licences, were essential safeguards of the integrity as well as the stability of the financial system.[80] This assessment was proved wrong by the failure of the constraints on competition to prevent future crises. Indeed, the scandals worsened over the next two decades. Cowperthwaite's mistrust of competition continued to influence policy for the rest of the century, nevertheless.

In the 1970s, Haddon-Cave decided to promote Hong Kong as an international financial centre and, as his first step, allowed a secondary banking sector to expand rapidly, unlicensed and unregulated. He was very aware of the mismanagement and misconduct that plagued these deposit-taking companies (DTCs) and of their contribution to property and share bubbles during the decade. The government decided to take no action out of fear that large numbers of DTCs would be unable to pass regulatory scrutiny and that their closure would hinder Hong Kong's expansion as a financial centre.[81] Chapter 2 showed that American and British regulators justified similar decisions in the run-up to 2007 by invoking the concept of virtuous markets. In Hong Kong, such a policy was no longer sustainable by the end of the 1970s, and minimalist oversight of DTCs was introduced reluctantly.[82]

In the 1980s, it seemed that the virtuous market concept would return to favour. A new Financial Secretary, Sir John Bremridge, had been recruited from the private sector in 1981 where he had run the business empire of the Swire family which had started its first Chinese venture in the 1860s. He was convinced that market forces were benign. Before his appointment, he had publicly praised 'those little men who have made fortunes by intelligent speculation', and he was unconvinced that regulation would enhance financial stability.[83] But unprecedented corporate scandals in 1982 and 1983 compelled him to change his mind. Dollar Credit, a small deposit-taking company, engaged in cheque-kiting to a total value of US$21.7 billion (US$50 billion in current terms). The fraud had gone unnoticed by the staff handling its transactions at HSBC, Citibank and Chemical Bank and by auditors and regulators.[84] The collapse of the Carrian Group in the following year led to criminal convictions of senior banking and legal executives and was followed by the murder of a Malaysian banker; the suicide of a prominent British lawyer; and the flight from justice of senior executives from HSBC's merchant bank, a British clearing bank and a German landesbank as well as several Hong Kong solicitors.[85]

Almost a hundred DTCs had closed by the end of the crisis, and the failure of seven licensed banks between 1982 and 1986 could be linked directly to the turmoil in the DTC sector.[86] The government spent almost US$500 million on rescuing and restructuring them.[87] The contribution to GDP from 'financing, insurance, real estate and business services' fell from 23 per cent in 1980 to 17 per cent in 1986.[88] That year, Bremridge announced his conversion to radical reforms to ensure that financial institutions 'are operated in a responsible, honest and business-like manner [and adopt] proper standards of conduct and sound business practice'.[89]

Moral hazard

A second pillar of the Anglo-American culture was the concept of moral hazard. This concept became an almost 'iron law' invoked by American and British regulators in the years before 2007 when declining to take action against questionable market practices, with costly consequences in the global financial crisis.[90] Moral hazard remained in vogue even at the height of the crisis. In 2008, for example, although British regulators accepted that bank collapses had brought 'the risk of creating severe collateral damage on the economy at large', they still insisted on leaving the market to penalise banking failures so that 'shareholders lose their money, creditors suffer losses and managers and employees seek new jobs'. This 'creative destruction' was essential, it was argued, to ensure that 'competition remains vibrant', which in turn was said to be a precondition of 'London's position as one of the world's leading financial centres'.[91] The dangers of such 'moral hazard fundamentalism' had been highlighted at the start of the global crisis by Lawrence Summers, a prominent American economist. Its advocates, he had warned, ignore the fact that 'moral hazard and confidence are opposite sides of the same coin'.

> Financial institutions can fail because they become insolvent, as misguided lending or borrowing causes their liabilities to exceed their assets. But solvent institutions can also fail because of illiquidity simply because creditors rush to withdraw their funds and assets cannot be liquidated fast enough. In this latter case the availability of external support averts needless panic and contagion.[92]

As with the concept of virtuous markets, Hong Kong had started out with an almost unconditional belief in moral hazard. 'We never intended to set ourselves up as nursemaids and governesses to silly people who put their money into shaky institutions', one official declared in 1950.[93] This attitude was based on two erroneous expatriate preconceptions. The

first was a conviction that Chinese depositors did not object to the loss of
their deposits because they were not looking for safety and stability from
their banks but for the maximum possible return. The official view was
that 'if the Chinese want security they can get it in the Western banks'.[94]
The second was the perception that regulation was unnecessary because
in the absence of public protests when deposits were lost, there was no
political risk in allowing banks to fail.[95] Such an unconditional commitment to moral hazard could not survive the onset of mass banking in
the early 1960s. The refusal in 1965 to save a bank with over 100,000
depositors led to street demonstrations which so alarmed the colonial
administration that henceforward no bank would be allowed to fail at
the depositors' expense.[96]

Officials were reluctant to abandon moral hazard altogether. In
the 1970s, Haddon-Cave as Financial Secretary remained loyal to the
concept while unlicensed DTCs mushroomed. He refused even to collect
data from non-bank DTCs until 1978 on the grounds that such a statistical exercise might imply a duty to ensure their prudent management,
which officials were determined to avoid.[97] The government's goal was
to escape any obligation to bail out unlicensed and unregulated DTCs
which lost their depositors' confidence. This repudiation of responsibility for DTCs meant that their 'imprudence, mismanagement, and malpractice' went unchecked according to a leading banking economist in
Hong Kong.[98]

In the 1980s, Bremridge came into office as Financial Secretary with
a deep personal conviction of the value of moral hazard as a guide to
policy. He had argued during his previous business career that it was
impossible to 'legislate for the complete protection of fools'. For this
reason, he had opposed calls to extend regulation to DTCs.[99] Now,
however, moral hazard became too much of a political liability to the
colonial administration. Public indignation mounted in the early 1980s
at the spate of financial scandals. Revelations of official indifference
towards illegal and incompetent management of DTCs coincided with
the first, indirect elections to the legislature in 1985. These made it
politically imperative to draft sweeping regulatory reforms, and their
introduction the following year brought to an end six decades of bank
crises and market collapses.[100]

Surviving values

Somewhat surprisingly, Hong Kong officials have never totally discarded
their attachment to the theoretical preconceptions with which the government first approached the oversight of the financial system and to
which their contemporary American and British counterparts remain

committed.[101] In 2007 Joseph Yam, the Hong Kong Monetary Authority's Chief Executive, invoked the concept of virtuous markets and the belief that market forces should determine the fate of financial enterprises.[102] But in Hong Kong, this principle had to be tempered with political pragmatism, and Yam accorded a much higher priority than his British counterparts to the case for avoiding bank failures on the grounds that they cause serious disruption to the economy at large.[103] Hong Kong officials continued to be attached to the theoretical merits of moral hazard and were anxious to retain the threat of liquidation as a penalty for mismanaged banks.[104] Thus, Yam cautioned depositors that an efficient banking system could not be entirely free from risk. But to meet the public's expectation of regulatory responsibility, this warning had to be accompanied by a reassurance that depositor protection would come first regardless of the doctrine of moral hazard.[105]

Fear of financial instability had fostered a continuing nervousness among officials about the impact of uncontrolled market forces on the financial system.[106] The anti-competition measures introduced in response to the 1965 banking crisis were increasingly difficult to justify after the 1986 regulatory reforms. They were not to disappear until the end of the century, though. The restrictions on competition were finally discarded only after it was shown that they were damaging Hong Kong's status as an international financial centre. The Asian financial crisis led the Hong Kong Monetary Authority to commission consultants to review the regulatory changes that would be needed in facing increasingly competitive global and markets.[107] This document stated that although 'compared to other Asian centres, Hong Kong appears to be more attractive', it fell behind both the United States and the United Kingdom on most of six tests of fair and well-regulated markets. To catch up, the consultants argued, Hong Kong needed to get rid of the barriers to competition inherited from the past. At the same time, it was noted, the Asian financial crisis had uncovered increasing risks to international as well as local stability.

The solution proposed was that banks should be given greater market opportunities, while the Hong Kong Monetary Authority's oversight of the financial system should be strengthened.[108] Implementation began swiftly. The last remnants of the interest-rate cartel disappeared in 2001. Restrictions on foreign bank branches were finally eliminated in the same year, and the gap between entry conditions for local and foreign banks was drastically reduced in 2002. The result was to bring Hong Kong up to much the same level as New York and London as measured by the consultants' criteria. In defiance of the conventional Anglo-American wisdom, however, increased competition in Hong Kong had come with greater regulation rather than less.

Conclusions

Overall, Hong Kong emerged from the global crisis with its international reputation in better shape than before. Old allegations that the last bastion of laissez faire was betraying its heritage with its hands-on approach to regulation faded. Its interventionist policies, this chapter has shown, had been vindicated not only by the stability of its financial system in both the Asian and the global crises but also by Hong Kong's sustained success as an international financial centre.

Ironically, its local reputation was not left unscathed by the events of 2007–08, and there were revelations that 'Lehman mini-bonds' and other complex products had been mis-sold to the public on the eve of the global crisis.[109] The government oversaw an agreement with the 16 retail banks involved to pay US$800 million to settle claims from unqualified retail investors who had bought such 'bonds'. Some sales staff were prosecuted or disciplined.[110] But in Hong Kong, instances of banking misconduct and failures to enforce the law have serious political implications well beyond the sums of money involved. The regulators and their performance in this affair came under continuous and hostile scrutiny because of the public's abiding intolerance of bureaucratic negligence and its intractable mistrust of government-business collusion.[111]

In parallel, the regulators were attacked on the grounds that their salaries and benefits were significantly higher than their counterparts in other jurisdictions. Hong Kong's superior performance during the global financial crisis by comparison with the regulatory record of the United States, the United Kingdom, France and Germany, for example, was not questioned. Also ignored was the considerable attention aroused in other financial centres by research findings that their regulators' failures to police market behaviour more effectively could be explained by an inability to 'attract and retain highly-skilled financial workers, because they could not compete with private sector wages'.[112] The critics simply argued that Hong Kong pay scales were excessive.

Historically bank runs and financial crises had caused only limited and short-term checks to Hong Kong's high growth rates.[113] Indeed, 'banking crises that result in a permanent GDP loss have never occurred in Hong Kong', a recent study has claimed.[114] In consequence, the most immediate and compelling incentive for government involvement in maintaining financial stability in Hong Kong has been the unacceptable political costs of widespread losses by depositors. Current constitutional arrangements have reinforced this historical legacy and increased the demands for accountability from the community. In the absence of a directly-elected government, there are no elected ministers to take responsibility for failing to prevent a financial crisis. Nor can the public blame the Chinese authorities because Hong Kong has been given such extensive autonomy in managing its financial and monetary affairs. The community is left with only its own financial officials to hold to account. The public's sensitivity to lapses in financial regulation was, arguably, increased by memories of past banking failures and market collapses which had not yet faded. Thus, its central bankers and financial regulators had no escape from accountability even for complaints that would arouse only limited criticism in other financial centres.[115]

In the last resort financial stability is not negotiable for Hong Kong. If its credibility as an international financial centre were endangered, its value to the Mainland would suffer immediately, and its unique role in the nation's financial affairs would be in jeopardy despite the constitutional guarantees set out in the Basic Law that its existing economic and financial arrangements should continue until 2047. This is the ultimate political pressure which dictates the priority of financial stability for Hong Kong.

Conclusions — Resisting Reforms

The international financial crisis of 2007–09 was arguably the worst 'in the two hundred year history of the modern capitalist system'.[1] A truly global phenomenon, it 'unfolded in an environment where financial institutions and other investors were excessively optimistic about asset prices and risk', the IMF has reported. 'Overall banking system leverage' was most alarming in the United Kingdom, the United States, Germany and Switzerland, but similar trends were observable in China (and India and Brazil as well), though to a much lesser degree.[2] The consequences for the real economy were dire: 'Banking contributed to a Great Recession on a scale last seen at the time of the Great Depression'.[3]

When growth comes first

Those in charge of the world's largest financial markets had gone for growth almost regardless of cost — a choice that met little opposition — and so were lulled into three miscalculations which account for much of the financial disaster that has occurred since 2007.

The history trap

The banking industry has a marked propensity to forget the unpleasant experiences of the past, and so have financial policy-makers.[4] Regulatory safeguards come to be regarded as relics of an earlier age, irrelevant to the mature markets of the present.[5] The danger is that during periods when earnings are buoyant and managements regularly exceed profit expectations, risk is seen as the real recipe for maximizing investors' returns. Thus, for example, 'LBOs, leveraged restructurings, takeovers, and venture capital firms' were lauded as a source of corporate salvation in the 1990s.[6] Chapter 2 and its case studies illustrated how the Anglo-American culture made officials reluctant to intervene even when confronted with evidence that financial stability was in danger. 'But human nature being what it is', banks cannot be left to their own devices, a 2009 OECD report argued. Easing of regulatory restraints on financial institutions was to have catastrophic consequences for their stability in 2007– 09, the OECD researchers commented, when Citibank and Deutsche Bank, for example, came to 'look much more like large highly leveraged hedge funds'.[7]

The reform trap

In the 1980s, 'developing country governments began to modernize and liberalize their regulatory systems in line with prevailing intellectual fashions and following the example of industrial countries', a well-known study observed. They set about dismantling administrative controls with enthusiasm but overlooked the need to put in place the regulatory and other institutional systems needed to maintain financial stability, it continued. The assumption was that market forces would achieve their own balance, through efficient management of lending especially.

The new banking entrepreneurs and their inexperienced regulators were thus left 'to feel their way to an assessment of what safe and sound banking would mean in practice'. All too often, liberalisation uncovered 'a long-standing underlying insolvency of the banking system', which became unavoidably clear as banks emerged from 'the sheltered environment that allowed or required them to cross-subsidize loss-making lines of business'.[8] Reform without regulation proved hazardous. Chapters 3 and 4 showed this miscalculation at work in contemporary China (as had been the case during Hong Kong's earlier development). This 'trap' is, of course, a very general experience of the emerging and Third World economies.

The growth trap

The general assumption that rapid growth worldwide would be more than enough to offset the costs of financial crises was always open to question. Among the research evidence available to guide policy-makers before 2007 was an impressive survey which calculated total damage suffered during crises in the closing decades of the 20th century. On average the losses were equivalent to 33 per cent of GDP, a far from trivial figure.[9] Supporters of the Anglo-American consensus were not daunted by estimates of this order, however, and believed the economic arithmetic favoured giving priority to growth. 'Although crises are costly and have severe recessionary effects, they are rare events', one large-scale study concluded, 'Over the long run, the pro-growth effects of greater financial deepening and more investment by far outweigh the detrimental growth effects of financial fragility and a greater incidence of crises'.[10] Thus was the 'growth trap' set, and regulation seemed redundant when reforms allowed markets the freedom to find optimal solutions which, it was believed, would be superior to financial officials' initiatives.

No alternative

The bias in favour of growth at all costs is likely to persist despite the risks of instability that may be involved. Impressive historical statistics have created a presumption in favour of the Anglo-American regulatory culture and its insistence that the right of financial services to generate profits should be constrained as little as possible even after the global crash. The estimate for the United Kingdom is that 'growth in financial sector value added has been more than double that of the economy as a whole' for 160 years. For the United States the estimated value added by the financial sector has risen 'from about 2% of total GDP in the 1950s to about 8%' by 2010.[11] It is fair to ask what could replace growth dynamic of this order.

The best of intentions

This book has argued that officials rather than their political masters made the fatal decisions. Central bankers and financial regulators everywhere are subject to political controls because in the last resort they can be removed if they lose the government's confidence. Yet, more and more political leaders have discovered how they can benefit from allowing these officials considerable autonomy. The issues for which they are responsible are almost always technical, esoteric and difficult to explain to the media and the public at large. Worse still, 'when your action means higher mortgage payments and higher costs of doing business', one central banker has pointed out, 'It is awfully difficult to say convincingly that this is all for the good of the community in the long run'.[12] Elected politicians have much to gain from allowing officials to take responsibility for painful financial and monetary decisions. Over recent decades, these officials in Washington and London have come to enjoy bipartisan support and won considerable freedom from political interference, arrangements which have survived the global financial crisis and the bitter political campaigning during an American presidential and a British general election together with the change in ruling parties that followed.

Andrew Sheng, one of Asia's most distinguished regulatory officials, has asked how the global financial crisis could happen 'since Western regulators all had increased resources, perceived independence of action and technical tools all in place'. He conjectures that regulators had become 'captive to lobbying power of the financial industry'. He quotes the research findings on the tendency for regulators to be 'captured' by the industries they are supposed to be overseeing.[13] By contrast with the attacks on cronyism's contribution to the 1997–98 Asian financial crisis, he suggests, there has been 'a deafening silence' on the links between regulators and business as a factor in the global collapse of 2007–09.[14]

This issue has been addressed directly in the case of Ireland, one of the worst-hit European economies where allegations of cronyism have been widespread. Regulators' deference to business and political leaders was investigated in a trenchant official review under the direction of Professor Patrick Honohan of why Irish banking fared so badly in the global crash. This report concluded that, at the very most, officials 'might have instinctively and almost unconsciously shied away from aggressive action' against the well-connected. The available evidence indicated, however, that regulators needed no persuasion to overlook improper and imprudent banking behaviour; still less did they need to be bribed. Officials believed that they could trust bankers to know their own business best and that the lightest touch regulation was in the national interest.[15]

As for the leading American and British central bankers and regulatory officials, what with hindsight can now be seen to have been disastrous mistakes started with a political and academic consensus widely shared before 2007 and subject to only limited revision since. The analysis presented in this book has recorded how the most glaring misjudgments were made in public with clear explanations of the official reasoning behind the decisions. This left a paper trail which chapter 2 followed and which does not support the suggestion that the regulators in Washington and London had changed roles and become the 'clients' or 'captives' of financial institutions. The officials involved were victims of the prevailing culture which made them defeatist about the effectiveness of regulation and naive about the behaviour of market participants. Thus, for example, in the negotiations over Basel II, officials can be accused of accepting proposals from the industry on how to calculate capital requirements which were so complex as to be daunting to supervise effectively.[16] In the case of the Bank of England, this prospect was openly defended as unavoidable on the grounds that 'any set of accounts, however drawn up, is likely to be considerably deficient … in terms of outlining the economic realities of risks within the balance sheet'.[17]

No less relevant were the mistaken 'good intentions' of policy-makers generally. In Washington the Securities and Exchange Commission has described the origins of the sub-prime mortgage debacle as the desire to fulfil the American dream of a nation of home owners. Its unintended consequences were the discarding of due diligence in processing applications for housing loans and a dangerous disregard for surging mortgage defaults.[18] In China similarly unimpeachable intentions inspired the economic stimulus package of 2008 and seemed to justify every measure possible to avoid a recession, chapter 3 explained. The unintended consequences here included a surge in non-performing loans as previous prudent policies were discarded and the law itself ignored.

Resisting reforms

Most damaging of all was a combination of ignorance and complacency. The British have admitted that 'the real failure was a lapse into hubris'.

> ... we came to believe that crises created by massive maturity transformation were problems that no longer applied to modern banking ... There was an inability to see through the veil of modern finance to the fact that the balance sheets of too many banks were an accident waiting to happen, with levels of leverage on a scale that could not resist even the slightest tremor to confidence about the uncertain value of bank assets.[19]

American officials regard the principal source of this unawareness as 'the shadow banking system' whose activities 'were not subject by law to strong consolidated supervision by federal regulators'.

> ... neither the investors, nor the rating agencies, nor the regulators, nor even the firms that designed the securities fully appreciated the risks that those securities entailed ... These risks grew rapidly in the period before the crisis, in part because the regulators — like most financial firms and investors — did not fully understand or appreciate them.[20]

Despite these confessions and the powerful case they made for reforms, changes were slow in coming. One IMF report pointed out, for example, that 'an institution can never have enough capital or liquidity if there are material flaws in its risk management practices'. It warned too that little serious attention was being given in 2010 to such basic precautions as 'oversight: supervision, governance, and market discipline'.[21] Regulation was perceived to be in conflict with growth, and enthusiasm for reforms after the global crisis was constrained by fears that they would slow down overall growth and reduce profit opportunities. An IMF review of 'regulatory reforms that were emerging in policy discussions' found that their focus was on 'lowering risks, raising costs, and thus, most likely, lowering returns' earned by the financial sector. If implemented, banks would be smaller and offer fewer, simpler and cheaper products although these would be more effective in meeting their customers' needs. The new financial system would probably 'look less innovative and dynamic and more old-fashioned'. Such downsizing and simplicity were hardly a vision of the future likely to win enthusiastic endorsement from the financial industry itself. At the same time, this IMF study warned, governments were likely to find that a more stable and more regulated system would be associated with slower growth for the entire economy.[22] This prospect was not a great encouragement for policy makers and politicians to embrace the proposals.

The crisis had shown that 'central bankers knew less than what they thought they did', the IMF has commented.[23] This lesson was particularly striking when it came to reliance on the markets as reliable guides to corporate quality. For example, those banks whose share prices had made them the market favourites in 2006 suffered the worst in 2007–08, according to one large-scale study.

> ... the attributes that the market valued in 2006, for instance, a successful securitization line of business, exposed banks to risks that led them to perform poorly when the crisis hit. The market did not expect these attributes to be a source of weakness for banks and did not expect the banks with these attributes to perform poorly as of 2006 ... banks were differentially exposed to various risks by the end of 2006. Some exposures that were rewarded by the markets in 2006 turned out to be unexpectedly costly for banks the following two years.[24]

Thus, '"old" certainties about the "new" financial landscape, shaped by lightly regulated entities and financial innovations that would allow them to "efficiently" allocate risks are waning and many of them are being dethroned', an OECD report optimistically asserted. Nevertheless, there was no great appetite for reversing deregulation. Mistrust of state involvement in economic management persisted, the OECD's comments made plain, and the importance of letting markets decide which institutions should fail remained an article of faith.[25]

Hostility towards government intervention intensified as memories of the first traumatic shocks of the global crisis receded. Demands for the authorities to repudiate all commitment to rescue financial institutions and even financial markets became insistent, and the dangers of moral hazard were frequently invoked. As chapter 1 noted, criticisms of state intervention were frequently misconceived or misleading and based on Anglo-American articles of faith. A remarkable example of such dogmatism was the assertion by an official inquiry into the 2008 Citigroup bailout that avoidance of moral hazard should have taken priority over the stability of United States' financial markets and the well-being of the global economy. The inquiry's report admitted in 2011 that the government's US$45 billion capital injection (plus a much larger guarantee) had 'not only achieved the primary goal of restoring market confidence in Citigroup, but also carefully controlled the overall risk of Government loss on the asset guarantee'. 'Citigroup did not fail, and the global economy avoided the catastrophic financial collapse that many feared would flow from a Citigroup failure', it added. Indeed, the report acknowledged, 'the Government incurred no losses, and even profited on its overall investment in Citigroup by more than $12 billion'. These impressive achievements were deemed insufficient to justify this rescue operation. The government had created a category of institution 'too big, too interconnected, and too essential to the global financial system to be allowed to fail', the report baldly asserted, and Citigroup's bailout 'undoubtedly contributed to the increased moral hazard that has been a direct byproduct of TARP'.

No factual evidence of TARP's corrupting effect on the conduct of banking business was produced to support the report's verdict: 'By standing behind Citigroup, [the government] did more than reassure troubled markets — it encouraged high-risk behavior by insulating the risk takers from the consequences of failure'.[26] Totally ignored was the acumen with which Federal Reserve officials had mounted an investment operation that would have won market acclaim if the deal had been put together by a commercial banker. Instead, they were pilloried, just as their Hong Kong counterparts had been in 1998 — ironically by the Federal Reserve Board itself — for a similar feat in calling the market so accurately (as the previous chapter recounted).

Fidelity to the central tenets of the Anglo-American culture was encouraged by a realisation that paradoxically, the world's financial system had proved far more stable than could have been prudently forecast in 2007–08. Financial markets may have seriously misgauged both risk and profit prospects before 2007, but they neither closed down nor descended into chaos. However traumatic for the real economy and society at large, the financial crisis itself seemed to become increasingly not only manageable but affordable as well. The robustness of the financial markets themselves and the resilience of financial corporations — albeit with government bailouts — meant that the heaviest losses would be borne by the rest of the business community and by the general public. Despite the political resentment that this state of affairs caused, once the immediate panic had abated, the pressure for rapid and radical reforms eased and progress slowed. For example, it was agreed that implementation of international initiatives included in Basel III would take place over a lengthy period,[27] and there was no great rush by the United Kingdom to implement its domestic reform package.[28]

Affordability was an unexpected outcome. The state outlay on rescuing the American and British banking systems was equivalent to around 1 per cent of GDP, the Bank of England calculated, and 'recouping these costs from banks would not place an unbearable strain on their finances'.[29] This resilience was not the result of any innate robustness but the outcome of state rescue packages which have proved less ruinous than had been predicted when the bailouts began. For example, in the United States, 'as voters rage and candidates put up ads against government bailouts, the reviled mother of them all — the $700 billion TARP [Troubled Asset Relief Program] lifeline to banks, insurance and auto companies could conceivably earn taxpayers a profit', it was being forecast in late 2010.[30] Such statistics help to clarify the background to government discussions on what regulatory reforms might reduce the risk of future global crises. They could be read as evidence that government intervention could resolve the most severe financial emergencies and that if disaster were to strike again, state rescue measures would be affordable and effective. On this analysis, there was no need for urgent changes to overhaul the system.

Manageability also came as a surprise. What proved the key factor in 2007–08 was institutional size, when a limited number of very large banks were found to be the most serious threat to financial stability and government rescue programmes had been able to ignore the woes of most smaller banks. Worldwide, '90 per cent of the support offered by governments during the course of the crisis' went to 145 banks which accounted for '85 per cent of the assets of the world's top 1,000 banks'. Their average assets were in excess of US$100 billion, and their failure would have been catastrophic.[31] Thus the chief priority in crisis management was believed to have shifted from the banking industry as a whole to a small group of dominant players on whom central bankers and financial regulators could concentrate their attention.

Too big to fail

The chief concerns for American and British officials after the crisis were system and size. In theory the Anglo-American regulatory culture had recognised that 'supervision (looking at the individual institutions and markets) and the systemic factors involving concentrations, interrelationships and behaviour in relation to the system as a whole' must both be regarded as 'an essential element in the provision of financial stability oversight'.[32] But the two were not of equal weight in the post-2007 political climate, and systemic risk was regarded as the more urgent priority. The Chairman of the Federal Reserve Board insisted during a 2009 discussion of regulatory reforms that 'strong and effective regulation and supervision of banking institutions' were not enough to reduce system risk. What was required, he argued, were much vaguer goals: 'reforms to the financial architecture, broadly conceived' and regulation of 'the financial system as a whole, in a holistic way, not just its individual components'.[33] This retreat into imprecision was understandable. As a British parliamentary report had noted a little earlier: 'There is no consensus about what financial stability means, how it should be measured and how the balance should be struck between the pursuit of a financial stability objective and other public policy objectives'.[34]

Moral hazard was a different issue, however, on which the Anglo-American consensus had unambiguous views, the most important of which was the need to ensure that this principle was incorporated into policy initiatives to deal with systemic risk and banks 'too large to fail'. In 2006 the Bank of England had explained why banks must be allowed to fail.

> ... the authorities cannot and should not be expected to intervene with a support package every time a bank — even a large one — gets into difficulties. The cost of such an interventionist approach, in terms of market discipline and fiscal burden, would be substantial. And it would in all likelihood compromise the efficient provision of financial services and inhibit the exit of weak firms from the industry.[35]

As the crisis in the United Kingdom intensified in 2008, the Bank continued to fight strenuously for the right to allow banks to go out of business 'to encourage prudent behaviour by others'.[36] There was wide political support for this stand. A parliamentary investigation into the collapse of British financial institutions described banks as 'special' organisations, 'similar in some ways to utility providers'. Nevertheless, its report stated, 'banks should be allowed to "fail" so as to preserve market discipline on financial institutions'. It was essential, the report added, 'to ensure that [the] framework for maintaining financial stability does not provide free insurance to banks' or a guarantee that no bank would be allowed to fail.[37] Moral hazard remained the regulators' gold standard.

Washington took an almost identical view. As President George Bush's administration was coming to an end in 2008, officials expressed apprehension that 'events have called it into question' the benefits generated by free and competitive markets. The public, therefore, should be left in no doubt that the massive rescue operations launched by the government were only temporary measures, and 'there has to be a deliberate design to eliminate them'.[38] This commitment to the market did not alter as President Barack Obama took office. The concept of moral hazard was sacred, and the right to let financial institutions fail was presented as non-negotiable. In 2009 the Chairman of the Federal Reserve Board used virtually the same wording as he had done in 2005 to reject any obligation to save even the largest banks. Even after the Lehman catastrophe, he remained determined to dispel the notion that the government would automatically 'prevent the failure of a large, highly interconnected financial firm' despite the disruption that the financial system and the broader economy might suffer in consequence. The price to be paid for classifying some firms as 'too big to fail' would be dire, he insisted.

> ... it reduces market discipline and encourages excessive risk-taking by the firm. It also provides an artificial incentive for firms to grow, in order to be perceived as too big to fail. And it creates an unlevel playing field with smaller firms, which may not be regarded as having implicit government support. Moreover, government rescues of too-big-to-fail firms can be costly to taxpayers, as we have seen recently. Indeed, in the present crisis, the too-big-to-fail issue has emerged as an enormous problem.[39]

Discussion of this issue was often one-sided and ill-informed.[40] As Lord Turner, a leading British regulator, was at pains to point out, history demonstrates how 'multiple small banks can fail as much as large and with as harmful effects'.[41] During the global crisis, the fragility of banks was not the result of their size, he insisted.

> The really big economic costs of the most recent crisis are not the explicit costs of big bank rescue, but the economic volatility resulting from the credit/asset price cycle, and such volatility could be generated from the competitive interaction of multiple medium size banks as much as from the actions of Too-Big-To-Fail banks.[42]

Replacement of the biggest financial institutions by a large number of small players would not lead to a more stable or more efficient financial system, according to an IMF study. 'The whole network, which is what matters for macroeconomic and financial stability, would probably be more, not less complex', the report continued, 'since it would take many linkages to perform some of the transactions that are internalized within and through larger institutions'. While 'each individual small bank would be simpler', the assumption that 'if these linkages instead were implemented by thousands of small institutions they would be much less complex and more transparent' is misleading.[43]

The Anglo-American focus on systemic risk and the moral hazard caused by the largest financial institutions involved more than managing the priorities for changes in regulatory policies and protocols. It was linked to the explanation being developed to account for the failure of American and British officials to respond to the growing vulnerability of their financial markets ahead of the 2007 crash. Among the most enduring doctrines propounded by Alan Greenspan, former Chairman of the Federal Reserve Board, was the assertion that officials could not be expected to have sufficient comprehension of financial markets to oversee them effectively, as the 'Introduction' explained. Before 2007, therefore, it would have been fruitless to try to adjust regulatory arrangements to changing market conditions. In the aftermath of the global financial crisis, central bankers and financial regulators have used this Greenspan doctrine to explain why they were taken unawares by the events of 2007. The principal threat to financial stability had become the leverage exerted by the very large, multinational firm which had multiple financial businesses operating in several regulatory and legal jurisdictions, they have averred.[44] The dangers of systemic risk and institutions 'too big to fail' had arisen unperceived, these officials have argued, camouflaged by the astonishing growth in the volume of the world's financial services and the complexity of its products since the 1970s.[45]

This argument allowed officials to shift blame on to the banking industry itself as they suggested that the largest financial institutions had powerful incentives to disregard the true risks involved in their business models. 'Everyone knows' that the biggest banks cannot be allowed to fail, the Bank of England stated. The result, it claims, is that 'highly risky banking institutions enjoy implicit public sector support ... [which] incentivises banks to take on yet more risk, knowing that, if things go well, they will reap the rewards while the public sector will foot the bill if things go wrong'.[46] American regulators claimed that not only were the biggest banks given privileged immunity from regulatory oversight, 'expectations of government support' meant that they ignored 'potential losses from risky behavior'.[47] This analysis is far from convincing. Neither American nor British officials have produced any evidence that financial institutions themselves were any better informed about the rapidly increasing vulnerability of their markets in the run-up to 2007 than investors or regulators. Systemic risk and institutions 'too big to fail' are challenges that arose after the market collapse in 2007. They were not its cause. As a United States Treasury official observed in 2009: 'This crisis has also clearly demonstrated that risks to the system can emerge from all corners of the financial markets and from any of our financial institutions'.[48]

Cultural convergence

Washington and London developed the regulatory strategy which did more to promote global prosperity than any rival approach. Furthermore, the damage done to advanced economies as a group by the disasters of 2007–09 was actually lower than in previous crises, the 'Introduction' explained. On this basis, the international financial crisis was just another unpleasant but not unexpected incident among the many that had occurred since 1970. But when it came to the United States and the United Kingdom, earlier chapters have shown, the costs of the 2007–09 crisis would not easily be made good by rapid economic recovery and sustained high growth thereafter. On the contrary, budget austerity and increased public borrowing were expected to be protracted. But these burdens on taxpayers and the general public did not generate sufficient political indignation to cause a repudiation of the Anglo-American regulatory culture and its attachment to free markets.

For all its faults, the Anglo-American culture had been an indispensable force in modernising financial markets and creating an international environment in which growth, especially in Asia, was rapid and sustained. China offers particularly important evidence of the survival value of this culture. That nation's regulators had a clear grasp of the Anglo-American regulatory arrangements and the way they functioned. Chinese financial officials believed that Anglo-American regulatory attitudes — rather than legal and institutional arrangements — determined whether or not the American and British financial markets would be able to withstand the global crisis.[49] Chinese officials shared the Anglo-American culture's commitment to market forces, to which they gave the credit for 'all progress' made by China's banking reforms.[50] Indeed, in the middle of a damning review of Washington's pre-2007 regulatory failures, the China Banking Regulatory Commission inserted a defence of liberalisation and echoed American warnings that without freedom to innovate, 'the market will lose its vitality'. But Chinese officials added an important reservation: the danger of being 'too obsessed with the market's self-correction function'.[51]

Chinese regulators were also in no doubt as to why autonomy mattered, and they presented their own discreet 'declaration of independence'. They saw themselves as part of a global confraternity with which China's cooperation was crucial for its own financial stability.[52] They claimed that the 'supervisory architecture' was not what counted most, but the freedom of national regulators to 'make independent and responsible supervisory decisions'. On this foundation alone would there be sufficient market and investor confidence for 'the financial sector to boost the real economy'. Furthermore, the China Banking

Regulatory Commission argued, greater independence was a worldwide goal of regulatory reform. Only by following this international trend and being willing to 'abide by globally shared transaction and supervisory rules' could China hope to establish its own international financial centre , the Commission warned in 2010.[53]

Freedom for China's regulators to enforce the measures required to maintain the integrity and the stability of the financial system was such a radical reform that inevitably it caused concern among political leaders. Experience showed that China at its current level of development could afford the losses incurred by banks through the failure to modernise the banking industry, its corporate governance and its credit culture. Less clear to the leadership especially after the financial crises of 1997–98 and 2007–09 was whether the financial system could survive future international crises if state controls were eliminated. An 'open door' policy had always seemed much more perilous — and less necessary — for banking and financial services than it had done for China's manufacturing industry, this book has recorded.

The Hong Kong alternative

That the China Banking Regulatory Commission was committed to an independent regulatory system was an important endorsement of Hong Kong, whose regulatory autonomy, it can be argued, was essential for it to survive as an international financial centre after 1997 and the end of British rule. The challenge lay in the political management of perceptions. How could the post-colonial administration and its financial officials quickly establish the sort of credibility which American and British central bankers had taken decades to build up to the point 'that interference in the work of the central bank is seen to be a political liability — you tend to lose rather than gain votes when you interfere', to quote the Hong Kong Monetary Authority? Its credibility issues were compounded by the limited democracy permitted to Hong Kong: 'Whether directly or indirectly elected, the politicians have the mandate of the people [but] do not actually have the authority to direct government policies', the Authority stated. The result was that legislators were always in opposition and never in power, which made a 'bipartisan' approach difficult to sustain. In any case, the Hong Kong Monetary Authority could not hope to achieve popularity because 'in managing monetary and financial systems, doing the right thing often involves inflicting pain on the majority of the people you serve'. Instead it set out to rank 'among the most transparent' central banks in the world. Because it could not rely on 'faith in an esoteric and aloof HKMA being professional and acting in the best interest of Hong Kong', it had to make itself accountable to the community at large.[54] Its constituents' first demand was freedom from the bank runs and financial collapses that had occurred in each decade until the mid-1980s, and laissez faire had been forced to give way to positive regulatory intervention.

The conviction that regulation is the enemy of growth has been challenged in this book by the experiences of Hong Kong. Chapter 5 described how its regulatory arrangements are among the strictest of any financial centre, and have been tightened steadily over the last decade. Yet, its financial system has flourished, its business volumes have grown, and it has continued to attract the world's leading banks. At the very least, Hong Kong's record over the last 30 years indicates that the Anglo-American regulatory culture is not the only formula for either economic freedom or prosperous and stable financial markets.

Notes

The following abbreviations are used in the Notes and Bibliography:

BIS: Bank for International Settlements
BofE: Bank of England
CBRC: China Banking Regulatory Commission
CD: *China Daily*
FDIC: Federal Deposit Insurance Corporation
FRB: Federal Reserve Board
FSA: Financial Services Authority
GIS: *Government Information Services* (Daily press releases of the Hong Kong government)
HH: *Hong Kong Hansard* (Official report of the proceedings of the Hong Kong Legislative Council)
HKMA: Hong Kong Monetary Authority (and its publication services)
HKRS: Government files in the Hong Kong Public Records Office
IMF: International Monetary Fund
NCNA: New China News Agency
OECD: Organisation for Economic Co-operation and Development
PBOC: People's Bank of China
PD: *People's Daily (Renmin Ribao)*
SEC: Securities and Exchange Commission

Introduction

1. This point is made by Professor Ricardo J. Caballero in 'Sudden Financial Arrest', *IMF Economic Review*, Vol. 58, Issue 1 (August 2010), pp. 11–3, 17–9.
2. 'All the more so given some of the burden will fall on Europe, Japan and even, to a much less extent, China,' he added. Zhou Xiaochuan, PBOC Governor, 'Instability and Evolution of the Financial System' (5 December 2007), p. 5.
3. Northern Rock's irrelevance to the global scene was argued by Verena Ross, FSA Director of Strategy and Risk, 'Lessons from the Financial Crisis', speech at the Chatham House Conference on Global Financial Regulation (24 March 2009); Lord Turner, FSA Chairman, 'The financial crisis and the future of financial regulation', The Economist's Inaugural City Lecture (21 January 2009).

4. Andrew G Haldane, BofE Executive Director Financial Stability, 'Rethinking the Financial Network', speech at the Financial Student Association, Amsterdam (28 April 2009), pp. 9, 10.
5. An excellent example of the regulators' astonishment at the crisis is Verena Ross, FSA Director of Strategy and Risk, 'Risk management governance and controls and their importance in banking system and financial sector stability', speech at the Financial Stability Institute and Executives' Meeting of East Asia-Pacific Central Banks (18 November 2008).
6. Lord Turner, FSA Chairman, Annual Public Meeting Speech (23 July 2009).
7. Sir John Gieve, BofE Deputy Governor, 'The City's Growth: The Crest of a Wave or Swimming with the Stream?', Society of Chartered Accountants, London (26 March 2007), p. 9.
8. Sir John Gieve, BofE Deputy Governor, 'Uncertainty, policy and financial markets', speech at the Barbican Centre (24 July 2007), p. 4. Earlier, in making a similar comparison, another British central banker had quoted Alan Greenspan, then FRB Chairman. Sir Andrew Large, BofE Deputy Governor, 'Convergence in Insurance and Banking: Some Financial Stability Issues', speech at the Mandarin Oriental Hotel (12 June 2003), p. 6.
9. The trend was well below the levels which had led to crises in 1987 and 1998, the Bank of England concluded. Sir John Gieve, BofE Deputy Governor, 'Financial System Risks in the UK — Issues and Challenges', speech at the Centre for the Study of Financial Innovation Roundtable (25 July 2006), pp. 6, 8–9.
10. Charles Bean, BofE Deputy Governor, 'Measuring Recession and Recovery: An Economic Perspective', speech at the RSS Statistics User Forum Conference (27 October 2010), p. 5.
11. Christopher Cox, SEC Chairman, Address to the Joint Meeting of the Exchequer Club and Women in Housing and Finance (4 December 2008).
12. IMF, 'IMF Executive Board Concludes 2009 Article IV Consultation with the United Kingdom', *Public Information Notice (PIN) No. 09/84* (16 July 2009).
13. Andrew G. Haldane, BofE Executive Director, 'Small Lessons from a Big Crisis', remarks at the Federal Reserve Bank of Chicago 45th Annual Conference (8 May 2009), pp. 1–2.
14. Mervyn King, BofE Governor, Address to the 2010 Trades Union Congress, Manchester (15 September 2010), p. 7.
15. Adam S. Posen, BofE Monetary Policy Committee External Member, 'The British Recovery in International Comparison', speech at the Society of Business Economists Annual Conference, London (30 June 2010), pp. 2–4.
16. For use of the term in this sense, see Alistair Darling, M.P., Chancellor of the Exchequer, in House of Commons Treasury Committee, *Banking Crisis*, Vol. I. Oral evidence (London: HMSO, HC 144-I, March 2009), pp. 8, 42.
17. In a retrospective on the global crisis, however, the Chairman of the Federal Reserve Board has claimed that 'the first lesson' from the Great Depression was that 'economic prosperity depends on financial stability'. Ben S. Bernanke, FRB Chairman, 'Economic Policy: Lessons from History', speech at the 43rd Annual Alexander Hamilton Awards Dinner, Center for the Study of the Presidency and Congress, Washington, DC (8 April 2010).

18. This conclusion was supported by a study of 60 countries for the period 1980–2002. Romain Ranciere, Aaron Tornell and Frank Westermann, 'Decomposing the effects of financial liberalization: Crises vs. Growth', *NBER Working Paper 12806* (December 2006), p. 16.

19. Charles Bean et al., BofE Deputy Governor, 'Monetary Policy after the Fall', paper presented at the Federal Reserve Bank of Kansas City Annual Conference (28 August 2010), p. 5.

20. Financial Crisis Inquiry Commission, *Final Report of the National Commission on the Causes of the Financial and Economic Crisis in the United States* (Official Government Edition, 21 January 2011), p. 401.

21. Mervyn King, BofE Governor, Speech given at the Civic Centre, Newcastle (25 January 2011), p. 4.

22. This table summarises the data in Luc Laeven and Fabian Valencia, 'Resolution of Banking Crises: The Good, the Bad, and the Ugly', *IMF Working Paper WP/10/146* (June 2010), Table 4. 'Summary of the Cost of Banking Crises over the period 1970–2009', p. 22.

23. Stijn Claessens, Giovanni Dell'Ariccia, Deniz Igan and Luc Laeven, 'Lessons and Policy Implications from the Global Financial Crisis', *IMF Working Paper WP/10/44* (February 2010), pp. 4–11.

24. House of Commons Treasury Committee, *Financial Stability and Transparency Sixth Report of Session 2007–08* (London: HMSO, HC 371, March 2008), p. 9.

25. See Claessens et al., 'Lessons and Policy Implications from the Global Financial Crisis', p. 9.

26. Washington provided substantial funding to British financial firms operating in American markets, however. Such assistance accounted for around 45 per cent of the US$3.3 trillion which the Federal Reserve system made available to support financial institutions during the global crisis. Richard Blackden and Harry Wilson, 'UK banks borrowed more than £640bn from US Federal Reserve', *Daily Telegraph*, 2 December 2010.

27. As measured by the US$2.8 trillion fall in banks' market capitalisation for 2007–09. Of this total, Eurozone and American banks each accounted for 28 per cent, while another 11 per cent was attributable to British banks. Gert Wehinger, 'The Turmoil and the Financial Industry: Developments and Policy Responses', *OECD Financial Trends*, Issue 1 (2009), Table 1. 'Banks' market value losses: Change in market value of largest G10 banks', p. 4.

28. Wim Fonteyne, Wouter Bossu, Luis Cortavarria-Checkley, Alessandro Giustiniani, Alessandro Gullo, Daniel Hardy and Seán Kerr, 'Crisis Management and Resolution for a European Banking System', *IMF Working Paper WP/10/70* (March 2010), pp. 7, 13.

29. Edmund L. Andrews, 'Fed shrugged as subprime crisis spread', *International Herald Tribune*, 18 December 2007.

30. Lord Turner, FSA Chairman, 'Priorities for the reform of global regulation — challenging past assumptions', speech at IOSCO 2009, Tel Aviv (11 June 2009).

31. Claessens et al., 'Lessons and Policy Implications from the Global Financial Crisis', p. 17.

32. Ross, 'Lessons from the Financial Crisis'.
33. Laura Kodres and Aditya Narain, 'Redesigning the Contours of the Future Financial System', *IMF Staff Position Note SPN/10/10* (16 August 2010), p. 4. An American official used much the same language. See Sheila C. Bair, FDIC Chairman, Testimony on Regulatory Perspectives on Financial Regulatory Reform Proposals before the House of Representatives Financial Services Committee (24 July 2009).
34. A senior British regulator has disputed the contribution made by the pre-2007 light touch regulatory régime to genuine wealth creation: 'If the [financial services] industry grew dramatically in the decade to 2007 [the Chicago School claims] that must be because it was performing value added services: if complex product innovations were able to sustain themselves economically, they must have been socially useful innovations. But after what has happened, I think we know that that is not the case'. Turner, 'The financial crisis and the future of financial regulation'.
35. He has also been one of the sharpest critics of the regulatory culture. Lord Turner, FSA Chairman, Speech at The Turner Review Conference (27 March 2009).
36. FSA, 'Memorandum from the Financial Services Authority (FSA)', in House of Commons Treasury Committee, *Banking Crisis*, Vol. II. Written evidence (London: HMSO, HC 144-II, March 2009), pp. EV 456–7 especially; Sheila C. Bair, FDIC Chairman, Testimony on Modernizing Bank Supervision and Regulation before the Senate Committee on Banking, Housing and Urban Affairs (19 March 2009).
37. Planning and state controls were a product of another kind of historical experience. World War II was widely regarded in Europe and Asia as having shown how governments could overcome the severest obstacles and mobilise resources, create modern industries and allocate output in the national interest far better than capitalism. The temptation to use state controls in the drive to create peacetime prosperity and build new nations was overwhelming quite apart from the ideological attractions of socialism. See Anne O. Krueger, 'Policy Lessons from Development Experience since the Second World War', in Jere Behrman and T. N. Srinivasan (eds.), *Development Economics*, Vol. IIIB (Amsterdam: Elsevier, 1995), pp. 2501, 2504.
38. Financial Crisis Inquiry Commission, *Final Report of the National Commission on the Causes of the Financial and Economic Crisis in the United States*, p. xviii.
39. Contemporary reporting of these developments in the official media is summarised in Leo F. Goodstadt, 'Control and Motivation of the Chinese Labour Force since the Cultural Revolution', in Lee Ngok and Leung Chi-keung (eds.), *China: Development and Challenge*. Proceedings of the Fifth Leverhulme Conference, Vol. 2 (Hong Kong: Centre of Asian Studies, 1979), pp. 84–87.
40. Professor Liu Guoguang, Peking University, and Deputy Director, CASS Institute of Economics, 'Seminar on China's economy in the 1980s', *Wen Wei Po*, 8 March 1980. His address offers a very frank summary of the confusion about how best to manage economic reform in China at this date.
41. The challenges faced by management were amply illustrated in Contributing Commentator, 'Strive to develop industrial production, communications

and transport with readjustment as the core', *Hongqi*, No. 8 (16 April 1981), pp. 2–4, 8.

42. Local officials had learnt to manage their own economic affairs when state planning and Finance Ministry authority had shrunk in the Cultural Revolution (1966–76). Susan L. Shirk, *The Political Logic of Economic Reform in China* (Berkeley: University of California Press, 1993), pp. 198–208.

43. The banks' position was weakened by the fact that they had been supposed to play a major part in the bid to restore the Ministry of Finance's authority, thus creating an image of the banking system as little more than an extension of the central control apparatus which was seen as stifling growth. On its role, see Leo F. Goodstadt, 'Taxation and Economic Modernization in Contemporary China', *Development and Change*, Vol. 10, No. 3 (July 1979), p. 412.

44. How the bankers and their authority survived the Cultural Revolution is discussed in Leo F. Goodstadt, *China's Search for Plenty. The Economics of Mao Tse-tung* (New York: Weatherhill, 1973), pp. 188–92

45. Leo Goodstadt, 'Rethink on Chinese bank reforms', *Asiabanking*, September 1984, pp. 37–8.

46. Zhou Xiaochuan, PBOC Governor, 'Opening to the Outside World: Past Experience and Prospects', speech at the conference to launch the *World Economic Development Declaration* (10 November 2003).

47. The published statistics on foreign exchange reserves before 1992 can seem confusing. SAFE records that the reserves totalled only US$ 167 million in 1978 and US$ 840 million the following year. (SAFE, 'Foreign Exchange Reserves, 1950–2005' (URL: http://www.safe.gov.cn/model_safe_en/tjsj_en/ tjsj_detail_en.jsp?ID=30303000000000000,14&id=4)). These SAFE figures exclude 'Bank of China Balances' that until 1991 were included in the published totals. (State Statistical Bureau, *China Statistical Yearbook 1992* (Beijing: Statistical Information and Consultancy Service Centre), T16.9. 'Gold and foreign exchange reserves', p. 603). The Bank of China's share exceeded, usually by very large amounts, the figure shown as 'Government Stock' in eight of the years between 1979 and 1991. SAFE's data thus considerably reduce the totals identified by the government at the time as official reserves. SAFE's practice, nevertheless, has prevailed since 1992 in China's publication of statistics on the reserves.

48. The international comparisons are based on State Statistical Bureau, *Statistical Yearbook of China 1984* (Hong Kong: Economic Information & Agency, 1984), p. 554.

49. This summary of 1978–2007 growth and the supporting statistics are derived from Zhou Jianxiong, 'China's Foreign Trade: A History', *Beijing Review*, 10 September 2009; and *NCNA*: 'National Bureau of Statistics: China takes 7.7% of world trade volume', 27 October 2008; 'China top contributor to world economic growth', 3 October 2009; and 'Backgrounder: China's forex reserves and investment', 9 March 2010.

50. Su Ning, PBOC Deputy Governor, 'Press ahead with Reform and Opening-up and Promote the Rapid and Healthy Development of the Financial Sector', speech at the Financial Summit Meeting (10 July 2006).

51. A good overview of the costly frustrations of banking reforms in the formerly centrally-planned Soviet Bloc nations when China was embarking on its own reforms can be found in Gary Gorton and Andrew Winton, 'Banking in Transition Economies: Does Efficiency Require Instability?', *Journal of Money, Credit and Banking*, Vol. 30, No. 3, Part 2 (August 1998), pp. 621–50.

52. Except where otherwise indicated, the analysis and quotations in this discussion of the 'transactional model' are drawn from the insightful review of China's strategy set in its wider international context by Katherina Pistor, 'Banking Reform in the Chinese Mirror', *Columbia Law and Economics Working Paper No. 354* (10 August 2009), pp. 5, 6, 7, 14, 15, 18, 22, 29.

53. The People's Bank took care to avoid any indication of which was regarded as most useful to China although the 'Anglo-Saxon' model came first in its list. Zhou Xiaochuan, PBOC Governor, 'Improve Corporate Governance and Develop Capital Market', speech at the *Euromoney* 'China Forum: Capital Market and Corporate Governance', Beijing (1 December 2004), p. 2.

54. Zhou, 'Instability and Evolution of the Financial System'.

55. CBRC, *2008 Annual Report* (n.d., n.p.), Box 2. 'Lessons from the global financial crisis', p. 32.

56. The quotations are from Gerard Caprio and Patrick Honohan, 'Restoring Banking Stability: Beyond Supervised Capital Requirements', *Journal of Economic Perspectives*, Vol. 13, No. 4 (Autumn 1999), p. 48. The authors did not identify any individual governments or suggest that they had China specifically in mind.

57. David Shambaugh, 'Is there a Chinese model?', *CD*, 1 March 2010.

58. Zhou, 'Instability and Evolution of the Financial System'.

59. A particularly impressive review of this mindset was presented by Zhou Xiaochuan, PBOC Governor, 'Learn Lessons from the Past for the Benefit of Future Endeavour', speech at the China Bond Market Development Summit, Beijing (20 October 2005), pp. 2, 5.

60. Real estate had slackened in 2007 (in response to tighter monetary policy), and industrial production had begun to fall from mid-2008 before the decline in export orders materialised. Thus, 'while the export slowdown exacerbated the economic slump, it was not the trigger'. Zhiwei Zhang and Honglin Wang, 'What triggered China's economic slowdown in 2008? The role of commodity price volatilities', *Hong Kong Monetary Authority Research Note 01/2010* (9 February 2010), pp. 2, 3 and 8.

61. Li Ruihan, Chinese People's Political Consultative Conference Chairman, *CD*, 7 November 2000.

62. See, for example, Cynthia Leung and Olaf Unteroberdoerster, 'Hong Kong SAR as a Financial Center for Asia: Trends and Implications', *IMF Working Paper WP/08/57* (March 2008), pp. 6, 9 and 13.

63. The report noted that 'some smaller joint stock commercial banks ... were as efficient as Hong Kong banks'. It concluded, nevertheless, that 'once Hong Kong banks are taken out [of the full study], the correlation between efficiency and profitability is close to zero for Chinese banks'. Tarhan Feyzioglu, 'Does Good Financial Performance Mean Good Financial Intermediation in China?', *IMF Working Paper WP/09/170* (August 2009), pp. 13, 17.

64. This striking feature of Hong Kong's banking was a topic of some admiration among Mainland economists quite soon after the economic reforms began. Yang Xin, 'Hong Kong's foreign banks energetically develop their China business', *Gang Ao Jingji*, No. 3 (25 March 1985), pp. 17–9.

65. For example, *PD*, 8 March 1985; Xu Dixin, 'On Hong Kong's Economic Relations with the Chinese Mainland', *Liaowang* (Overseas edition), No. 1 (16 September 1985), pp. 22–3; Peng Naidian, 'Reflections on Deepening Economic and Trade Cooperation between Guangdong, Hong Kong, Macao', *Guoji Maoyi*, No. 6 (27 June 1988), pp. 13–6.

66. Pak-wai Liu, Richard Yue-chim Wong, Yun-wing Sung and Pui-king Lau, *China's Economic Reform and Development Strategy of Pearl River Delta* (Hong Kong, Nanyang Commercial Bank Ltd, 1992), p. 127.

67. For a round-up of the sort of difficulties which bankers in Hong Kong were tackling, see Leo Goodstadt, 'A market place for funds and formulae', *Asian Banking*, July 1980, pp. 45–7.

68. Randall S. Jones, Robert E. King and Michael Klein, 'Economic Integration between Hong Kong, Taiwan and the Coastal Provinces of China', *OECD Economic Studies No. 20* (Spring 1993), pp. 116–7, 134 and 138.

69. Joseph Yam, HKMA Chief Executive, 'Speech British Chamber of Commerce', *HKMA*, 20 October 2006; and 'Hong Kong — New Opportunities as an International Financial Centre', *HKMA*, 8 May 2007.

70. The principal parallels are noted throughout Leo F. Goodstadt, "Regulation and Financial Stability in Laissez-Faire Hong Kong: A Reassuring Record', in Greg N. Gregoriou (ed.), *The Banking Crisis Handbook* (London: CRC Press, 2010).

71. The sources of official economic thinking are reviewed in Leo F. Goodstadt, 'A Fragile Prosperity: Government Policy and the Management of Hong Kong's Economic and Social Development', *HKIMR Working Paper No. 1/2009* (January 2009).

72. For the data on these crises and their impact on Hong Kong's currency and financial markets, see Matthew S. Yiu, Wai-Yip Alex Ho and Lu Jin, 'A measure of financial stress in Hong Kong financial market — The financial stress index', *Hong Kong Monetary Authority Research Note 02/2010* (3 March 2010), pp. 2–8.

73. 'Few political economists' would accept this cultural approach 'as a central explanation for policy diffusion'. See Beth A. Simmons and Zachary Elkins, 'The Globalization of Liberalization: Policy Diffusion in the International Political Economy', *American Political Science Review*, Vol. 98, No. 1 (February 2004), pp. 172, 175–6, 187.

74. Note the warnings in a study of culture defined as a much wider concept: 'Could it be that politics are the driving force and that culture just provides excuses? Culture would then provide arguments that help rationalize political arguments'. René M. Stulz and Rohan Williamson, 'Culture, openness, and finance', *Journal of Financial Economics*, Vol. 70 (2003), pp. 346, 347.

75. For a critical evaluation of their relationship, see Andrew Sheng, *From Asian to Global Financial Crisis: An Asian Regulator's View of Unfettered Finance in the 1990s and 2000s* (New York: Cambridge University Press, 2009), p. 110.

76. Claudio Borio and Gianni Toniolo, 'One hundred and thirty years of central bank cooperation: a BIS perspective', *BIS Working Papers No. 197* (February 2006), p. 23.
77. The irrelevance of the 'Washington consensus' to India and to China and other high-growth Asian economies is argued in Dani Rodrik, 'Goodbye Washington Consensus, Hello Washington Confusion? A Review of the World Bank's "Economic Growth in the 1990s: Learning from a Decade of Reform"', *Journal of Economic Literature*, Vol. 44, No. 4 (December 2006), pp. 975, 979–80, 984–5.
78. Pistor, 'Banking Reform in the Chinese Mirror', p. 9.
79. See, for example, China's central bank view: 'Investing in US Treasury bills is "an important component of China's foreign currency reserve investments," People's Bank of China Vice-Governor Hu Xiaolian told a news conference … the credit risk in continuing to buy US Treasuries is low in overall terms. Given that the US dollar is still the leading currency for international settlements, valuation and payment of trade, China will pay closer attention to the supervision of the international monetary system based on the US dollar'. Zhang Ran, 'Purchase of US Treasuries to continue', *CD*, 24 March 2009.
80. Zhou, 'Learn Lessons from the Past for the Benefit of Future Endeavour', pp. 4–5; 'Reform of the internal control and internal incentive systems of the commercial banks', speech at the *Beijing Finance Expo*, Beijing (1 September 2005), p. 1.
81. 'Examples of the [American exports] have included joint venture laws and regulations with regard to profit remission, labor provision, business contracts, patents, trademarks, and copyrights, etc., demanded by foreign multinationals for their own protection, along with new laws that developed as PRC property and business was privatized'. Meredith Woo-Cumings, 'Diverse Paths toward "the Right Institutions": Law, the State, and Economic Reform in East Asia', *ADB Institute Working Paper 18* (April 2001), pp. 11, 17. It should be said that Professor Woo does not commend 'Anglo-American discourse and experience, generalizing on the basis of a set of governmental institutions that are themselves anomalous survivors in the 21st century'. (p. 30)
82. The full text is 663-pages long including dissenting members' statements. In addition, the Commission has created a public archive containing the interview records, staff papers and all the other documentary and digital information obtained by the Commission or generated by its staff..
83. The potential overlap of roles has long been pointed out in Hong Kong in the case of prudential supervision in maintaining monetary as well as financial stability, even after the 1983 linked exchange rate with the American dollar. Sir John Cowperthwaite, Financial Secretary, *HH*, 26 March 1969, p. 205; Papa N'Diaye, 'Macroeconomic Implications for Hong Kong SAR of Accommodative U.S. Monetary Policy', *IMF Working Paper WP/09/256* (November 2009), pp. 13–4.
84. This process and its consequences have been described by Ben S. Bernanke, FRB Chairman, 'Central Bank Independence, Transparency, and

Accountability', speech at the Institute for Monetary and Economic Studies International Conference, Tokyo (25 May 2010).

85. Not that these dangers can be excluded entirely. In a 2009 account of its response to the financial crisis, for example, the Securities and Exchange Commission stated: 'Charged Fannie Mae and Freddie Mac with accounting fraud in 2006 and 2007 respectively, and the companies paid more than $450 million in penalties to settle the SEC's charges'. Few readers could be expected to follow the links shown to other webpages that revealed how both enforcement actions related to offences committed in 2004 or earlier and were thus unrelated to the current crisis. SEC, 'SEC Actions During Turmoil in Credit Markets' (22 January 2009) (URL: http://www.sec.gov/news/press/sec-actions.htm).

86. See, for example, its central bankers' awareness of the implications of the international financial media's views on its monetary policies and performance. Zhou Xiaochuan, PBOC Governor, 'Some Issues Concerning the Reform of the State-owned Commercial Banks', speech at the IIF Spring Membership Conference, Shanghai (16 April 2004).

Chapter 1

1. Andrew G Haldane, BofE Executive Director, 'Rethinking the Financial Network', speech at the Financial Student Association, Amsterdam (28 April 2009), pp. 9, 10.
2. Hector Sants, FSA Chief Executive, 'The challenges facing bank regulation', speech to the Association of Corporate Treasurers (14 May 2009).
3. Adrian Blundell-Wignall, Gert Wehinger and Patrick Slovik, 'The Elephant in the Room: The Need to Deal with What Banks Do', *OECD Journal: Financial Market Trends*, Vol. 2009, Issue 2, Table 2. 'Major financial institutions' write-downs and credit losses', p. 11.
4. Sheila C. Bair, FDIC Chairman, Testimony on Regulatory Perspectives on Financial Regulatory Reform Proposals before the House of Representatives Financial Services Committee (24 July 2009).
5. Lord Turner, FSA Chairman in House of Commons Treasury Committee, *Banking Crisis*, Vol. I Oral evidence (London: HMSO, HC 144–I, March 2009), pp. EV280, 281.
6. Before the global crisis, this conclusion was supported by data derived from 60 countries relating to crises which occurred between 1980 and 2002 and presented in Romain Ranciere, Aaron Tornell and Frank Westermann, 'Decomposing the Effects of Financial Liberalization:Crises vs. Growth', *National Bureau of Economic Research Working Paper 12806* (December 2006). Some central bankers, nevertheless, acknowledged the very heavy costs that financial crises could inflict on an economy, e.g., David Clementi, BofE Deputy Governor, 'Banks and Systemic Risk — Theory and Evidence', speech at the Bank of England Conference (23 May 2001).
7. An impressive example of an evidence-based presentation in favour of the market's wisdom was Mark J. Flannery, 'Using Market Information in Prudential Bank Supervision: A Review of the U.S. Empirical Evidence', *Journal of Money, Credit and Banking*, Vol. 30, No. 3, Part 1 (August 1998), pp. 297–8.

8. The classic expressions of this outlook came from Ben S. Bernanke as a governor of the Federal Reserve Board in 'On Milton Friedman's Ninetieth Birthday', remarks at the Conference to Honor Milton Friedman, University of Chicago (8 November 2002); and Remarks at the Federal Reserve Bank of Dallas Conference on 'The Legacy of Milton and Rose Friedman's *Free to Choose*', Dallas (24 October 2003).

9. The Bank of England denied that 'the *Inflation Targeting* regime ... imposed a straightjacket on central banks including ours by setting too narrow a remit'. Sir John Gieve, BofE Deputy Governor, 'Seven lessons from the last three years' (19 February 2009), pp. 13–4.

10. Washington and London used almost identical wording on this issue, although in the British case, the bank closures since 2007 were without parallel since the nineteenth century. Ben S. Bernanke, FRB Chairman, 'Financial Reform to Address Systemic Risk', speech at the Council on Foreign Relations, Washington, DC (10 March 2009); House of Commons Treasury Committee, *Re–appointment of Mervyn King as Governor of the Bank of England Tenth Report of Session 2007–08*, Vol. II. Oral and written evidence (London: HMSO, HC 524-II, June 2008), p. EV4.

11. Clementi, 'Banks and Systemic Risk — Theory and Evidence'. This view was shared by one of Asia's most experienced regulators after an extensive survey of evidence from the last century. But his finding was challenged by an impressive essay in the same volume. Andrew Sheng, 'Bank Restructuring Revisited' and Geoffrey P. Miller, 'Banking Crises in Perspective: Two Causes and One Cure', in Gerard Caprio, Jr. et al. (eds.), *Preventing Bank Crises: Lessons from Recent Global Bank Failures* (Washington, DC: World Bank, 1998), pp. 280, 325.

12. Professor David Blanchflower, BofE Monetary Policy Committee Member, 'The Future of Monetary Policy', Open Lecture at Cardiff University (March 2009), pp. 1, 9.

13. This finding reflects a study of the principal regulatory issues in the light of data gathered from 107 countries at the end of the previous century presented in James R. Barth, Gerard Caprio, Jr. and Ross Levine, 'Bank Regulation and Supervision: What Works Best?', *National Bureau of Economic Research Working Paper Series, Working Paper 9323* (November 2002).

14. For a summary of the key issues, see Sanghoon Ahn and Philip Hemmings, 'Policy Influences on Economic Growth in OECD Countries: An Evaluation of the Evidence', *Economics Department Working Papers No. 246* (Paris: OECD, 2000), pp. 41–3.

15. Paul Tucker, BofE Deputy Governor, 'Financial Crisis and G20 Financial Regulatory Reform: An Overview', remarks at the FSB and Korean G20 Presidential Committee Conference, Korea (3 September 2010), p. 3.

16. 'Financial economics. Efficiency and beyond', *Economist*, 16 July 2009. This verdict was promptly challenged by the University of Chicago's Professor Robert Lucas, 'In defence of the dismal science', *Economist*, 6 August 2009.

17. Not until almost two years after leaving office did President George W. Bush publicly attack officials for their light-touch regulation before 2007. '"We were blindsided by a financial crisis that had been more than a decade in the making": his focus, he writes [in his newly-published autobiography],

"had been kitchen-table economic issues like jobs and inflation. I assumed any major credit troubles would have been flagged by the regulators or rating agencies.'" Michiko Kakutani, 'In Bush Memoir, Policy Intersects With Personality', *New York Times*, 4 November 2010.

18. US Treasury, 'The Role of the Federal Reserve in Preserving Financial and Monetary Stability: Joint Statement by the Department of the Treasury and the Federal Reserve' (23 March 2009).

19. House of Commons Treasury Committee, *Re–appointment of Mervyn King as Governor of the Bank of England Tenth Report of Session 2007–08*, Vol. I. Report together with formal minutes (London: HMSO, April 2008), p. 11.

20. British politicians were not so convinced, however, about the importance of the financial sector in the British economy judged by international standards. See House of Commons Treasury Committee, *Banking Crisis: regulation and supervision, Fourteenth Report of Session 2008–09* (London: HMSO, HC 767, 21 July 2009), pp. 48, 49.

21. 'Over the past few months there has been renewed talk of London overtaking New York as the world's leading financial centre. And it has reflected fears in the US as much as self congratulation in this country.' Sir John Gieve, BofE Deputy Governor, 'The City's Growth: The Crest of a Wave or Swimming with the Stream?', speech to the Society of Chartered Accountants, London (26 March 2007), p. 2.

22. Craig Doidge, G. Andrew Karolyi and René M. Stulz, 'Has New York become less competitive in global markets? Evaluating foreign listing choices over time', *Journal of Financial Economics*, Vol. 91, Issue No. 3 (March 2009), pp. 254, 255, 256–7.

23. Joe Nocera, 'Talking Business: New York and London: Twins in Finance and Folly', *New York Times*, 9 May 2009.

24. Claudio Borio and Gianni Toniolo, 'One hundred and thirty years of central bank cooperation: a BIS perspective', *BIS Working Papers No. 197* (February 2006), p. 21.

25. Ethan B. Kapstein, 'Resolving the Regulator's Dilemma: International Coordination of Banking Regulations', *International Organization*, Vol. 43, No. 2 (Spring 1989), pp. 328–9.

26. The analysis in this paragraph is based on an impressive analysis of the early stages of the Anglo-American consensus at work in David Andrew Singer, 'Capital Rules: The Domestic Politics of International Regulatory Harmonization', *International Organization*, Vol. 58, No. 3 (Summer 2004), pp. 550–1, 554–60. The author does not use this terminology, however.

27. Joan E. Spero, 'Guiding Global Finance', *Foreign Policy*, No. 73 (Winter, 1988–89), pp. 115–6.

28. Gerard Carpio and Patrick Honohan, 'Restoring Banking Stability: Beyond Supervised Capital Requirements', *Journal of Economic Perspectives*, Vol. 13, No. 4 (Autumn 1999), p. 51.

29. Heath Price Tarbert, 'Are International Capital Adequacy Rules Adequate? The Basle Accord and beyond', *University of Pennsylvania Law Review*, Vol. 148, No. 5 (May 2000), pp. 1782, 1784–5.

30. Camille M. Caesar, 'Capital-Based Regulation and U. S. Banking Reform', *Yale Law Journal*, Vol. 101, No. 7 (May 1992), pp. 1534–5.

31. Michael R. King and Timothy J. Sinclair, 'Private Actors and Public Policy: A Requiem for the New Basel Capital Accord', *International Political Science Review/Revue internationale de science politique*, Vol. 24, No. 3 (July 2003), pp. 349, 351, 356.

32. On these differences and their significance, see Howell E. Jackson, 'An American Perspective on the U.K. Financial Services Authority: Politics, Goals & Regulatory Intensity', *Harvard Law School Discussion Paper No. 522* (08/2005), pp. 4, 12 especially.

33. 'The time has long past where we can calmly accept that the role of the central bank is let asset price bubbles burst and pick up the pieces afterwards. That was the Fed's mantra; it can no longer be the case ... some would attribute the asset price bubble at least partly to the Fed's own actions, specifically its policy of holding interest rates at extremely low levels for nearly three years (from the end of 2001 to the end of 2004).' Thomas Huertas, FSA Banking Sector Director, 'The Outlook for Banking and Banking Regulation', speech at the ICFR Inaugural Summit, London (1 April 2009).

34. The SEC chairman described how 'as the regulators of two of the world's major market centres, the SEC and the FSA have a strong interest in collaborating [to] ... achieve coherent oversight of global actors and limit opportunities for playing the regulatory seams'. In a joint statement, the FSA Chief Executive declared that 'the strategic dialogue with the SEC is a valuable component of the discussions around these reforms, particularly in areas of joint interest and in identifying potential regulatory gaps.' Hector Sants, FSA Chief Executive, and Mary Schapiro, SEC Chairman, 'FSA and SEC discuss approaches to global regulatory requirements', *FSA Press Release FSA/PN/124/2009 916* (16 September 2009).

35. Beth A. Simmons and Zachary Elkins, 'The Globalization of Liberalization: Policy Diffusion in the International Political Economy', *American Political Science Review*, Vol. 98, No. 1 (February 2004), pp. 180, 186, 187.

36. But American pressures on the region's weaker governments in the run-up to the 1997–98 Asian financial crisis and during its management should not be ignored. See John Williamson, 'The Years of Emerging Market Crises: A Review of Feldstein', *Journal of Economic Literature*, Vol. 42, No. 3 (September 2004), pp. 822–37.

37. Beth A. Simmons, 'The International Politics of Harmonization: The Case of Capital Market Regulation', *International Organization*, Vol. 55, No. 3 (Summer, 2001), pp. 592–5. This process did not imply that at the level of the firm (rather than the regulatory environment), Anglo-American norms would set the rules. The complexity of the response of foreign corporations to the norms of American boardroom culture as globalisation accelerated was well illustrated by Gerald F. Davis and Christopher Marquis, 'The Globalization of Stock Markets and Convergence in Corporate Governance', in Victor Nee and Richard Swedberg (eds.), *The Economic Sociology of Capitalism* (Princeton: Princeton University Press, 2005), pp. 360, 362, 364, 385–6 in particular.

38. Darryl Crawford, 'Globalisation and Guanxi: The Ethos of Hong Kong Finance', *New Political Economy*, Vol. 6, No. 1 (2001), p. 47.

39. James R. Barth, Gerard Caprio, Jr. and Ross Levine, 'Bank Regulation and Supervision: What Works Best?', *National Bureau of Economic Research Working Paper Series, Working Paper 9323* (November 2002), p. 1.

40. A typical example of such reassurance to the world at large was an American central banker's detailed review of financial innovation which advised that 'the potential for the new instruments and techniques [i.e., mortgage-based and other derivatives] to produce instability has been overestimated'. Roger W. Ferguson, Jr., FRB Vice Chairman, 'Financial Engineering and Financial Stability', remarks at the Annual Conference on the Securities Industry, American Institute of Certified Public Accountants and the Financial Management Division of the Securities Industry Association, New York (20 November 2002).

41. Richard Spillenkothen, FRB Director, 'Oversight of investment banks' response to the lessons of Enron', testimony before the Senate Permanent Subcommittee on Investigations of the Committee on Governmental Affairs (11 December 2002).

42. On the difference in constraints on regulators and legislators, see Singer, 'Capital Rules: The Domestic Politics of International Regulatory Harmonization', *International Organization*, p. 543.

43. The conflicting national interests among Eurozone leaders were very public. See for example the reporting in Carter Dougherty, 'European Central Bank resists rush to print more money', *International Herald Tribune*, 24 March 2009; *Economist*: 'The European Union's week from hell', 9 October 2008 and 'Central banks' exit strategies: This way out', 4 June 2009.

44. Data on the varied impact of the global crisis on the United States, the United Kingdom and individual members of the EU, and their very national responses, are summarised in Mark Horton et al., 'The State of Public Finances: A Cross-Country Fiscal Monitor', *IMF Staff Position Note SPN/09/21* (30 July 2009), pp. 28–30.

45. This hostility was well reported in Jack Ewing and Steve Erlanger, 'Trichet Faces Growing Criticism in Europe Crisis', *New York Times*, 21 May 2010.

46. For a post-global crisis summary of the British regulators' sense of Greenspan's influence, see Lord Turner's comments in House of Commons Treasury Committee, *Banking Crisis*, pp. EV280, 281.

47. Alan Greenspan, *The Age of Turbulence: Adventures in a New World* (New York: Penguin Press, 2007), p. 489.

48. Ben S. Bernanke, FRB Chairman, 'Hedge Funds and Systemic Risk', speech at the Federal Reserve Bank of Atlanta's 2006 Financial Markets Conference, Georgia (16 May 2006).

49. Greenspan, *The Age of Turbulence: Adventures in a New World*, pp. 375–6.

50. But note that earlier in this speech, he had declared: 'We must ensure that an institutional memory is maintained so that the lessons from the crisis are not forgotten and those impediments to excessive risk-taking are not swept away once memories of the crisis recede.' Mervyn King, BofE Governor, 'Finance: A Return from Risk', speech to the Worshipful Company of International Bankers (17 March 2009), pp. 4, 15.

51. Charles W. Calomiris, 'The Political Lessons of Depression-Era Banking Reform' (April 2010), *Oxford Review of Economic Policy* (forthcoming), pp. 29–30.

52. Significantly, while he pledged that 'authorities should (and will) try to ensure that the lapses in risk management of 1998 do not happen again', he warned that this 'systemic risk' could not be eliminated: 'To try to do so would likely stifle innovation without achieving the intended goal.' Bernanke, 'Hedge Funds and Systemic Risk'.

53. Sheila C. Bair, FDIC Chairman, Testimony on Modernizing Bank Supervision and Regulation before the Senate Committee on Banking, Housing and Urban Affairs (19 March 2009).

54. Robert Z. Aliber, 'Financial Innovation and the Boundaries of Banking', *Managerial and Decision Economics*, Vol. 8, No. 1 (March 1987), pp. 67–8.

55. See the prescient observations in Joan E. Spero, 'Guiding Global Finance', *Foreign Policy*, No. 73 (Winter 1988–89), pp. 114–5, 117–8, 121–2.

56. Simmons and Elkins, 'The Globalization of Liberalization: Policy Diffusion in the International Political Economy', *American Political Science Review*, p. 171.

57. Dani Rodrik, 'Goodbye Washington Consensus, Hello Washington Confusion? A Review of the World Bank's "Economic Growth in the 1990s: Learning from a Decade of Reform"', *Journal of Economic Literature*, Vol. 44, No. 4 (December 2006), p. 975.

58. See the comments based on a reference frame of '86 episodes of banking insolvency in 69 countries between the late 1970s and the early 1990s' in King and Sinclair, 'Private Actors and Public Policy: A Requiem for the New Basel Capital Accord', *International Political Science Review*, p. 349.

59. C. A. E. Goodhart, 'Why Do Banks Need a Central Bank?', *Oxford Economic Papers*, Vol. 39, No. 1 (March 1987), pp. 87–8; Gary Gorton and Andrew Winton, 'Banking in Transition Economies: Does Efficiency Require Instability?', *Journal of Money, Credit and Banking*, Vol. 30, No. 3, Part 2 (August 1998), p. 625.

60. A study of 24 emerging economies between 1975 and 1997 concluded that the estimated losses they suffered 'should alarm policymakers'. Michael M. Hutchison and Ilan Noy, 'How Bad are Twins? Output Costs of Currency and Banking Crises', *Journal of Money, Credit, and Banking*, Vol. 37, No. 4 (August 2005), p. 748.

61. 'A Short History of Modern Finance', *Economist*, 16 October 2008.

62. Elizabeth A. Duke, FRB Governor, 'Credit availability and prudent lending standards', testimony before the House of Representatives Committee on Financial Services (25 March 2009).

63. Kevin Warsh, FRB Governor, 'The Panic of 2008', speech at the Council of Institutional Investors 2009 Spring Meeting, Washington, DC (6 April 2009).

64. Huertas, 'The Outlook for Banking and Banking Regulation'.

65. Andrea Beltratti and René M. Stulz, 'The Credit Crisis Around the Globe: Why Did Some Banks Perform Better?', *Dice Center WP 2010–05* (March 2010), pp. 13–4.

66. Lord Turner, FSA Chairman, *The Turner Review: A regulatory response to the global banking crisis* (London: Financial Services Authority, March 2009), pp. 45–6.

67. Warsh, 'The Panic of 2008'.

68. 'But the blunt fact is that even if we had had a better supervisory process in place, it would have made only a small difference to the evolution of the financial crisis in the UK.' Lord Turner, FSA Chairman, 'Building a more stable global banking system', speech at the Global Financial Forum, New York (27 April 2009).

69. Paul Tucker, BofE Deputy Governor, Remarks at The Turner Review Conference (27 March 2009).

70. Kevin Warsh, FRB Governor, 'Regulation and Its Discontents', speech at the New York Association for Business Economics, New York (3 February 2010).

71. Mervyn King, BofE Governor, 'Banking: From Bagehot to Basel, and Back Again', speech to the Buttonwood Gathering, New York (25 October 2010), p. 17.

72. The Federal Reserve Board Chairman, himself a distinguished academic, concluded a proposed agenda for economic research with the assertion: 'The financial crisis did not discredit the usefulness of economic research and analysis by any means; indeed, both older and more recent ideas drawn from economic research have proved invaluable to policymakers attempting to diagnose and respond to the financial crisis.' Ben S. Bernanke, FRB Chairman, 'Implications of the Financial Crisis for Economics', speech at the Conference Co-sponsored by the Center for Economic Policy Studies and the Bendheim Center for Finance, Princeton University (24 September 2010).

Chapter 2

1. Editorial, 'It's the Regulations, Not the Regulator', *New York Times*, 18 March 2009.

2. Ken Hogg, FSA Insurance Sector Director, 'Key priorities in regulation — outlining the FSA's strategy', speech at the Future of Life Assurance IEA Conference (19 May 2010).

3. Financial Crisis Inquiry Commission, *Final Report of the National Commission on the Causes of the Financial and Economic Crisis in the United States* (Official Government Edition, 21 January 2011), chapter 1, 'Before our very eyes'.

4. Mervyn King, BofE Chairman, 'Finance: A Return from Risk', speech to the Worshipful Company of International Bankers (17 March 2009), p. 15.

5. Sheila C. Bair, FDIC Chairman, Testimony on Modernizing Bank Supervision and Regulation before the Senate Committee on Banking, Housing and Urban Affairs (19 March 2009).

6. ibid.

7. Lord Turner, FSA Chairman, 'Protecting Consumers and Winning Trust', speech at the British Bankers' Association Conference (13 July 2010).

8. King, 'Finance: A Return from Risk'.

9. Ben S. Bernanke, FRB Chairman, 'Financial Reform to Address Systemic Risk', speech at the Council on Foreign Relations, Washington, DC (10 March 2009).

10. This point was made in an early reaction to 'big bang' deregulation of British financial markets. John Kay et al., 'Regulatory reform in Britain', *Economic Policy*, Vol. 3, No. 7 (October 1988), p. 288.

11. William J. Baumol, 'Entrepreneurship: Productive, Unproductive, and Destructive', *Journal of Political Economy*, Vol. 98, No. 5 (October 1990), pp. 895, 899, 917.

12. Karin Knorr Cetina and Urs Bruegger, 'Global Microstructures: The Virtual Societies of Financial Markets', *American Journal of Sociology*, Vol. 107, No. 4 (January 2002), pp. 906, 910–1, 939, 942–4.

13. Identification of these behaviour patterns as a cultural outcome of regulatory policies is acknowledged, albeit less explicitly than here, in IMF, 'Cross-Cutting Themes in Economies with Large Banking Systems' (16 April 2010), pp. 19–20; Table 3. 'Large Complex Financial Institutions (UK and Asia)', p. 26.

14. Hector Sants, FSA Chief Executive, 'Do regulators have a role to play in judging culture and ethics?', speech at the Chartered Institute of Securities and Investments Conference (17 June 2010).

15. Lord Turner, FSA Chairman, 'Priorities for the reform of global regulation — challenging past assumptions', speech at IOSCO 2009, Tel Aviv (11 June 2009).

16. For a belated acknowledgment of the parallels, see Bernanke, 'Financial Reform to Address Systemic Risk'.

17. Among the regulators' challenges in the Asian financial crisis (which were to prove no less menacing in the current global crisis) were the quality of corporate information and the severe pressure on bank credit triggered by sharp falls in share prices. Alastair Clark, BofE Executive Director, 'Accounting Standards and International Financial Markets', speech at the Institute of Chartered Accountants in Banking, Dublin (3 May 2000); David Clementi, BofE Deputy Governor, 'Banks and Systemic Risk — Theory and Evidence', speech at the Bank of England Conference (23 May 2001).

18. World Bank, *The East Asian Miracle. Economic Growth and Public Policy* (New York: Oxford University Press, 1993), pp. 1–2.

19. This topic is analysed in some depth in World Bank, *Managing Capital Inflows in East Asia* (Washington: World Bank, 1995). See also Manuel Guitián, 'The Challenge of Managing Global Capital Flows', *Finance and Development*, Vol. 35, No. 2 (June 1998), pp. 14–7.

20. Stijin Claessens and Simeon Djankov, 'Publicly-Listed East Asian Corporates: Growth, Financing and Risks', paper presented to the Regional Conference on Asian Corporate Recovery: Corporate Governance, Government Policy (World Bank, 15 March 1999).

21. The analysis in this paragraph, together with the accompanying quotation, is drawn from J. A. Kregel, 'Derivatives and global capital flows: applications to Asia', *Cambridge Journal of Economics*, Vol. 22, No. 6 (November 1998), pp. 678, 679, 690.

22. For an excellent overview of China's domestic and international financial situation in this period, see Nicholas R. Lardy, 'The case of China', in Chung H. Lee (ed.), *Financial Liberalization and the Economic Crisis in Asia* (London: Routledge Curzon, 2003).

23. A good summary of the ITICs, their history, role and problems can be found in Solomon Smith Barney, 'Fixed Income – Local Government ITIC Credits', 26 November 1998.

24. See Markus Taube, 'Economic Relations between the PRC and the States of Europe', *China Quarterly*, No. 169 (March 2002), p. 103.

25. Alistair Darling, M.P., Chancellor of the Exchequer, in House of Commons Treasury Committee, *Banking Crisis*, Vol. I. Oral evidence (London: HMSO, HC 144-I, March 2009), p. EV366. It should be noted that officials offered another, less compressed and more objective listing of the external factors: 'Large current account surpluses accumulated in the oil-exporting countries, Japan and some other east Asian developing nations, while fiscal and current account deficits grew in the US, UK and some members of the Eurozone'. FSA, 'Memorandum from the Financial Services Authority (FSA)', in House of Commons Treasury Committee, *Banking Crisis*, Vol. II. Written evidence (London: HMSO, HC 144-II, March 2009), p. EV 456.

26. Charles Bean, BofE Deputy Governor, 'Some Lessons for Monetary Policy from the Recent Financial Turmoil', remarks at the Conference on Globalisation, Inflation and Monetary Policy (22 November 2008), pp. 2–3.

27. Ben S. Bernanke, FRB Chairman, 'Four Questions about the Financial Crisis' speech at the Morehouse College, Atlanta, Georgia (14 April 2009).

28. Bernanke, 'Financial Reform to Address Systemic Risk'. As early as 1996, China had the world's fourth largest foreign exchange reserves. *NCNA*, 21 April 1996.

29. King, 'Finance: A Return from Risk', p. 15.

30. Christopher Cox, SEC Chairman, Address to the Joint Meeting of the Exchequer Club and Women in Housing and Finance (4 December 2008).

31. These figures are derived from Bank of England estimates published in House of Commons Treasury Committee, *Financial Stability and Transparency Sixth Report of Session 2007–08* (London: HMSO, HC 371, March 2008), p. 17.

32. Sir John Gieve, BofE Deputy Governor, 'Uncertainty, policy and financial markets', speech at the Barbican Centre (24 July 2007), pp. 7–8.

33. House of Commons Treasury Committee, *Financial Stability and Transparency Sixth Report of Session 2007–08*, p. 5.

34. FSA, 'Memorandum from the Financial Services Authority (FSA)', *Banking Crisis*, Vol. II, p. EV 457.

35. Yuliya S. Demyanyk and Otto Van Hemert, 'Understanding the Sub-prime Mortgage Crisis', (5 December 2008), p. 5 (URL: http://papers.ssrn.com/sol3/papers.cfm?abstract_id=1020396).

36. Karl E. Case, Edward L. Glaeser and Jonathan A. Parker, 'Real Estate and the Macroeconomy', *Brookings Papers on Economic Activity*, Vol. 2000, No. 2 (2000), pp. 132–3, 136, 144.

37. Sheila C. Bair, FDIC Chairman, Remarks to the Global Association of Risk Professionals, New York (25 February 2008).

38. Data on the declining quality of these mortgages and their market impact were provided by Sheila C. Bair, FDIC Chairman, Testimony on the State of the Banking Industry before the Senate Committee on Banking, Housing and Urban Affairs (4 March 2008).

39. The decline in standards of loan screening was substantiated in a study based on data covering 90 per cent of all sub-prime loans that were securitised. Benjamin J. Keys et al., 'Did Securitisation Lead to Lax Screening? Evidence

from Sub-prime Loans', *EFA 2008 Athens Meetings Paper* (December 2008), pp. 1, 5, 28.

40. David Clementi, BofE Deputy Governor, 'Property and the Economy', speech at the Chartered Surveyors Livery Company International Dinner (29 April 2002), pp. 2–3, 4–5, 10.

41. House of Commons Treasury Committee, *The run on the Rock Fifth Report of Session 2007–08*, Vol. I (London: HMSO, HC56-I, January 2008), p. 35.

42. Cox, Joint Meeting of the Exchequer Club and Women in Housing and Finance.

43. Kathleen L. Casey, SEC Commissioner, 'Remarks at the Commission Open Meeting' (3 December 2008).

44. Note, for example, how the British Accountancy & Actuarial Discipline Board launched investigations into allegations against auditors: 'AADB Investigating Auditors' Role in Relation to JP Morgan Securities Ltd.'s Compliance with FSA Client Asset Rules', *AADB PN 24* (4 October 2010); 'AADB Investigating Auditors' Role in Relation to Lehman Brothers' Compliance with FSA Client Asset Rules', *AADB PN 25* (4 October 2010). There have been complaints, however, that the accounting profession's own audit standards were badly flawed and led bank executives to unwittingly over-estimate their financial stability. Louise Armitstead, 'Coalition admits concerns over "flawed" IFRS', *Daily Telegraph*, 27 August 2010. In addition, the approach that auditors ought to take is a matter of dispute between financial and securities regulators. See Lord Turner, FSA Chairman, 'Banks are different: should accounting reflect that fact?', speech at the Institute of Chartered Accountants in England and Wales, London (21 January 2010).

45. The analysis and quotations in this paragraph are drawn from a useful summary of the ratings agencies' historical role in American and other financial markets, together with a prescient review of the dangers inherent in the expanded role which the Basel arrangements conferred on them, in King and Sinclair, 'Private Actors and Public Policy: A Requiem for the New Basel Capital Accord', *International Political Science Review*, pp. 351–3, 358–9.

46. The quotations are from Basel Committee on Banking Supervision, *A New Capital Adequacy Framework, Consultative Paper* (Basel: Bank for International Settlements, June 1999), pp. 13, 26, 36.

47. This case is made by Vanessa Redak, 'Risks, Ratings and Regulation: Toward a Reorganization of Credit via Basel II?', in Peter Mooslechner et al. (eds.), *The Political Economy Of Financial Market Regulation: The Dynamics of Inclusion and Exclusion* (Cheltenham: Edward Elgar Publishing Ltd, 2006), pp. 199–200.

48. 'Just as Basel I created incentives for behavior in the financial markets which undermined the intent of the initial Capital Adequacy Accord, the political economy of bond rating ... may be the weakest link in the Basel II proposals'. Michael R. King and Timothy J. Sinclair, 'Private Actors and Public Policy: A Requiem for the New Basel Capital Accord', *International Political Science Review/Revue internationale de science politique*, Vol. 24, No. 3 (July 2003), p. 358.

49. Sir Andrew Large, BofE Deputy Governor, 'Financial Stability Oversight, Past & Present', speech at the London School of Economics (22 January 2004), pp. 14–5.

50. Sheila C. Bair, FDIC Chairman, Remarks at the Bear Stearns Mortgage and Structured Product Conference, New York (17 January 2008).
51. Nigel Jenkinson, BofE Financial Stability Executive Director, et al., 'Financial Innovation: What Have We Learnt?', Reserve Bank of Australia Conference on Lessons from the Financial Turmoil of 2007 and 2008 (14–15 July 2008), pp. 10–11.
52. Casey, 'Remarks at the Commission Open Meeting'.
53. Bernanke, 'Four Questions about the Financial Crisis'.
54. There is some confusion about the links between banking and insurance. A leading British regulator stated, for example, that 'in general, insurance companies did not play a major role' in the international financial crisis and then went on to list an extensive range of insurance activities directly linked to banking stability. Lord Turner, FSA Chairman, Address to the IAIS Annual Conference, Dubai (27 October 2010).
55. House of Commons Treasury Committee, *Financial Stability and Transparency Sixth Report of Session 2007–08*, pp. 18, 20, 23, 25.
56. David Clementi, BofE Deputy Governor, 'Crisis prevention and resolution — two aspects of financial stability', Inaugural Lecture at the South Bank University Centre for Monetary and Financial Economics (6 September 2000).
57. Sir Andrew Large, BofE Deputy Governor, 'Convergence in Insurance and Banking: Some Financial Stability Issues', speech at the Mandarin Oriental Hotel (12 June 2003), pp. 4–5.
58. This analysis of the American outlook, together with the quotations, is drawn from Roger W. Ferguson, Jr., FRB Vice Chairman, 'Financial Engineering and Financial Stability', remarks at the Annual Conference on the Securities Industry, American Institute of Certified Public Accountants and the Financial Management Division of the Securities Industry Association, New York (20 November 2002).
59. Bair, Testimony on Modernizing Bank Supervision and Regulation before the Senate Committee on Banking, Housing and Urban Affairs.
60. Adrian Blundell-Wignall, Gert Wehinger and Patrick Slovik, 'The Elephant in the Room: The Need to Deal with What Banks Do', *OECD Journal: Financial Market Trends*, Vol. 2009, Issue 2, Table 2. 'Major financial institutions' write-downs and credit losses', p. 11.
61. Cox, Address to the Joint Meeting of the Exchequer Club and Women in Housing and Finance.
62. Details of the criminal activities were provided by Elisse B. Walter, SEC Commissioner, Testimony Concerning Securities Law Enforcement in the Current Financial Crisis before the United States House of Representatives Committee on Financial Services, 20 March 2009.
63. King, 'Finance: A Return from Risk', p. 6.
64. Kevin Warsh, FRB Governor, 'The Panic of 2008', speech at the Council of Institutional Investors 2009 Spring Meeting, Washington, DC (6 April 2009).
65. Bair, Testimony on Modernizing Bank Supervision and Regulation before the Senate Committee on Banking, Housing and Urban Affairs.

66. Daniel K. Tarullo, FRB Governor, 'Financial Regulatory Reform', speech at the U.S. Monetary Policy Forum, New York (26 February 2010).

67. Sheila C. Bair, FDIC Chairman, 'Restoring the Strength and Vitality of the U.S. Financial System', remarks before the Risk Management Association, Baltimore (18 October 2010).

68. Consumer protection was presented literally as 'a word' concluding the Chairman's congressional testimony. Ben S. Bernanke FRB Chairman, 'Regulatory restructuring', testimony before the House of Representatives Committee on Financial Services (24 July 2009).

69. See the patronising reference to 'a nostalgic elegy for a past age of innocence and stability: with Captain Mainwaring back behind the desk in the branch at Walmington-on-Sea casting a censorious eye over any householder or small-business man silly enough to want to take on too much credit, while the wide boys of the City and Wall Street are free to speculate but well away from sober middle England'. Lord Turner, FSA Chairman, 'The financial crisis and the future of financial regulation', The Economist's Inaugural City Lecture (21 January 2009).

70. HMG, *Reforming financial markets* (Cm 7667/2009), p. 14.

71. Ben S. Bernanke, FRB Chairman, 'Financial Innovation and Consumer Protection', speech at the Sixth Biennial Community Affairs Research Conference, Washington, DC (17 April 2009).

72. Elizabeth A. Duke, FRB Governor, 'Consumer protection', testimony before the House of Representatives Subcommittee on Domestic Monetary Policy and Technology, Committee on Financial Services (16 July 2009).

73. These criticisms of the Federal Reserve's performance are summarised from Sheila C. Bair, FDIC Chairman, Statement on the Causes and Current State of the Financial Crisis before the Financial Crisis Inquiry Commission (14 January 2010).

74. Mervyn King, BofE Governor, Speech at the Lord Mayor's Banquet for Bankers and Merchants, London (16 June 2010), p. 5.

75. Lord Turner, FSA Chairman, Mansion House Speech, London (21 September 2010).

76. For examples of litigation relating to anti-arthritic drugs, pain-killers and anti-depressants and the manufacturers' failures to respond to warnings from their own executives, see *New York Times*: Stephanie Saul, 'Merck Wrote Drug Studies for Doctors', 16 April 2008; Barry Meier, '3 Executives Spared Prison in OxyContin Case', 21 July 2007; Barry Meier and Benedict Carey, 'Drug maker is accused of fraud', 26 February 2009; Gardiner Harris and Duff Wilson, 'Whistle-blower cases rock drug industry', 28 October 2010.

77. King, 'Finance: A Return from Risk', p. 6.

78. A saving clause was added: 'If we cannot afford to have them fail, then they should be regulated so as to prevent imposing systemic risk.' Ethiopis Tafara, SEC Director, 'A Few Observations Based On International Regulatory Conversations', speech at the CESR Conference, Paris (23 February 2009).

79. Sheila C. Bair, FDIC Chairman, Statement on Implementing the Dodd-Frank Wall Street Reform and Consumer Protection Act before the Senate Committee on Banking, Housing, and Urban Affairs (30 September 2010).

80. Kevin Warsh, FRB Governor, 'Regulation and Its Discontents', speech at the New York Association for Business Economics, New York (3 February 2010).
81. King, Speech at the Lord Mayor's Banquet for Bankers and Merchants, p. 5
82. This affair was part of the collective memory of British regulators on the eve of the global crisis. See Ian Bond, BofE Financial Crisis Management Division Head, 'Managing a Bank-specific Crisis: A UK Perspective', BBA workshop on managing a bank-specific crisis (26 October 2006), p. 1.
83. Norma Cohen, 'Regulation: Doubts over political resolve for reform', *Financial Times*, 5 October 2009. Dismay about the slow pace of reform has been voiced, albeit diplomatically, by the IMF Managing Director. Dominique Strauss-Kahn, 'Beyond the Crisis: Sustainable Growth and a Stable International Monetary System', Sixth Annual Bundesbank Lecture (4 September 2009).

Chapter 3

1. This author points out that this view was always implausible. Guy de Jonquières, 'China and the global economic crisis', *ECIPE Policy Briefs No. 02/2009*, p. 1. The *Economist* recorded the prevalence of this mood in 2008: e.g., 'From Mao to the mall: Amid all the global gloom, the good news is that China is turning into a nation of spenders, as well as sellers', 14 February 2008; 'The credit crunch China moves to centre stage: In a whirl of financial summitry, China ponders how to wield its new-found clout', 30 October 2008; 'Reflating the dragon: Can the world's fastest-growing economy avoid a sharp downturn?', 13 November 2008.
2. Wang Xiuqiong and Chang Ai'ling, 'Premier Wen says financial crisis not bottom out, impact spreading', *NCNA*, 28 February 2009.
3. For example, 'President Hu: China's economic development faces challenges', *NCNA*, 29 November 2008; Ambrose Evans-Pritchard, 'Global investors see Chinese green shoots', *Daily Telegraph*, 19 February 2009.
4. This attitude seemed clear enough among China's central bankers in 2007. See Zhou Xiaochuan, PBOC Governor, 'Instability and Evolution of the Financial System' (5 December 2007), pp. 1–7.
5. People's Bank of China, *Annual Report 2008* (n.d., n.p.), p. 36.
6. The vulnerability was being described in sombre terms even after the global crisis itself was over. 'The banking industry still faces great risks. Banks should be clear about the situation and make relentless efforts to manage risks'. Liu Mingkang, CBRC Chairman, 'Chinese regulators highlight precautions against financial risks before Seoul Summit', *NCNA*, 11 November 2010.
7. 'The correlation between efficiency and profitability is close to zero for Chinese banks'. Tarhan Feyzioglu, 'Does Good Financial Performance Mean Good Financial Intermediation in China?', *IMF Working Paper WP/09/170* (August 2009), pp. 17, 19, 26.
8. Based on Feyzioglu, 'Does Good Financial Performance Mean Good Financial Intermediation in China?', *IMF Working Paper WP/09/170*, pp. 20–1 and Table 6. 'The Banking System, 2008', p. 22. Numbers of rural credit cooperatives and finance companies are as shown in China Banking Regulatory Commission, *2008 Annual Report* (n.d., n.p.), p. 148.

9. 'China has established a comprehensive socialist legal system that governs all sectors of social life and provides a legal basis for the nation's economic and social construction ... The system ensures, legally and institutionally, that the Communist Party of China (CPC) will always be at the core of the leadership'. Wu Bangguo, Standing Committee Chairman of the National People's Congress, 'China will stick to socialism as required by law: top legislator', *NCNA*, 25 January 2011.

10. A well-illustrated analysis of how and why the economic reforms did not undermine the institutional dominance traditionally exercised by the Chinese Communist Party is Lance L. P. Gore, 'The Communist Legacy in Post-Mao Economic Growth', *China Journal*, No. 41 (January 1999), pp. 25–54.

11. Zhou Xiaochuan, PBOC Governor, 'Improve Corporate Governance and Develop Capital Market', speech at the *Euromoney* 'China Forum: Capital Market and Corporate Governance', Beijing (1 December 2004), pp. 1, 2.

12. Zhou Xiaochuan, PBOC Governor, Address at the Global Think-tank Summit (3 July 2009), p. 6.

13. For example, by 2010, all private law firms had their own Party organisations, as did 'more than 62 per cent of the country's accounting firms' (compared with only 20 per cent a year earlier). Li Yuanchao, Party Organisation Department Head, 'Senior official calls for enhanced Party building in new social strata, professions', *NCNA*, 27 January 2010.

14. David Murphy, 'Bank on Zhou: China's tough stockmarket regulator becomes central bank chief to boost confidence', *Far Eastern Economic Review*, 9 January 2003.

15. On the status and related problems of the PBOC and the CBRC, see Hui Huang, 'Institutional structure of financial regulation in China: Lessons from the global financial crisis', *Journal of Corporate Law Studies*, Vol. 10, Part 1 (April 2010), pp. 234–5.

16. Pan Yue, State Environmental Protection Administration (SEPA) Vice Director, 'More efforts needed to implement environmentally-friendly loan policy', *NCNA*, 13 February 2008.

17. In fact the banks had already been subject to a PBOC directive in 2008 setting out several, similar restrictions to the 'Guidance'. Hu Xiaolian, PBOC Deputy Governor, Speech at the Buenos Aires Money and Banking Conference, Buenos Aires (1 September 2008).

18. The 'Guidance' directed enforcement of 'strict controls on market access, reinforced environmental supervision, and tougher controls over land use. *Banks were ordered to lend money for these sectors in strict accordance with present industrial policies'.* (emphasis added) 'China to address overcapacity in emerging sectors', *NCNA*, 26 August 2009. Similar examples could be cited from other policy areas, including relocation of existing manufacturing facilities from Shanghai and Guangdong to Western provinces and pricing policies for fuel and power.

19. 'China to speed up elimination of outdated production capacity', *NCNA*, 21 January 2010. The Prime Minister's remarks were reported in 'China's overcapacity no relation to central government investment', *NCNA*, 27 December 2009.

20. See, for example, Zhou, 'Improve Corporate Governance and Develop Capital Market', pp. 1–6. A strong case for this principle in banking was also made by Wu Xiaoling, PBOC Deputy Governor, Remarks on the International Seminar on the Tenth Anniversary of the Asian Financial Crisis (21 June 2007), p. 4.

21. Chen Bin, National Development and Reform Commission, 'Top planner warns of overcapacity', *CD*, 21 September 2009; 'Official warns of overcapacity under industry recovery', *NCNA*, 3 December 2009.

22. *NCNA* covered the car manufacturers' resistance in some detail: Chen Bin, National Development and Reform Commission, 'Unchecked auto industry growth could harm China's economy: official', 4 September 2010; Chen Bin and Xu Changming, State Information Centre, 'China's auto makers reject "excess capacity" warning', 5 September 2010; 'China's auto industry not overheated, industry analysts argue', 17 October 2010. The campaign to rein in the industry switched from economic issues (where the industry's data were persuasive) to highlighting pollution and road congestion (complaints which were harder for the industry to counter), e.g., Liu Shijin, State Council Development Research Centre Deputy Director, 'Chinese think tank calls for refocus of auto industry development', *NCNA*, 23 October 2010. Overcapacity in this industry was a long-standing preoccupation of state planners, e.g., 'New moves to steer China's car sector stability', *PD*, 31 May 2006.

23 Even in a frank analysis of the problems ahead, for example, past progress was presented as almost spontaneous: 'More than ten years of reform efforts have resulted in three fundamental changes in the Chinese economy. The first change is the shift from shortage to surplus in the goods market. The second change is the successful transition from a centrally planned system to a market-base system. The third change is the opening of the economy to the rest of the world. All these achievements are attributable to the operation of a socialist market economy with Chinese characteristics'. Dai Xianglong, PBOC Governor, 'China's Financial Industry at the Threshold of the 21st Century', address at Stanford University (17 October 2000).

24. Liu Mingkang, CBRC Chairman, *2008 Annual Report*, p. 8.

25. Significantly, an excellent overview of reform debates during the first decade of reform has no discussion of either banking or financial issues although it has brief mentions of controversies about the importation of 'foreign capital'. Robert C. Hsu, *Economic Theories in China, 1979–88* (Cambridge: Cambridge University Press, 1991), pp. 26, 134–6, 139.

26. Dai, 'China's Financial Industry at the Threshold of the 21st Century'.

27. Zhou, 'Reform of the internal control and internal incentive systems of the commercial banks'.

28. 'Though Chinese law prohibited local governments from raising capital through bond issues, the central government was considering allowing "local governments raise funds by loan transfers or through appropriate channels or measures with central approval"'. Mu Hong, National Development and Reform Commission Vice Director, *NCNA*, 14 November 2008.

29. Zhou, 'Instability and Evolution of the Financial System', pp. 6–7.

30. 'The fact that the report, known as an Article IV review, was released at all marks an improvement in the sometimes-testy relationship between China and the Fund. China had blocked the IMF from publishing a review since 2006. The dispute was only resolved when the IMF backed away from calling China's currency "fundamentally misaligned," and substituted the term "substantially undervalued."' Andrew Batson, *Wall Street Journal*, 30 July 2010. Against this background, Zhou's special endorsement of the IMF's 'Article IV Consultations' has added interest.

31. Gore, 'The Communist Legacy in Post-Mao Economic Growth', pp. 36–8.

32. This state of affairs persisted until 2007, according to Shimin Chen, Zheng Sun, Song Tang and Donghui Wu, 'Government intervention and investment efficiency: Evidence from China', *Journal of Corporate Finance* (2010), p. 12 (doi:10.1016/j.jcorpfin.2010.08.004).

33. Zhou, 'Instability and Evolution of the Financial System', pp. 2–3.

34. Zhou Xiaochuan, PBOC Governor, 'Some Issues Concerning the Reform of the State-owned Commercial Banks', speech at the IIF Spring Membership Conference, Shanghai (16 April 2004).

35. ibid.

36 The official view, however, was that the level of corruption and malpractice depended very much on the success or otherwise of reforms to financial regulation and corporate governance. White Paper, *China's Efforts to Combat Corruption and Build a Clean Government* (Beijing: State Council Information Office, 2010), chapter v, 'Prevention of Corruption through System Reform and Institutional Innovation'.

37. Zheng Xinli, Party Policy and Research Office Deputy Director, 'Senior official warns against graft in 4-trillion-yuan gov't-funded projects', *NCNA*, 29 November 2008.

38. A typical denunciation of such misconduct in the pre-reform era was Xia Liji, 'Monetary transactions and the current class struggle', *PD*, 16 June 1975 (originally published in *Hongqi*, No. 6 (June 1975)).

39. An impressive analysis of this process can be found in Melanie Manion, *Corruption by Design: Building Clean Government in Mainland China and Hong Kong* (Cambridge, Mass.: Harvard University Press, 2004), especially pp. 97–101.

40. ibid.

41. Xiaoqiang Cheng and Patrick Van Cayseele, 'State Aid and Competition in Banking: The Case of China in the Late Nineties', *LICOS Discussion Paper 250/2009*, pp. 3–4, 7.

42. Feyzioglu, 'Does Good Financial Performance Mean Good Financial Intermediation in China?', *IMF Working Paper WP/09/170*, pp. 16, 17, 19–20, 22–4.

43. Zhijun Zhao, Yue Ma, Yak-yeow Kueh, Shu-ki Tsang, Matthew S. Yiu, and Shucheng Liu, 'Banking Deregulation and Macroeconomic Impact in China: A Theoretical Analysis and Implications of WTO Accession to the Mainland and Hong Kong', *HKIMR Working Paper No.8/2002* (April 2002), pp. 1, 32.

44. Zhou, 'Improve Legal System and Financial Ecology', pp. 8–9.

45. The account of the Maoist era that follows, together with the quotations, is based on the analysis published in the early reform period by a well-known liberal economist from the State Council's Development Research Centre. Yang Peixin, 'Banking', in Yu Guangyuan (ed.), *China's Socialist Modernization* (Beijing: Foreign Languages Press, 1984), pp. 409–13, 414–20 in particular.

46. Typical 1975 examples were reported in provincial radio services: Guizhou, 23 December 1975; Liaoning, 8 June 1975; Hupei, 15 July 1975.

47. Commentator, 'The Construction Bank must guard the passes well', *PD*, 4 July 1978.

48. Li was to become Vice Chairman of the Financial and Economic Commission set up later in 1979. The other four headed the State Planning, State Economic, State Capital Construction and State Agricultural Commissions.

49. This summary of the conference is based on the report in *NCNA*, 8 March 1979.

50. *NCNA*, 1 November 1980.

51. For examples of these initiatives, see Leo Goodstadt, 'Banking on Change', *Asiabanking*, June 1986, p. 28.

52. Hou Yunchun, 'Improve regional cooperation by making the best use of local conditions and retaining advantages while eliminating disadvantages', *PD*, 2 August 1985.

53. A People's Bank official was quoted as expressing doubt about whether the technical resources could be found for a national cheque service even for business enterprises. *CD*, 30 October 1984.

54. The best overview of this phenomenon is Yasheng Huang, *Capitalism with Chinese Characteristics: Entrepreneurship and the State* (Cambridge: Cambridge University Press, 2008), pp. 138–9, 144–5, 147–50.

55. Joseph Fewsmith, *Dilemmas of Reform in China: Political Conflict and Economic Debate* (Armonk: M. E. Sharpe, 1994), p. 167.

56. An excellent summary of the early transition to modern banking is Nicholas R. Lardy, *China's Unfinished Economic Revolution* (Washington, DC: Brooking Institution Press, 1998), chapter 3.

57. Huang, *Capitalism with Chinese Characteristics: Entrepreneurship and the State*, p. 139.

58. See Audrey Donnithorne, *China's Economic System* (London: George Allen & Unwin Ltd, 1967), pp. 403, 406, 412, 418–24, 429.

59. A participant's account of the Chinese Communist Party's decision to adopt this slogan can be found in Ruan Ming, *Deng Xiaoping: Chronicle of an Empire* (Boulder: Westview Press, 1994), pp. 29–37.

60. Kristen Parris, 'The Rise of Private Business Interests', in Merle Goldman and Roderick MacFarquhar (eds.), *The Paradox of China's Post-Mao Reforms* (Cambridge, Mass.: Harvard University Press, 1999), pp. 262, 271–5.

61. Deng Xiaoping, *Fundamental Issues in Present-day China* (Beijing: Foreign Languages Press, 1987), pp. 55, 123. The data are from Joseph C. H. Chai, *China: Transition to a Market Economy* (Oxford: Clarendon Press, 1997), Table 10.7. 'Share of Non-State sector in the Chinese Economy, 1980–1994', p. 179.

62. 'The law approved by the national legislature in March after repeated revisions and unprecedented eight readings … had met with doubts and opposition from people who argued private property should not be leveled with state property'. 'Landmark property law takes effect', *NCNA*, 1 October 2007.

63. In October 2008, the Party Central Committee agreed 'to allow farmers to "lease their contracted farmland or transfer their land use rights" [to third parties] to boost the scale of operation for farm production and provide funds to start new businesses'. 'Chronology of the CPC's decision on rural reform, development', *NCNA*, 20 October 2008.

64. Liao Jili, 'The relationship between structural reform and horizontal and vertical integration', *PD*, 26 August 1980.

65. Hsu, *Economic Theories in China. 1979–88*, pp. 33–4.

66. Significantly, as late as 1996, the need for legislative and regulatory measures was not recognised in an otherwise probing Asian Development Bank review of banking developments. Christine P. W. Wong, 'Part One: People's Republic of China', in Pradumna B. Rana and Naved Hamid (eds.), *From Centrally Planned to Market Economies: The Asian Approach*, Vol. 2 (Hong Kong: Oxford University Press, 1996), pp. 175–80.

67. An excellent summary of the rural struggles can be found in Kate Xiao Zhou, *How the Farmers Changed China: Power of the People* (Boulder: Westview Press, 1996), pp. 60–71.

68. Indeed, the growth of the private sector created new opportunities for officials to exercise authority 'because they were still in control of essential economic elements (capital goods, financial capital, land and information)', and they frequently competed to profit from these powers both institutionally and personally. Eun Kyung Choi and Kate Xiao Zhou, 'Entrepreneurs and Politics in the Chinese Transitional Economy: Political Connections and Rent-seeking', *China Review*, Vol. 1, No. 1 (Fall 2001), p. 123.

69. For a review of the obstacles to reforms in the 1990s, see Jun Ma, *The Chinese Economy in the 1990s* (Basingstoke: Macmillan Press Ltd, 2000), pp. 69–71. On the perverse consequences for the banks of reforms in other parts of the system, see Susan L. Shirk, *The Political Logic of Economic Reform in China* (Berkeley: University of California Press, 1993), pp. 184, 217.

70. 'Full text of Chinese Vice President Xi Jinping's speech at World Investment Forum 2010', *NCNA*, 7 September 2010.

71. Wu Xiaoling, PBOC Deputy Governor, 'Strengthen China's Financial Industry in the Process of Opening up' (14 February 2006), pp. 3, 4.

72. Song Jingli, 'Foreign banks' assets share in China slides again', *CD*, 6 April 2010. The CBRC listed 84 foreign banks as operating in China in 2010 (URL: http://www.cbrc.gov.cn/chinese/home/jsp/docView.jsp?docID=2045).

73. A typical summary of the Chinese approach to development finance in the era before the 'open door' policies can be found in *NCNA*, 23 September 1974.

74. *NCNA*, 6 September 1976.

75. The Russians' transgressions included a welcome for American consumerism symbolised by approval for Pepsi Cola to start Russian factories, see *NCNA*, 16 September 1976. Pepsi started operations in China in 1982 but 20

years later confessed that it had always operated at a loss despite investing a total of US$500 million in its Chinese business. Peter Thompson, Pepsi International Group President, *PD*, 9 April 2002.

76. The classic account of the long battle by key Chinese Communist Party leaders to make full use of international trade and finance to accelerate China's modernisation and of their final triumph through Deng Xiaoping's 1978 initiatives is Lawrence C. Reardon, *The Reluctant Dragon: Crisis Cycles in Chinese Economic Policy* (Hong Kong: Hong Kong University Press, 2002), pp. 160–65, 169–70, 185–202 in particular.

77. *Financial Times*, 30 June 1978.

78. Tianjin city radio service, 28 November 1978.

79. Leo Goodstadt, 'China's glad farewell to behind-schedule socialism', *Euromoney*, January 1977, p. 87.

80. For a review of contemporary Chinese discussions of the ideological and technical obstacles to expanding foreign trade and banking in the 1970s, see Leo F. Goodstadt, 'China's Foreign Debts', *International Currency Review*, Vol. 10, No. 2 (May 1978), pp. 56–8, in particular.

81. This account is from Wu, 'Strengthen China's Financial Industry in the Process of Opening up', pp. 1, 2.

82. *NCNA*, 4 February 1981.

83. These complications were very evident, for example, in what was regarded as a path-breaking refinery deal first proposed in 1978 and only completed in 1981. Leo Goodstadt, 'Yan Shan's long trek for funds ends at Amex', *Asian Banking*, November 1981, pp. 66–71. Its promoter was later punished for corruption. Shao-Chuan Leng and Hungdah Chiu, *Criminal Justice in Post-Mao China: Analysis and Documents* (Albany: State University of New York Press, 1985), p. 140.

84. Leo Goodstadt, 'Lending to China: A spread of ½% may sound better in Chinese', *Euromoney*, May 1980, pp. 76–80. The obstacles persisted. Leo Goodstadt, 'It's Tough Getting over the Wall', *Euromoney*, April 1986, pp. 36–41.

85. Yan Guangguo, 'Shanghai faces multiple problems while opening up to the outside world', *Shijie Jingji Daobao*, 6 January 1986.

86. The vulnerability of the private sector generally to such behaviour is summarised in Charles J. P. Chen, Zengquan Li, Xijia Su and Zheng Sun, 'Rent-seeking incentives, corporate political connections, and the control structure of private firms: Chinese evidence', *Journal of Corporate Finance* (2010), p. 3 (doi:10.1016/j.jcorpfin.2010.09.009).

87. This discrimination and the weight given to the objective creditworthiness of the borrower are analysed in Michael Firth, Chen Lin, Ping Liu and Sonia M. L. Wong, 'Inside the black box: Bank credit allocation in China's private sector', *Journal of Banking & Finance*, Vol. 33, Issue 6 (June 2009), pp. 1144–55.

88. An instructive case study of the complex political environment which even Hong Kong manufacturers faced in Guangdong province can be found in Leslie Yip Sai-Ching and G. P. Walters, 'Wah Hoi Industrial Company', *Entrepreneurship: Theory and Practice*, Vol. 22, No. 3 (1998), pp. 87–99.

89. This survival was facilitated by the fact that the cultural values encouraged by the founding fathers of modern Chinese banking before 1949 and the start of the Chinese Communist Party's rule were 'superficially … not incompatible with aspects of Communist indoctrination'. Andrea MacElderry, 'Confucian Capitalism? Corporate Values in Republican Banking', *Modern China*, Vol. 12, No. 3 (July 1986), p. 415. A concrete example of the cultural 'inheritance' is provided by Wen-Hsin Yeh, 'Corporate Space, Communal Time: Everyday Life in China's Bank of China', *American Historical Review*, Vol. 100, No. 1 (February 1995), p. 99.

90. Special Correspondent, 'China's overseas banks' deposits exceed $3 billion', *Ta Kung Pao*, 6 March 1981.

91. Zhiu Xiao, *Zhongguo Xinwen She*, 16 November 1985.

92. 'The problem of the aging of our cadres' was regarded as a major challenge not just for banking but also for all levels of the Party and state leadership as the reform era got underway. Ren Tao, State Council Economic Research Centre, 'Consistency in Policies', in Su Wenning (ed.), *Modernization — the Chinese Way* (Beijing: Beijing Review, 1983), pp. 118–20.

93. Cai Esheng, PBOC Assistant Governor, 'Financial supervision in China: framework, methods and current issues', paper presented in the Joint BIS/PBC Conference: 'Strengthening the banking system in China: issues and experience', *BIS Policy Papers No. 7* (October 1999), pp. 167–72.

94. The *NCNA* reported, for example, the arrival of visiting bankers from the Australian Reserve Bank (17 April 1974), Bank of Tokyo (10 August 1974) and Austria (27 April 1975); while the Bank of China visited Canada (*NCNA*, 26 April 1976). For an extreme example of past political risks, see Samejima, *Nihon Kezai Shinbun*, 7 January 1967.

95. Leo F. Goodstadt, *Profits, Politics and Panics: Hong Kong's Banks and the Making of a Miracle Economy, 1935–1985* (Hong Kong: Hong Kong University Press, 2007), p. 94.

96 Damian Tobin, 'Austerity and Moral Compromise: Lessons from the Development of China's Banking System', *World Development* (2010), p. 10 (doi:10.1016/j.worlddev.2010.10.002).

97. On Hong Kong's standing with the Mainland, see the analysis by Charles Li, HKEx Chief Executive, 'Six Questions Regarding the Internationalisation of the Renminbi' (21 September 2010) (URL: http://www.hkex.com.hk/eng/newsconsul/speech/2010/sp100920.htm).

Chapter 4

1. Wang Chen, State Council Information Office Director, 'China registers historic progress in human rights', *NCNA*, 9 December 2008.

2. But note a contrary opinion: 'Beijing certainly does not want to place its [financial] bet only on Hong Kong, especially in light of the facts that Hong Kong is an economy that is de facto independent from and "foreign" to China, and that Hong Kong's political future remains unclear in light of expected full universal suffrage after 2017'. JiangYu Wang, 'Regulatory competition and cooperation between securities markets in Hong Kong and Mainland China', *Capital Markets Law Journal*, Vol. 4, No. 3 (July 2009), p. 389. This assertion seems to assume that China's leaders mistrust their

own Basic Law which incorporates the preservation of an entirely separate, capitalist economy in Hong Kong in addition to the pledge of universal suffrage.

3. Hong Kong as a special case of colonial autonomy because of its dependence on China is discussed in Leo F. Goodstadt, 'Fiscal Freedom and the Making of Hong Kong's Capitalist Society', *China Information*, Vol. 24, No. 3 (November 2010), pp. 273–94.

4. Gerard Caprio and Patrick Honohan, 'Restoring Banking Stability: Beyond Supervised Capital Requirements', *Journal of Economic Perspectives*, Vol. 13, No. 4 (Autumn 1999), pp. 49–50.

5. Y. K. Mo 'A review of recent banking reforms in China', paper presented in Joint BIS/PBC Conference: 'Strengthening the banking system in China: issues and experience', *BIS Policy Papers No. 7* (October 1999), pp. 99–100.

6. People's Bank of China, *China Financial Outlook 2000* (n.d., n.p.), pp. 19, 25.

7. An illustration of this culture clash was recorded in Leo Goodstadt, 'The Hotel with Five Red Stars', *Euromoney*, February 1984, pp. 14–5.

8. Leo Goodstadt, 'How safe is your China contract?', *Insight*, June 1979, p. 9.

9. See Markus Taube, 'Economic Relations between the PRC and the States of Europe', *China Quarterly*, No. 169 (March 2002), p. 103.

10. *Financial Times*, 28 January and 22 April 1999.

11. For a good contemporary overview of the ITICs affair and its business and banking ramifications, see Faith Keenan, 'Finance: Picking up The Pieces', *Far Eastern Economic Review*, 6 May 1999.

12. Prime Minister Zhu Rongji stated: 'If Chinese companies cannot afford to pay their debts, they must apply to the People's Bank of China and court to be made bankrupt … The Chinese Government will protect the rights and interests of foreign creditors according to the law'. *CD*, 17 October 2000.

13. Bloomberg News, *International Herald Tribune*, 8 August 2000; Xiao Xu, *CD*, 20 October 2001; Xia Bin, Financial Institute of the Development and Research Centre, *PD*, 27 July 2004.

14. Xiaoqiang Cheng and Patrick Van Cayseele, 'State Aid and Competition in Banking: The Case of China in the Late Nineties', *LICOS Discussion Paper 250/2009*, pp. 3–4.

15. People's Bank of China, *China Financial Outlook 2000*, Table 1-3. 'Closed or Bankrupt Financial Institutions during 1997–1998', p. 19.

16. Zhou Xiaochuan, PBOC Governor, 'Some Issues Concerning the Reform of the State-owned Commercial Banks', speech at the IIF Spring Membership Conference, Shanghai (16 April 2004).

17. Zhou Xiaochuan, PBOC Governor, 'Improve Legal System and Financial Ecology', speech at the 'Forum of 50 Chinese Economists' (2 December 2004), pp. 1–3.

18. The regulatory developments are summarised in Hui Huang, 'Institutional structure of financial regulation in China: Lessons from the global financial crisis', *Journal of Corporate Law Studies*, Vol. 10, Part 1 (April 2010), pp. 222–3.

19. Wu Xiaoling, PBOC Deputy Governor, Remarks on the International Seminar on the Tenth Anniversary of the Asian Financial Crisis (21 June 2007), pp. 3–5.

20. IMF, *People's Republic of China Staff Report for the 2010 Article IV Consultation* (9 July 2010), p. 16.
21. The press conference and his remarks were reported in 'Top official: Severe challenge for China to stop slowdown in economic growth', *NCNA*, 14 November 2008.
22. IMF, *People's Republic of China Staff Report for the 2010 Article IV Consultation*, p. 15.
23. A National Audit Office study of land sales in 11 cities between 2004 and 2006 discovered that they had evaded reporting 70 per cent of their net proceeds from land sales (equivalent to US$12.52 billion). 'NAO says violations found in land proceeds management, land sales in 11 cities', *NCNA*, 4 June 2008. Details of subsequent violations were reported in National Audit Office, 'No. 6 Announcement of 2010: Audit Investigation Findings on Collection, Application and Management of Special Funds Earmarked for Land and Requisition and Transfer of Land in 40 Municipalities, Regions and Prefectures and 56 Counties and Districts under Their Jurisdiction', Audit Reports (17 September 2010) (URL: http://www.cnao.gov.cn/main/articleshow_ArtID_1092.htm).
24. Illegal holdings worth US$1.8 billion were seized within a year. 'China increases reward for tipsters of unauthorized departmental coffers', *NCNA*, 25 August 2010.
25. 'China to monitor possible mass layoffs, large-scale labor disputes', *NCNA*, 18 November 2008.
26. This financial programme launched by the Guangzhou Development District was not as widely publicised as Dongguan's initiative. 'China to inject 30 billion yuan into major economic development district', *NCNA*, 12 December 2008.
27. Xie Liqun, Zhejiang Provincial Audit Department Director, 'Local government debts detrimental to state treasury: Chinese legislator', *PD*, 12 March 2005.
28. IMF, *People's Republic of China Staff Report for the 2010 Article IV Consultation*, p. 27.
29. Era Dabla-Norris, 'Issues in Intergovernmental Fiscal Relations in China', *IMF Working Paper WP/05/30* (February 2005), p. 15.
30. 'Chinese gov't investigating rural authority debts', *NCNA*, 28 November 2006.
31. These were issued in the form of 'book-entry national treasury bonds tradable ... on the inter-bank market and securities exchanges'. 'Local bonds of Liaoning, Tianjin set for sale', *PD*, 14 April 2009; '9b yuan Sichuan province local bond sale to open on Wed.', *NCNA*, 8 April 2009; 'China to sell local gov't bonds next week', *NCNA*, 18 June 2010.
32. Jing Ji, 'Local govts may be allowed to issue bonds', *CD*, 23 October 2008.
33. National Development and Reform Commission, 'NDRC to review status of stimulus driven projects', *CD*, 18 September 2010.
34. IMF, *People's Republic of China Staff Report for the 2010 Article IV Consultation*, p. 15.
35. Ibid., pp. 15, 16, 27.

36. 'China's local gov'ts 3 trillion yuan in red with infrastructure, stimulus spending', *NCNA*, 23 June 2010.
37. Wang Bo, 'Regulator sees no risks from local govt loans', *CD*, 28 July 2010; '"No systemic risk" for local borrowings', *CD*, 20 August 2010.
38. For example, market nervousness about the China Construction Bank's exposure. 'CCB downplays default risks', *CD*, 24 August 2010.
39. Hu Xiaolian, PBOC Deputy Governor, Speech at the Symposium on Judicial Interpretation of Law on Real Rights (31 May 2010).
40. IMF, *People's Republic of China Staff Report for the 2010 Article IV Consultation*, p. 26.
41. Xiang Junbo, PBOC Deputy Governor, 'Improve the Legal System to Prevent Financial Risks', speech at the '2005 High-level Forum of China's Financial Reform' (26 April 2005), pp. 3, 6.
42. Hao Mingjin, Vice Minister of Supervision, 'Land, construction management "high-risk" posts for official corruption: watchdog', *NCNA*, 29 May 2010.
43. 'Backgrounder: A timeline of China's recent economic-stimulus measures', *NCNA*, 9 October 2008; 'China property stimulus plan targets low-income housing ownership', *NCNA*, 17 December 2008.
44. Xiao Gang, Bank of China Chairman, 'Top Chinese banker warns of lending risks', *NCNA*, 9 November 2009.
45. The negative consequences were reported in some detail for an international audience by *CD*: e.g., Wang Zhuoqiong, 'Officials punished for misuse of funds', 16 October 2009; Hao Yan, 'Local govts "want land sales" to pay back loans', 23 June 2010; 'Proceed cautiously on land-based funds', 13 October 2009.
46. 'China's local governments land sale revenue close to 233 bln. USD in 2009 on property mkt. surge', *NCNA*, 2 February 2010.
47. For a theoretical discussion of this issue, see Guillermo Rosas, 'Bagehot or Bailout? An Analysis of Government Responses to Banking Crises', *American Journal of Political Science*, Vol. 50, No. 1 (January 2006), pp. 186, 188.
48. Liu Mingkang, CBRC Chairman, 'Chinese Bankers Carry Hopes for Future Balances', speech delivered in Hong Kong (20 January 2010).
49. 'China regulates local gov't financing companies', *NCNA*, 14 June 2010.
50. Liu Mingkang, CBRC Chairman, Address at the third economic and financial situation briefing of CBRC (20 July 2010); Wang, *CD*, 28 July 2010.
51. Jia Kang, Ministry of Finance Institute of Fiscal Science Research Director, 'China should be aware of local govt debt risks: Official', *NCNA*, 2 November 2010.
52. 'Banking regulator urges structural reforms', *NCNA*, 24 October 2010.
53. Liu Mingkang, CBRC Chairman, 'Six Things that Make Us Concern[ed]', Keynote Speech at the 16th International Conference on Banking Supervision, Singapore (23 September 2010).
54. White Paper, *China's Efforts to Combat Corruption and Build a Clean Government* (Beijing: State Council Information Office 2010), chapter v, 'Prevention of Corruption through System Reform and Institutional Innovation'.
55. Xiao Gang, BoC Chairman, 'Liberalize interest rates further', *CD*, 7 January 2011. Such reforms had long been promised, however. See, for example,

'China's state-owned commercial banks to enjoy greater autonomy this year', *Zhongguo Xinwen She*, 25 March 1996.

56. The justification for such protectionist measures included a desire to safeguard Chinese depositors and defend the financial system against imported instability as the nation's banking system was opened up to the outside world. 'Overseas bankers raise concerns', *PD*, 24 August 2006.

57. The agreement was never finalised because Guangdong officials were heavily involved in smuggling activities and thus profited from the new tariffs. Norman Miners, *Hong Kong Under Imperial Rule, 1912–1941* (Hong Kong: Oxford University Press, 1987), pp. 21–2.

58. Treaty Series No. 9 (1949), *Exchange of Notes ... for the Prevention of Smuggling between Hong Kong and Chinese Ports* (London: Cmd 7615/1949).

59. *Report of the Commission ... to Enquire into the Causes and Effects of the Present Trade Recession ...* (Hong Kong: Noronha & Co., 1935), pp. 76–7, 79, 81, 89–90.

60. A full account of the negotiations can be found in HKRS163-1-402/3, 'China Trade And Commerce — Aide Memoire re Closer Cooperation between China and Hong Kong in Connection with Trade and Exchange Control'. The stubborn defiance of London's wishes is recorded in HKRS170-1-307, 'Banking Legislation ... ' and HKRS41-1-6691, 'Banking Operations Legislation for Control of ... '.

61. Commander in Chief Hong Kong telegram to War Office, 1 November 1945 (HKRS169-2-53, 'Rehabilitation of Business'); War Office secret telegram to Commander in Chief Hong Kong, no. 522263 F5, 22 March 1946 (HKRS169-2-26, 'Currency and Banking'); Officer Administering the Government telegram to Secretary of State for the Colonies, no. 958, 6 June 1947; S (later Sir Sidney) Caine (Colonial Office) telegram to D. M. MacDougall (Hong Kong), no. 982, 21 June 1947 (HKRS163-1-442, 'Import and Exchange Control in Hong Kong Proposed Visit of a H.K. Govt. Officer to the U.K. in Connection with ... '). Zhong-ping Feng, *The British Government's China Policy 1945–1950* (Keele: Ryburn Publishing, 1994), pp. 34–6.

62. Cai Beihua, Shanghai Municipal People's Congress, 'Expectations for developing economic relations with Hong Kong', *Shehui Kexue*, No. 7 (15 July 1988), pp. 11, 12.

63. An impressive analysis of Hong Kong's role in the pre-reform period and its political as well as its economic complexity is provided by Catherine R. Schenk, 'Banking and Exchange Rate Relations between Hong Kong and Mainland China in Historical Perspective: 1965–75', in Catherine R. Schenk (ed.), *Hong Kong SAR's Monetary and Exchange Rate Challenges: Historical Perspectives* (Basingstoke: Palgrave Macmillan, 2009).

64. Lawrence C. Reardon, *The Reluctant Dragon: Crisis Cycles in Chinese Economic Policy* (Hong Kong: Hong Kong University Press, 2002), pp. 160–1.

65. For example, Qu Shunping, 'Policy Measures for the Utilisation of Foreign Capital in Guangdong', *Guoji Maoyi Wenti*, No. 1 (January–February 1986), pp. 5–11; Feng Bangyan, 'The Role of Hong Kong in China's Modernisation Process', *Jingji Yanjiu*, No. 4 (20 April 1989), pp. 64–5

66. Yao Yufang, Li Fuqiang and Wang Haiyan, 'China's Regional Economic Development: The Factor Analytic Approach', in Roger C. K. Chan, Tientung Hsueh and Chiu-ming Lok (eds.), *China's Regional Economic Development* (Hong Kong: Hong Kong Institute of Asia-Pacific Studies, 1996), Table 4. 'Composite factor scores of per capita economic development levels by provinces, 1952–1989', p. 162.

67. Yang Qinquan and Jiang Zhiyuan, Guangzhou Party Propaganda Department, 'Analysis of the results of Guangzhou's foreign economic cooperation and future strategy', *Guangzhou Yanjiu*, No. 5 (September–October 1985), pp. 35–7.

68. In 1992 the Exchange Fund Ordinance (cap. 66) was amended through the addition of s. (1A) to give the Financial Secretary sweeping powers to maintain Hong Kong as an international financial centre. Under article 109 of the post-1997 Basic Law, 'the Government of the Hong Kong Special Administrative Region shall provide an appropriate economic and legal environment for the maintenance of the status of Hong Kong as an international financial centre'.

69. Douglas W. Arner et al., 'The Global Financial Crisis and the Future of Financial Regulation in Hong Kong', *AIIFL Working Paper No. 4* (February 2009), p. 87.

70. Xu Dixin, 'On Hong Kong's economic relations with the Chinese Mainland', *Liaowang* (Overseas edition), No. 1 (16 September 1985), pp. 22–3.

71. Katherina Pistor, 'Banking Reform in the Chinese Mirror', *Columbia Law and Economics Working Paper No. 354* (10 August 2009), p. 2.

72. Henry Tang, Financial Secretary, *GIS*, 15 October 2005.

73. Wang, 'Regulatory competition and cooperation between securities markets in Hong Kong and Mainland China', *Capital Markets Law Journal*, p. 396.

74. 'Agricultural Bank's IPO: Agricultural revolution', *Economist*, 8 July 2010; Peter Stein, 'AgBank Prospectus Highlights Reasons for Caution', *Wall Street Journal*, 6 June 2010.

75. 'Mideast sovereign funds eye Agricultural Bank IP', *NCNA*, 1 June 2010; Jamil Anderlini, 'Fundraisings cast shadow on Agricultural IPO', *Financial Times*, 2 June 2010.

76. 'Agricultural Bank of China: Listing or capsizing?', *Economist*, 13 June 2010.

77. Pistor, 'Banking Reform in the Chinese Mirror', *Columbia Law and Economics Working Paper No. 354*, p. 20.

78. This change in attitude was not easy to admit. In 2010, RBS publicly expressed regret at having sold off its share holding in Bank of China. But RBS presented a very different assessment of its Mainland prospects barely a month later when it announced the decision to give away its retail operations in China to a Singapore Bank (DBS) for nothing. Naomi Rovnick and Lulu Chen, 'RBS chief regrets sale of 4.3pc stake in Bank of China', *South China Morning Post*, 10 November 2010; Zhou Yan, 'From Scotland to Singapore', *CD*, 16 December 2010.

79. Jonathan Anderson, 'The Great Chinese Bank Sale', *Far Eastern Economic Review*, September 2005, p. 12. However, while Chinese regulators have played down the fundraising role of these IPOs, they admit that 'the introduction

of foreign strategic investment was initially a pure capital investment'. Liu Mingkang, CBRC Chairman, *2008 Annual Report*, p. 9.

80. The chapter 'Getting credit' in the 2006 survey began with China's deficiencies. The same chapter four years on did not report substantial improvements. World Bank, *Doing Business in 2006: Creating Jobs* (Washington, DC: World Bank, 2006); *Doing Business 2010: Reforming through Difficult Times* (Washington, DC: World Bank, 2009).

81. Wu Xiaoling, PBOC Deputy Governor, Remarks at the International Seminar on the Tenth Anniversary of the Asian Financial Crisis, p. 4.

82. The China Banking Regulatory Commission's defences of the pricing were reported in *PD*: Liu Mingkang, Chairman, 6 December 2005; Tang Shuangning, Vice Chairman, 10 March 2006. Criticism had first been provoked by the pre-listing terms for foreigners in the flotation of the Bank of Communications, with a respected Hong Kong business daily expressing sympathy for Mainland investors and alleging favouritism for foreigners. *Hong Kong Economic Journal*, 7 December 2005.

83. A useful overview of the special problems of company flotations in China is Bill B. Francis, Iftekhar Hasana and Xian Sun, 'Political connections and the process of going public: Evidence from China', *Journal of International Money and Finance*, Vol. 28, Issue 4 (June 2009), pp. 696–719.

84. Only the Bank of Communications, not one of the 'big four' and an earlier transaction, was seriously mispriced. World Bank Beijing, *Quarterly Update* (May 2007), pp. 18–20 and Table 3. 'China: Selected IPOs 2005–7'. On listing strategy, see Zhou Xiaochuan, PBOC Governor, 'Exclusive Interview with the People's Daily', *PD*, 8 May 2005.

85. This article offered an impressive summary of Hong Kong's banking relationship with the Mainland after the first five years of economic reforms. Yang Xin, 'Hong Kong's foreign banks energetically develop their China business', *Gang Ao Jingji*, No. 3 (25 March 1985), pp. 17–9.

86. Feng Bangyan, 'Hong Kong's role and the process of China's modernisation', *Jingji Yanjiu*, p. 67.

87. A detailed review of the legal and institutional relationship between the Hong Kong authorities and their Mainland counterparts is presented in Duncan Alford, 'The Influence of Hong Kong Banking Law on Banking Reform in the PRC', *East Asia Law Review*, Vol. 3, No. 1 (Summer 2008), especially pp. 35–6, 43–8.

88. Liu Mingkang, CBRC Chairman, 'Chinese Bankers Carry Hopes for Future Balances'.

89. Alford, 'The Influence of Hong Kong Banking Law on Banking Reform in the PRC', *East Asia Law Review*, p. 42.

90. Joseph Yam, HKMA Chief Executive, 'Speech British Chamber of Commerce', *HKMA*, 20 October 2006.

91. Prime Minister Zhou died in 1976 but his instructions were quoted the following year by Deputy Premier Li to defeat ideological hostility towards giving special economic priority to Hong Kong. Reardon, *The Reluctant Dragon: Crisis Cycles in Chinese Economic Policy*, pp. 79–83, 147, 182.

92. 'Wen: Economy shows positive changes', *NCNA*, 11 April 2009.

Chapter 5

1. Andrew Whitfield, *Hong Kong, Empire and the Anglo-American Alliance at War, 1941–1945* (Basingstoke: Palgrave, 2001), p. 218.

2. See Henry Wai-chung Yeung, *Transnational Corporations and Business Networks. Hong Kong firms in the Asian Region* (London: Routledge, 1998), pp. 130, 206–7.

3. Gordon Redding, 'Culture and Business in Hong Kong', in Wang Gangwu and Wong Siu Lun (eds.), *Dynamic Hong Kong: Business & Culture* (Hong Kong: Centre of Asian Studies, 1997), p. 102.

4. W. F. Jenner, *The Tyranny of History. The Roots of China's Crisis* (London: Penguin Books, 1992), p. 191.

5. Jose Viñals and Jonathan Fiechter, 'The Making of Good Supervision: Learning to Say "No"', *IMF Staff Position Note SPN/10/08* (18 May 2010), p. 5.

6. IMF, 'IMF Executive Board Concludes 2008 Article IV Consultation Discussions with People's Republic of China — Hong Kong Special Administrative Region', *Public Information Notice (PIN) No. 08/145* (8 December 2008), pp. 2–3.

7. IMF, 'Cross-Cutting Themes in Economies with Large Banking Systems' (16 April 2010), p. 19.

8. Douglas W. Arner et al., 'The Global Financial Crisis and the Future of Financial Regulation in Hong Kong', *AIIFL Working Paper No. 4* (February 2009), pp. 32–3.

9. The data are from John C. Tsang, Financial Secretary, *GIS*, 20 May, 7 June, 23 July and 1 September 2010; Au King-chi, Permanent Secretary for Financial Services and the Treasury, *GIS*, 21 September 2010.

10. Dong He et al., 'Hong Kong's Financial Market Interactions with the US and Mainland China in Crisis and Tranquil Times', *Hong Kong Monetary Authority Working Paper 10/2009* (16 June 2009). See also the overall conclusions from the research papers presented in Hans Genberg and Dong He (eds.), *Macroeconomic Linkages between Hong Kong and Mainland China* (Hong Kong: City University of Hong Kong Press, 2008).

11. Sir John Gieve, BofE Deputy Governor, 'Seven lessons from the last three years' (19 February 2009), p. 17. But another senior British regulator indicated that such quantitative restrictions were no longer suitable except for 'emerging countries (e.g. Hong Kong and Singapore)'. Lord Turner, *The Turner Review: A regulatory response to the global banking crisis* (London: Financial Services Authority, March 2009), p. 70.

12. House of Commons Treasury Committee, *Banking Crisis: regulation and supervision, Fourteenth Report of Session 2008–09* (London: HMSO, HC 767, 21 July 2009), pp. 36–7. Significantly, a 2007 BIS study failed to test against Hong Kong's experience the assumption that quantitative restrictions were 'bound to be less effective in economies that have highly developed capital markets, or institutions outside the scope of regulation, and that are very open to cross-border capital flows'. Claudio E V Borio and Ilhyock Shim, 'What can (macro-)prudential policy do to support monetary policy?', *BIS Working Papers No 242* (December 2007), pp. 13, 17.

13. Stephen Knowles and Arlene Garces-Ozanne, 'Government Intervention and Economic Performance in East Asia', *Economic Development and Cultural Change*, Vol. 51, No. 2 (January 2003), pp. 451–77.

14. Charles K. Rowley and Nathanael Smith, *Economic Contractions in the United States: A Failure of Government* (Fairfax: The Locke Institute, 2009), pp. 55–6.

15. Milton Friedman, 'Hong Kong Wrong: What would Cowperthwaite say?', *Wall Street Journal*, 6 October 2006.

16. M. 4. Acting Director of Supplies, Commerce and Industry to Labour Officer, 31 July 1947 (HKRS163-1-305,'Retail Price & Wages Index. Preparation of … '); Acting Financial Secretary minute to Colonial Secretary, 25 April 1957 (HKRS163-1-634, 'Public Utilities Companies Proposed Control of the Charges and Dividends Levied by … ').

17. Measurable family hardship caused by rising rents was not acute. But the public mood, Cowperthwaite intimated, demanded immediate statutory controls (*HH*, 26 September 1962, pp. 280–2) 'Completely new industries' were his actual words (*HH*, 30 March 1962, pp. 131–4 and 26 February 1964, p. 45).

18. Compare Cowperthwaite, *HH*, 30 March 1967, p. 251 and Haddon-Cave, *HH*, 5 January 1972, p. 318. There was no economic case for such loans. Industry Development Branch, 'The Case for Improved Access to Loans for Re-equipment Purposes by Small Scale Industry' (*Department of Commerce and Industry, IND 2/903*, 27 October 1969, mimeo) and 'Memorandum to the Loans for Small Industry Committee' (*Commerce and Industry Department, IND 2/903*, 4 November 1969, mimeo). The scheme failed and was wound up in 1976. H. C. Y. Ho, *The Fiscal System of Hong Kong* (London: Croom Helm, 1979), p. 62.

19. *Report of the Advisory Committee on Diversification 1979* (Hong Kong: Government Printer, 1979), p. 167; *HH*, 13 April 1978, p. 812.

20. This point was made in the Hong Kong context when the colonial administration was making a last stand against regulatory reforms in the middle of market collapses and a runaway money supply. A. J. Youngson, *Hong Kong's Economic Growth and Policy* (Hong Kong: Oxford University Press, 1982), p. 131.

21. Joseph Yam, HKMA Chief Executive, 'Towards a Stronger Financial System', speech to the Hong Kong Society of Accountants, *HKMA*, 29 October 1999. This presentation includes a lucid review of the case for more active regulation and intervention in a small open economy like Hong Kong.

22. The discussion in this paragraph reflects in particular the analysis presented in Joseph Yam, HKMA Chief Executive, 'Hong Kong and Asia: Strategies for Recovery', *Far Eastern Economic Review* Conference, *HKMA*, 16 June 1999 and 'Issues in Monetary Policy' Hong Kong University Speech, *HKMA*, 19 January 2004.

23. Of Hong Kong's total trade in financial services during 2008, the United States accounted for 34 per cent of exports and 22 per cent of imports, while the United Kingdom accounted for 23 per cent of exports and 17 per cents of imports. Census and Statistics Department, *Report on Hong Kong Trade in Services Statistics for 2008* (Hong Kong: Census and Statistics Department, 2010), pp. 36, 43.

24. Y. C. Jao, 'Hong Kong as a Financial Centre of China and the World', in Lok Sang Ho and Robert Ash (eds.), *China, Hong Kong and the World Economy. Studies in Globalization* (New York: Palgrave Macmillan, 2006), pp. 123–4, 130, 132; Howard Curtis Reed, 'The Ascent of Tokyo as an International Financial Center', *Journal of International Business Studies*, Vol. 11, No. 3 (Winter 1980), Table 3. 'Rankings of Asian International Bank Centers', p. 28.

25. Significantly, the first HKMA Chief Executive quoted the latest comments of the Chairman of the United States Federal Reserve Board at some length when explaining why Hong Kong would follow a different course. Joseph Yam, HKMA Chief Executive, 'Viewpoint', *HKMA*, 19 March 2009.

26. K. Y. Yeung, Secretary for the Treasury, 'The Role of the Hong Kong Government in Industrial Development', in Edward K. Y. Chen et al. (eds.), *Industrial and Trade Development in Hong Kong* (Hong Kong: Centre of Asian Studies, 1991), p. 49.

27. As late as 1999, however, standards for the securities industry and corporate governance still fell short of international benchmarks. *A Policy Paper on Securities and Futures Markets Reform* (Hong Kong: HKSARG, 1999), pp. 16–9.

28. Neil Gunningham, 'Moving the Goalposts: Financial Market Regulation in Hong Kong and the Crash of October 1987', *Law & Social Inquiry*, Vol. 15, No. 1 (Winter, 1990), pp. 46, 53.

29. Donald Tsang Yam-kuen, Financial Secretary, *GIS*, 16 June 2000.

30. Charles Goodhart and Lu Dai, *Intervention to Save Hong Kong: Counter-Speculation in Financial Markets* (Oxford: Oxford University Press, 2003), pp. 2, 4.

31. Alan Greenspan, FRB Chairman, Testimony before the House of Representatives, Committee on Banking and Financial Services (16 September 1998), p. 310.

32. Donald Tsang, Financial Secretary, *GIS*, 23 September 1999.

33. IMF, *Concluding Statement for the Article IV Consultation with the People's Republic of China in respect of the Hong Kong Special Administrative Region* (30 October 1998).

34. Alkman Granitsas et al., 'Politics and the Peg: Hong Kong fends off speculators at the price of credibility', *Far Eastern Economic Review*, 27 August 1998.

35. Louise Lucas, 'Hong Kong: State defence of currency under attack', *Financial Times*, 29 August 1998.

36. Jame DiBiasio, 'Hong Kong's Cultural Revolution', *FinanceAsia* (September 2000), p. 28.

37. Edmund R. Thompson, 'Dangers of Differential Comprehensions of Hong Kong's Competitive Advantages: Evidence from Firms and Public Servants', *China Quarterly*, Vol. 167 (September 2001), p. 707.

38. Lord Turner, FSA Chairman in House of Commons Treasury Committee, *Banking Crisis*, Vol. I. Oral evidence (HMSO: HC 144–I, March 2009), p. EV280.

39. Alan Greenspan, *The Age of Turbulence: Adventures in a New World* (New York: Penguin Press, 2007), p. 371.

40. Dora Iakova, 'How Hong Kong SAR Banks Survived the Asian Crisis', in Jahangir Aziz, Jeanne Gobat, Dora Iakova, William Lee and Peter Breuer, *People's Republic of China — Hong Kong Special Administrative Region. Selected Issues and Statistical Appendix*, IMF Country Report No. 01/146 (August 2001), pp. 23–8. 'Good luck' got two 'headline' mentions (pp. 24, 29).

41. Scott Lanman, 'Greenspan Says Hong Kong's Yam Was Right to Buy Stocks in 1998', *Bloomberg*, 19 May 2009.

42. This acknowledgment was presented in an unflattering context, however. Paul Tucker, BoE Deputy Governor, Remarks at the Institute of International Bankers Annual Breakfast Regulatory Dialogue, Washington, DC (11 October 2010), p. 3.

43. For example, throughout the previous century, Hong Kong was dominated by international and Chinese Mainland banks, a fact which had not weakened its capacity to regulate them effectively. Yet, the IMF commented: '*The size of the banking sector needs to match the resources of the home regulator. The small fiscal resources of Hong Kong SAR and Singapore, the main Asian money centers, may have constrained the scale of banks they can credibly place under their supervisory umbrella*'. (Emphasis in the original) IMF, 'Cross-Cutting Themes in Economies with Large Banking Systems', p. 23.

44. A. G. Hopkins, 'Back to the Future: From National History to Imperial History', *Past & Present*, No. 164 (August 1999), pp. 235, 238. The article does not suggest, however, that this phenomenon could occur in the contemporary world and specifically not in financial services.

45. This was the traditional view of British colonial economies. Ida Greaves, 'The Character of British Colonial Trade', *Journal of Political Economy*, Vol. 62, No. 1 (February 1954), pp. 3, 4–6.

46. Tang Shu-hung, 'The Economy', in Joseph Y. S. Cheng and Sonny S. H. Lo (eds.), *From Colony to SAR: Hong Kong's Challenges Ahead* (Hong Kong: Chinese University Press, 1995), p. 130.

47. Y. C. Richard Wong, 'Public Policies in the Hong Kong Economy: Emphasis on Manufacturing', in F. Gerard Adams and William E. James (eds.), *Public Policies in East Asian Development: Facing New Challenges* (Westport: Praeger Publishers, 1999), p. 146.

48. On the economists' hostility to government intervention to protect the exchange rate and the financial markets in 1998, see Y. C. Jao, *The Asian Financial Crisis and the Ordeal of Hong Kong* (Westport: Quorum Books, 2001), p. 87. They had succeeded in blocking government plans for an old age pension scheme in 1994. Francis T. Lui, *Retirement Protection: A Plan for Hong Kong* (Hong Kong: City University of Hong Kong Press, 1998), pp. 6–7.

49. The strength of this aversion to Keynes is not always recognised, and there is sometimes an assumption that Hong Kong officials will adopt much the same measures as governments elsewhere. See, for example, the assertion that 'high fiscal surpluses accumulated during the good times allowed the [Hong Kong] government to engage in countercyclical fiscal policy during the Asian crisis' (whereas, in reality, the government struggled hard to cut its spending). W. Max Corden, 'Exchange Rate Regimes for Emerging

Market Economies: Lessons from Asia', *Annals*, Vol. 579 (January 2002), p. 33.

50. See H. W. Singer, 'The Distribution of Gains between Investing and Borrowing Countries', *American Economic Review*, Vol. 40, No. 2 (May 1950), p. 473; Hla Myint, 'Economic Theory and the Underdeveloped Countries', *Journal of Political Economy*, Vol. 73, No. 5 (October 1965), pp. 477–8.

51. Sir Robert Black, Governor, letter to Sir Hilton Poynton (Colonial Office), 19 July 1958 (HKRS270-5-44, 'Commercial and Industrial Development — Major Policy'); Cowperthwaite, *HH*, 26 February 1964, p. 47; 24 February 1966, p. 57.

52. In Hong Kong, he insisted, public finance could not seek to 'pursue social justice or to manipulate — or rather try to manipulate — the rate and pattern of economic growth'. Haddon-Cave, *HH*, 7 April 1976, p. 802. He seemed not to know that the 1964 Banking Ordinance included among its aims: 'to regulate such [banking] business for monetary policy purposes'.

53. Tung Chee Hwa, Chief Executive, *GIS*, 10 August 2000.

54. (79) Cowperthwaite letter to W. F. Searle, Chief Statistician (Colonial Office), 8 June 1955 (HKRS163-9-88, 'Trade — Balance of Payment Statistics. Policy Regarding Preparation of ... ').

55. For example, *HH*: Cowperthwaite, 27 February 1963, p. 41; 10 March 1966, p. 57; 8 October 1969, p. 85; Haddon-Cave, 28 March 1973, p. 645; 26 February 1975, p. 484, f.n. 53; 3 April 1975, p. 691, f.n. 4; and *GIS*, 1 February 1982.

56. Tony Latter, 'Rules versus Discretion in Managing the Hong Kong dollar, 1983–2006', *HKIMR Working Paper No. 2/2007* (January 2007), p. 9.

57. It should be noted that most Hong Kong academics assume the opposite. Financial policy is presented as a major instance of United Kingdom exploitation of the colonial relationship, in Alex H. Choi, 'State-Business Relations and Industrial Restructuring', in Tak-Wing Ngo (ed.), *Hong Kong's History. State and society under colonial rule* (London: Routledge, 1999), pp. 149–50.

58. *Report of the Commission ... to Enquire into the Causes and Effects of the Present Trade Recession ...* (Hong Kong: Noronha & Co., 1935), pp. 82–3, 86.

59. Sir Lesley Robinson (Board of Trade), (12) Minutes of the Sixth Meeting, 22 August 1961 (HKRS270-5-56, 'Cotton Advisory Board. Minutes of Meeting').

60. Frank H. H. King, *The Hong Kong Bank in the Period of Development and Nationalism, 1941–1984. From Regional Bank to Multinational Group* (Cambridge: Cambridge University Press, 1991), pp. 345–6.

61. Economic Secretary minute to Financial Secretary, 17 May 1952; (79) Cowperthwaite to Searle, 8 June 1955; (294) Cowperthwaite letter to Searle, 11 August 1959 (HKRS163-9-88).

62. The best account of Hong Kong's struggle for financial autonomy is Catherine R. Schenk, 'The empire strikes back: Hong Kong and the decline of sterling', *Economic History Review*, Vol. LVII, No. 3 (August 2004), pp. 570–3.

63. A confidential British Treasury statement said that it was 'inappropriate for [the United Kingdom government] to enter into specific commitments

to provide assistance to Hong Kong' in a financial crisis. Alastair Mackay (British Treasury) letter to Financial Secretary, 22 July 1971 (HKRS163-9-217, '(A) Meeting of Senior Commonwealth Finance Officials 1970. Sterling Area Balance Of Payments — Developments and Prospects To Mid-1971 (B) Overseas Sterling Area Countries Statistics').

64. Gordon A. Hughes et al., 'Protection and Developing Countries' Exports of Manufactures', *Economic Policy*, Vol. 1, No. 2 (April 1986), pp. 412, 422; Matthew Turner, 'Hong Kong Design and the Roots of Sino-American Trade Disputes', *Annals*, Vol. 547 (September 1999), pp. 37–53.

65. See the comments of Suzanne Berger and Richard K. Lester (eds.), *Made By Hong Kong* (Hong Kong: Oxford University Press, 1997), pp. 152, 163; *GIS*, 6 August 1997 and 9 August 1999; Chau Tak Hay, Secretary for Trade and Industry, *GIS*, 2 May 1998.

66. Mark S. Gaylord, 'The Chinese Laundry: International Drug Trafficking and Hong Kong's Banking Industry', in Harold H. Traver and Mark S. Gaylord (eds.), *Drugs, Law and the State* (Hong Kong: Hong Kong University Press, 1992), p. 90. *GIS*, 4 July 1999; David Carse, HKMA Deputy Chief Executive, *GIS*, 15 September 1999.

67. Examples of the scope of this campaign were reported in *Far Eastern Economic Review*: 'Hongkong Company Meetings', 20 May 1954 and Derek Davies, 'Hongkong Affairs: The Hong Kong Hilton', 4 July 1963. See also Richard I. Devane, 'The United States and China: Claims and Assets', *Asian Survey*, Vol. 18, No. 12 (December 1978); Chi-kwan Mark, 'American "China Hands" in the 1950s', in Cindy Yik-yi Chu (ed.), *Foreign Communities in Hong Kong, 1940s–1950s* (New York: Palgrave Macmillan, 2005), pp. 176–8, 181–4.

68. Secretary of State for the Colonies savingram to Officer Administering the Government, 'United States Investment Guarantee', 19 October 1965; (20) Financial Secretary note, 18 June 1966 (HKRS163-3-269, 'Investment Guarantees by the United States Government').

69. For an example of Hong Kong's assertion of the right to disagree with London, see Bremridge, Financial Secretary, *HH*, 27 February 1985, p. 680.

70. This point was made by an official who had served as commissioner of banking and also for securities. Robert Fell, *Crisis and Change. The Maturing of Hong Kong's Financial Markets* (Hong Kong: Longman, 1992), p. 150. It must also be noted that the legislation was based on recommendations by a Bank of England official whose services as an advisor had been sought by Hong Kong. See H. J. Tomkins, *Report on the Hong Kong Banking System and Recommendations for the Replacement of the Banking Ordinance 1948* (Hong Kong: Government Printer, 1962). Hong Kong officials, nevertheless, regarded themselves as the decision-makers.

71. On the impact of the new banking model on Hong Kong and on regulatory challenges generally, see Y. C. Jao, 'The Rise of Hong Kong as a Financial Centre', *Asian Survey*, Vol. 19, No. 7 (July 1979), p. 688; Robert Z. Aliber, 'Financial Innovation and the Boundaries of Banking', *Managerial and Decision Economics*, Vol. 8, No. 1 (March 1987), pp. 67–9.

72. Hong Kong's formal dialogue with the Chinese government on the continuity of the financial system began in May 1987 and continued throughout the

next decade. Joseph Yam, HKMA Chief Executive, 'Viewpoint', *HKMA*, 3 May 2007.

73. Roger W. Ferguson, Jr., FRB Vice Chairman, 'Financial Engineering and Financial Stability', remarks at the Annual Conference on the Securities Industry, American Institute of Certified Public Accountants and the Financial Management Division of the Securities Industry Association, New York (20 November 2002).

74. Ben S. Bernanke, FRB Chairman, 'Financial Innovation and Consumer Protection', speech at the Sixth Biennial Community Affairs Research Conference, Washington, DC (17 April 2009).

75. HMG, *Reforming financial markets* (London: HMSO, Cm 7667/2009), p. 140.

76. Cowperthwaite, *HH*, 8 October 1969, p. 85; Haddon-Cave, *HH*, 13 December 1972, pp. 218–29; 14 November 1974, p. 218.

77. In an earlier passage, Cowperthwaite had declared: 'The trouble is that economic analysis of future events is a matter, not of demonstrable fact, but of judgment and opinion … Government should not in general interfere with the course of the economy merely on the strength of its own commercial judgment. If we cannot rely on the judgment of individual businessmen, taking their own risks, we have no future anyway'. *HH*, 24 March 1966, pp. 215, 216.

78. Policy-makers had similar misgivings about the merits of unfettered competition in other markets, including export manufacturing. See (3) Director of Commerce and Industry (H. A. Angus) letter to Wilkinson and Grist, 25 July 1962 (HKRS163-1-2861, 'Cotton Textiles Allocation of Quota to Restricted Markets'); *Hong Kong Report for the Year 1969* (Hong Kong: Government Press, 1970), p. 50.

79. See Catherine R. Schenk, 'The origins of Anti-competitive Regulation: Was Hong Kong "Over-banked" in the 1960s?', *HKIMR Working Paper No. 9/2006* (July 2006), pp. 8–9, 11, 15.

80. The change in attitude between Cowperthwaite and his predecessor as Financial Secretary is evident from a comparison of Circular No. 68, 'Deutsch-Asiatische Bank,' 10 December 1957, with Circular No. 95, 'Banking Ordinance — chapter 155 Bank Negara Indonesia', 16 June 1961 (HKRS 163-1-679, 'Banking Advisory Committee').

81. Haddon-Cave, *HH*, 8 January 1975, pp. 340, 341–2; 15 March 1978, pp. 623–4.

82. Fuller details of the regulatory problems of the decade can be found in Leo F. Goodstadt, 'Dangerous Business Models: Bankers, Bureaucrats & Hong Kong's Economic Transformation, 1948–86', *HKIMR Working Paper No. 8/2006* (June 2006), pp. 15–21.

83. His arguments against regulation also included the difficulties of enforcement in an open economy like Hong Kong. Bremridge, *HH*, 30 July 1975, pp. 948–51.

84. Fell, *Crisis and Change*, p. 158; Leo Goodstadt, 'Mum's the Word', *Asian Banking*, January 1983, p. 32. The criminal features of the financial scandals of this period are summarised in R. T. Naylor, *Hot Money and the Politics of Debt*, 3rd ed. (Montreal: McGill-Queen's University Press, 2004), pp. 208–22.

85. Contemporary reporting of these events is recorded in Philip Bowring and Robert Cottrell, *The Carrian File* (Hong Kong: Far Eastern Economic Review Ltd, 1984).

86. Customer deposits with 241 DTCs were equivalent to 17 per cent of the total with licensed banks in 1978, 22 per cent in 1982, but only 10 per cent in 1987. Census and Statistics Department, *Hong Kong Annual Digest of Statistics*, 1988 ed. (Hong Kong: Census and Statistics Department, 1988), pp. 125–8.

87. T. K. Ghose, *The Banking System of Hong Kong* (Singapore: Butterworths, 1987), p. 96. The actual exposure of the Exchange Fund in supporting these banks was probably significantly larger at the height of the crisis.

88. Census and Statistics Department, *2003 Gross Domestic Product* (Hong Kong: Census and Statistics Department, 2004), p. 81.

89. Bremridge, *HH*, 19 March 1986, p. 771.

90. The Bank of England was castigated by a parliamentary inquiry for its over-emphasis on moral hazard during the first stage of the global financial crisis. This official report, nevertheless, remained true to this principle in its recommendations. House of Commons Treasury Committee, *The run on the Rock Fifth Report of Session 2007–08*, Vol. I (London: HMSO, HC56-I, January 2008), pp. 43, 77.

91. Thomas Huertas, FSA Banking Sector Director, 'Competition in Banking: The Role of Orderly Entry and Orderly Exit', speech at the Chatham House Conference, London (20 June 2008).

92. Lawrence Summers, 'Beware moral hazard fundamentalists', *Financial Times*, 23 September 2007.

93. This statement was made in the context of discussion among officials about whether the 1948 Banking Ordinance ought to be enforced with any diligence. See HKRS41-1-3044, 'The Nam Sang Bank — 1. Application from ... for a Banking Licence. 2. Balance Sheet of ... 3. Cancellation of the Licence of ... '.

94. This view was regarded as racist nonsense by a leading expatriate businessman at the time. Colonial Treasurer memorandum, 25 August 1936; Patterson minute to Colonial Secretary, 31 August 1938 (HKRS170-1-307, 'Banking Legislation — 1. General Supervision of Banking Concerns in Hong Kong ... ').

95. The pre-war allegation of Chinese indifference to bank failures was repeated two decades later: 'The Government itself does not seem to have received complaints, direct or indirect, from depositors who have lost their money'. (86) Financial Secretary, 23 October 1959 (HKRS 163-1-679).

96. The one exception was the Hong Kong branch of the BCCI in 1991. Its local operations were solvent but it could not survive its overseas parent's collapse. Its failure provoked brief runs on four other banks, including Standard Chartered, a note-issuer. See Michael Taylor, 'Hongkong: Exchange of Views', *Far Eastern Economic Review*, 17 October 1991.

97. Haddon-Cave, *HH*, 8 January 1975, pp. 342–3; F. W. Li, appointed member, *HH*, 15 November 1978, p. 172.

98. Y. C. Jao, 'Monetary system and banking structure', in H. C. Y. Ho and L. C. Chau (eds.), *The Economic System of Hong Kong* (Hong Kong: Asian Research Service, 1988), p. 59.

99. Albeit while he was still a businessman. Bremridge, *HH*, 30 July 1975, p. 949.
100. See Bremridge, *HH*, 9 April 1986, pp. 981–7.
101. A Commissioner for Securities writing in 1990, close to the ignominious collapse in 1987, was still anxiously lobbying for minimal regulation. Robert Owen, 'Hong Kong Maintains Tradition of Light-Handed Regulation', in Securities and Futures Commission, *Securities Regulation in Hong Kong* (Hong Kong: Securities and Futures Commission, 2002), pp. 71–2, 76.
102. Joseph Yam, HKMA Chief Executive, 'Viewpoint', *HKMA*, 18 October 2007.
103. The British view was that moral hazard should be preserved. House of Commons Treasury Committee, *The run on the Rock*, pp. 74, 77.
104. 'There is a further argument for maintaining a degree of constructive ambiguity in order to avoid encouraging moral hazard by setting out too clearly the terms on which support might be forthcoming. This is a valid point. But it is also worth noting that the problem of moral hazard, while it can never be entirely eradicated, has been considerably reduced in Hong Kong in recent years'. Joseph Yam, HKMA Chief Executive, 'The Lender of Last Resort', speech to the Hong Kong Association of Banks, *HKMA*, 29 June 1999.
105. Yam, 'Viewpoint', *HKMA*, 18 October 2007.
106. Donald Tsang Yam-kuen, Financial Secretary, *GIS*, 12 June 1997. The research evidence showed that this nervousness was unjustified. See Guorong Jiang et al., 'Banking Sector Competition in Hong Kong — Measurement and Evolution Over Time', *Hong Kong Monetary Authority Research Memoranda* (20 April 2004). Note the continuing concern about competition expressed by Joseph Yam, HKMA Chief Executive, 'View Point', *HKMA*, 31 August 2006.
107. A persuasive account of why the Hong Kong Monetary Authority did not believe that financial markets could be left to find their own remedies for instability after the Asian financial crisis was presented in 1998 by the current HKMA Chief Executive. Norman Chan, HKMA Deputy Chief Executive, 'The Asian Financial Crisis: What have we Learnt?', speech to the Oxford University Asia-Pacific Affairs Society (7 June 1999).
108. KPMG and Barents Group LLC, *Hong Kong Banking into the New Millennium*, Hong Kong Banking Sector Consultancy Study (December 1998), Table 1.6.1. 'Sector-level key success performance comparison', pp. 9, 17; Table 1.10.1. 'Proposed implementation approach for key recommendations', p. 42; and Table 1.10.2. 'High-level implementation plan — key regulatory and supervisory recommendations', p. 43; HKMA, 'Policy Response to the Banking Sector Consultancy Study' (June 1999).
109. For an excellent summary of the Lehman mini-bonds, what they were, how they were marketed and why their failure provoked widespread criticism of the regulators, see Arner et al., 'The Global Financial Crisis and the Future of Financial Regulation in Hong Kong', *AIIFL Working Paper No. 4*, pp. 33 *et seq.*
110. The largest distributor of these securities was the Hong Kong arm of the Bank of China. For details of its involvement, see Fu Lei, 'Banker goes to trial over minibonds', *CD*, 26 November 2011.

111. On this feature of Hong Kong's political landscape, see Leo F. Goodstadt, *Uneasy Partners: The Conflict between Public Interest and Private Profit in Hong Kong*, 2nd ed. (Hong Kong: Hong Kong University Press, 2009), pp. xiv–xvi.

112. The evidence in support of this conclusion is based on research from the run-up to the crises of both 1930–33 and 2007–08. Thomas Philippon and Ariell Reshef, 'Wages and Human Capital in the U.S. Financial Industry: 1909–2006' (December 2008), p. 30 (URL: http://pages.stern.nyu.edu/~tphilipp/papers/pr_rev15.pdf). The impact of this paper is indicated by the attention it received from the *Economist*, for example: 'Paying the piper', 5 February 2009 and 'The coming recovery', 28 May 2009.

113. This resilience was particularly evident in the sustained growth of the export sector and the continuing (albeit lower) growth in real GDP in the 1960s despite a banking crisis and violent anti-colonial clashes. The pattern was repeated in the following decade (with the services sector coming to the fore) despite serious defects in regulatory performance and monetary management. For the data, see Census and Statistics Department, *Hong Kong Statistics 1947–1967* (Hong Kong: Government Printer, 1969), p. 88 and *2003 Gross Domestic Product* (Hong Kong: Census and Statistics Department, 2004), pp. 14–6, 20, 78–9.

114. Eric Wong, Tom Fong, Ka-fai Li and Henry Choi, 'An assessment of the long-term economic impact of the new regulatory reform on Hong Kong', *Hong Kong Monetary Authority Research Note 05/2010* (9 November 2010), p. 4 and repeated verbatim p. 9.

115. Joseph Yam, Chief Executive HKMA, 'The Political Process of Monetary Management', Hong Kong Management Association 13th Susan Yuen Memorial Lecture, *HKMA*, 20 October 1998.

Conclusions

1.   Lord Turner, FSA Chairman, 'Something old and something new: Novel and familiar drivers of the latest crisis', speech to the European Association of Banking and Financial History, Brussels (21 May 2010).

2.   Laura Kodres and Aditya Narain, 'Redesigning the Contours of the Future Financial System', *IMF Staff Position Note SPN/10/10* (16 August 2010), p. 4.

3.   Andrew G. Haldane, BofE Executive Director, 'The Contribution of the Financial Sector: Miracle or Mirage?', speech at the Future of Finance Conference, London (14 July 2010), p. 2.

4.   Before the global crash, China's central bankers were alarmed that the younger generation took stability for granted: 'The more likely norm is that a financial system faces instability or turbulences of varying degree every few years; freedom from all such instability would be, in fact, abnormal'. Zhou Xiaochuan, PBOC Governor, 'Instability and Evolution of the Financial System' (5 December 2007), p. 1. After the crash, the regulators' language became blunter: 'People in this business always have short memories'. Liu Mingkang, CBRC Chairman, 'Six Things that Make Us Concern[ed]', Keynote Speech at the 16th International Conference on Banking Supervision, Singapore (23 September 2010).

5. This point has been made forcibly in the context of the United States and the 'Great Crash'. Gertrude Tumpel-Gugerell, European Central Bank Executive Board Member, 'Business Models in Banking: Is There a Best Practice', paper presented in the CAREFIN Conference, Milan (21 September 2009), pp. 2, 4, 5, 8.

6. This argument was presented very powerfully by Michael C. Jensen, 'The Modern Industrial Revolution, Exit, and the Failure of Internal Control Systems', *Journal of Finance*, Vol. 48, No. 3 (July 1993), pp. 864-6, 867-9.

7. Adrian Blundell-Wignall, Gert Wehinger and Patrick Slovik, 'The Elephant in the Room: The Need to Deal with What Banks Do', *OECD Journal: Financial Market Trends*, Vol. 2009, Issue 2, pp. 2, 10.

8. Gerard Caprio and Patrick Honohan, 'Restoring Banking Stability: Beyond Supervised Capital Requirements', *Journal of Economic Perspectives*, Vol. 13, No. 4 (Autumn 1999), p. 48.

9. Franklin Allen and Douglas Gale, 'Competition and Financial Stability', *Journal of Money, Credit and Banking*, Vol. 36, No. 3, Part 2 (June 2004), Table 1. 'Average cumulative fiscal costs of banking crises in 24 crises, 1977–2000' and Table 2. 'Output losses associated with banking crises, 1977–98', pp. 454–5.

10. This conclusion was based on a study of 60 countries for the period 1980–2002. Romain Ranciere, Aaron Tornell and Frank Westermann, 'Decomposing the effects of financial liberalization: Crises vs. Growth', *National Bureau of Economic Research Working Paper 12806* (December 2006), p. 16.

11. Haldane, 'The Contribution of the Financial Sector: Miracle or Mirage?', pp. 4–5. Haldane's paper stands up very well to complaints from the Governor of the Bank of England that these sorts of estimates are misleading; have not been adjusted for the real costs of the risks involved in this industry; and over-estimate both its profits and its productivity. Mervyn King, BofE Governor, 'Banking: From Bagehot to Basel, and Back Again', Buttonwood Gathering, New York (25 October 2010), pp. 6–7.

12. Joseph Yam, HKMA Chief Executive, 'Viewpoint: Alan Greenspan and the Federal Reserve', *HKMA*, 1 February 2001.

13. Andrew Sheng, *From Asian to Global Financial Crisis: An Asian Regulator's View of Unfettered Finance in the 1990s and 2000s* (New York: Cambridge University Press, 2009), p. 391. He was not alone in voicing such suspicions. See, for example, 'Basel brush: Regulators' new blueprint for bank supervision avoids the trickiest bits', *Economist*, 2 April 2009.

14. The silence was not universal. Professor M. D. Nalapat stated that the reason for Washington and London 'relaxing their already weak regulations' was that 'in the UK, the monetary authorities have close ties with financial institutions and individuals who make most of their profits from speculation, in the US, high-level officials are almost always chosen from among people who are experts in market-distorting activities'. See his 'Yuan target of greedy speculators', *CD*, 21 May 2010.

15. *The Irish Banking Crisis Regulatory and Financial Stability Policy 2003–2008. A Report to the Minister for Finance by the Governor of the Central Bank* (31 May

2010), pp. 16–7. This assessment is supported by the analysis in Klaus Regling and Max Watson, *A Preliminary Report on The Sources of Ireland's Banking Crisis* (Dublin: Government Publications, 2010), pp. 36–42.

16. The case for viewing officials as captured by leading financial institutions in the Basel II discussions is well argued in Jasper G. W. Blom, 'Governance pattern and market structure: the case of banking supervision under the Basel Capital Accords', *GARNET Working Paper No: 66/09* (June 2009), pp. 8–9, 16–21 and 26 especially. However, the agreement to concessions sought by banking interests can also be interpreted as no more than the compromises necessary for a successful outcome to international negotiations on economic issues in a global environment dominated by a conviction that free and competitive markets are the surest way to prosperity.

17. 'And disclosure itself is arguably inadequate at present in relation to both off- as well as on-balance sheet activity. However much it may be a matter of regret, and despite best intentions, the transparency of today's accounts has become less and the opacity greater than was the case in former days, thereby giving a less than complete or reliable view of overall risks'. Andrew Large, BofE Deputy Governor, 'Basel II and Systemic Stability', British Bankers' Association — Basel II/Cad 3 Conference (13 March 2003), p. 6.

18. Christopher Cox, SEC Chairman, Address to the Joint Meeting of the Exchequer Club and Women in Housing and Finance (4 December 2008).

19. King, 'Banking: From Bagehot to Basel, and Back Again', p. 9.

20. Ben S. Bernanke, FRB Chairman, 'Economic Challenges: Past, Present, and Future', speech at the Dallas Regional Chamber (7 April 2010).

21. Jose Viñals and Jonathan Fiechter, 'The Making of Good Supervision: Learning to Say "No"', *IMF Staff Position Note SPN/10/08* (18 May 2010), p. 5.

22. Kodres and Narain, 'Redesigning the Contours of the Future Financial System', *IMF Staff Position Note SPN/10/10*, pp. 4, 17–8.

23. Stijn Claessens, Giovanni Dell'Ariccia, Deniz Igan and Luc Laeven, 'Lessons and Policy Implications from the Global Financial Crisis', *IMF Working Paper WP/10/44* (February 2010), p. 17.

24. The survey covered '165 banks with assets in excess of US$50 billion and 386 banks with assets in excess of US$10 billion'. Andrea Beltratti and René M. Stulz, 'Why Did Some Banks Perform Better during the Credit Crisis? A Cross-Country Study of the Impact of Governance and Regulation', *Dice Center WP 2009-12* (July 2009), pp. 2, 3, 21.

25. Gert Wehinger, 'The Turmoil and the Financial Industry: Developments and Policy Responses', *OECD Financial Trends*, Issue 1 (2009), pp. 7, 15.

26 Special Inspector General for the Troubled Asset Relief Program, 'Extraordinary Financial Assistance Provided to Citigroup, Inc.', Washington DC (13 January 2011), pp. 41, 42, 43.

27. King, 'Banking: From Bagehot to Basel, and Back Again', pp. 10–4.

28. Andrew Bailey, BofE Executive Director, 'Financial Reform', London (21 September 2010), p. 5.

29. Andrew G. Haldane, BofE Executive Director, 'The $100 Billion Dollar Question', comments given at the Institute of Regulation & Risk, Hong Kong (30 March 2010), pp. 3, 4.

30. Even the AIG rescue package may prove profitable. Jackie Calmes, 'TARP Bailout to Cost Less Than Once Anticipated' and Mary Williams Walsh, 'A.I.G. Reaches Deal to Repay Treasury and Fed for Bailout', *New York Times*, 30 September 2010. 'Clearly, it was not apparent when the TARP was created two years ago that the cost would turn out to be this low. At that time, the U.S. financial system was in a precarious condition ... However, the cost has come out toward the low end of the range of possible outcomes anticipated when the program was launched'. Congressional Budget Office, *Report on the Troubled Asset Relief Program — November 2010* (Washington DC: CBO Report, 2010), p. 2.

31. Haldane, 'The $100 Billion Dollar Question', p. 19.

32. Sir Andrew Large, BofE Deputy Governor, 'Financial Stability Oversight, Past & Present', speech at the London School of Economics (22 January 2004), p. 19.

33. Bernanke, 'Financial Reform to Address Systemic Risk'.

34. House of Commons Treasury Committee, *Banking Reform Seventeenth Report of Session 2007–08* (London: HMSO, HC 1008, September 2008), pp. 100–2.

35. An exception would be made only 'to avoid serious disturbance' to the national economy. Ian Bond, BofE Financial Crisis Management Division Head, 'Managing a Bank-specific Crisis: A UK Perspective', BBA workshop on managing a bank-specific crisis (26 October 2006), p. 3.

36 Mervyn King, BofE Governor, 'Banking and the Bank of England', speech to the British Bankers Association, London (10 June 2008), pp. 3–4.

37. But note the criticism of the Bank of England for invoking moral hazard in the same report: 'We are unconvinced that the Bank of England's focus on moral hazard was appropriate for the circumstances in August [2007]. In our view, the lack of confidence in the money markets was a practical problem and the Bank of England should have adopted a more proactive response'. House of Commons Treasury Committee, *The run on the Rock Fifth Report of Session 2007–08*, Vol. I. (London: HMSO, HC56-I, January 2008), pp. 43, 74, 77.

38. Cox, Address to the Joint Meeting of the Exchequer Club and Women in Housing and Finance.

39. An exception would be made only when collapse might cause 'further serious destabilization of the financial system'. Bernanke, 'Financial Reform to Address Systemic Risk'.

40. A good example was the way 'systemic risk' was defined in 2009 as including an 'imbalance' created by 'unintentionally favor[ing] large systemically important institutions over smaller, more nimble competitors, reducing the system's ability to innovate and adapt to change'. Mary L. Schapiro, SEC Chairman, Testimony concerning Regulation of Systemic Risk before the Senate Committee on Banking, Housing and Urban Affairs (23 July 2009). Innovation had been a prominent feature of the largest firms' business models before the crisis, of course.

41. Turner, 'Something old and something new: Novel and familiar drivers of the latest crisis'.

42. Lord Turner, 'What do banks do, what should they do and what public policies are needed to ensure best results for the real economy?', Speech at the CASS Business School (17 March 2010), p. 30. See also his observation that 'some of the most profitable market making activities … are actually relatively low risk', p. 26, f.n. 26.

43. Ricardo J. Caballero, 'Sudden Financial Arrest', *IMF Economic Review*, Vol. 58, Issue 1 (August 2010), p. 24.

44. 'A material contributor to this crisis was the failure of the official regimes for overseeing the financial system — the intellectual framework, the machinery, and regulation and supervision — to keep up with the extraordinary evolution of our capital markets over the past two decades or more'. Paul Tucker, BofE Deputy Governor, Remarks at the Institute of International Bankers Annual Breakfast Regulatory Dialogue, Washington, DC (11 October 2010), p. 2.

45. See, for example, Sheila C. Bair, FDIC Chairman, Statement on the Causes and Current State of the Financial Crisis before the Financial Crisis Inquiry Commission (14 January 2010); King, 'Banking: From Bagehot to Basel, and Back Again', pp. 3–6.

46. King, 'Banking: From Bagehot to Basel, and Back Again', p. 9.

47. Daniel K. Tarullo, FRB Governor, 'Involving Markets and the Public in Financial Regulation', speech at the Council of Institutional Investors Meeting, Washington, DC (13 April 2010).

48. Michael Barr, US Treasury Assistant Secretary for Financial Institutions, Remarks on Regulatory Reform to the Exchequer Club, Washington, DC (15 July 2009).

49. Wang Huaqing, CBRC Vice Chairman, Speech at the 2010 Lujiazui Forum (26 June 2010).

50. Jiang Dingzhi, CBRC Vice Chairman, 'Reform and development of China's banking industry in the past thirty years', speech at the CCISSR Forum, Peking University (10 April 2008).

51. Cai Esheng, CBRC Vice Chairman, Speech at the China Financial Summit Meeting (19 May 2009).

52. Jiang, 'Reform and development of Chinas banking industry in the past thirty years'.

53. Wang, Speech at the 2010 Lujiazui Forum.

54. Yam, 'The Political Process of Monetary Management'; 'Viewpoint: Alan Greenspan and the Federal Reserve'; and 'Viewpoint: The roles of the HKMA', *HKMA*, 8 June 2000.

Bibliography

Books and Monographs

Berger, Suzanne and Richard K. Lester (eds.), *Made By Hong Kong* (Hong Kong: Oxford University Press, 1997).

Bowring, Philip and Robert Cottrell, *The Carrian File* (Hong Kong: Far Eastern Economic Review Ltd, 1984).

Chai, Joseph C. H., *China: Transition to a Market Economy* (Oxford: Clarendon Press, 1997).

Donnithorne, Audrey, *China's Economic System* (London: George Allen & Unwin Ltd, 1967).

Fell, Robert, *Crisis and Change. The Maturing of Hong Kong's Financial Markets* (Hong Kong: Longman, 1992).

Feng, Zhong-ping, *The British Government's China Policy 1945–1950* (Keele: Ryburn Publishing, 1994).

Fewsmith, Joseph, *Dilemmas of Reform in China: Political Conflict and Economic Debate* (Armonk: M. E. Sharpe, 1994).

Genberg, Hans and Dong He (eds.), *Macroeconomic Linkages between Hong Kong and Mainland China* (Hong Kong: City University of Hong Kong Press, 2008).

Ghose, T. K., *The Banking System of Hong Kong* (Singapore: Butterworths, 1987).

Goodhart, Charles and Lu Dai, *Intervention to Save Hong Kong: Counter-Speculation in Financial Markets* (Oxford: Oxford University Press, 2003).

Goodstadt, Leo F., *China's Search for Plenty. The Economics of Mao Tse-tung* (New York: Weatherhill, 1973).

———, *Profits, Politics and Panics: Hong Kong's Banks and the Making of a Miracle Economy, 1935–1985* (Hong Kong: Hong Kong University Press, 2007).

———, *Uneasy Partners: The Conflict between Public Interest and Private Profit in Hong Kong*, 2nd ed. (Hong Kong: Hong Kong University Press, 2009).

Greenspan, Alan, *The Age of Turbulence: Adventures in a New World* (New York: Penguin Press, 2007).

Ho, H. C. Y., *The Fiscal System of Hong Kong* (London: Croom Helm, 1979).

Hsu, Robert C., *Economic Theories in China, 1979–88* (Cambridge: Cambridge University Press, 1991).

Huang, Yasheng, *Capitalism with Chinese Characteristics: Entrepreneurship and the State* (Cambridge: Cambridge University Press, 2008).

Jao, Y. C., *The Asian Financial Crisis and the Ordeal of Hong Kong* (Westport: Quorum Books, 2001).

Jenner, W. F., *The Tyranny of History. The Roots of China's Crisis* (London: Penguin Books, 1992).

King, Frank H. H., *The Hong Kong Bank in the Period of Development and Nationalism, 1941–1984. From Regional Bank to Multinational Group* (Cambridge: Cambridge University Press, 1991).

Kwong, Julia, *The Political Economy of Corruption in China* (Armonk: M. E. Sharpe, 1997).

Lardy, Nicholas R., *China's Unfinished Economic Revolution* (Washington, DC: Brooking Institution Press, 1998).

Leng, Shao-Chuan and Hungdah Chiu, *Criminal Justice in Post-Mao China: Analysis and Documents* (Albany: State University of New York Press, 1985).

Liu, Pak-wai, Richard Yue-chim Wong, Yun-wing Sung and Pui-king Lau, *China's Economic Reform and Development Strategy of Pearl River Delta* (Hong Kong: Nanyang Commercial Bank Ltd, 1992).

Lui, Francis T., *Retirement Protection: A Plan for Hong Kong* (Hong Kong: City University of Hong Kong Press, 1998).

Ma, Jun, *The Chinese Economy in the 1990s* (Basingstoke: Macmillan Press Ltd, 2000).

Manion, Melanie, *Corruption by Design: Building Clean Government in Mainland China and Hong Kong* (Cambridge, Mass.: Harvard University Press, 2004).

Miners, Norman, *Hong Kong Under Imperial Rule, 1912–1941* (Hong Kong: Oxford University Press, 1987).

Ming, Ruan, *Deng Xiaoping: Chronicle of an Empire* (Boulder: Westview Press, 1994).

Naylor, R. T., *Hot Money and the Politics of Debt*, 3rd ed. (Montreal: McGill-Queen's University Press, 2004).

Reardon, Lawrence C., *The Reluctant Dragon: Crisis Cycles in Chinese Economic Policy* (Hong Kong: Hong Kong University Press, 2002).

Rowley, Charles K. and Nathanael Smith, *Economic Contractions in the United States: A Failure of Government* (Fairfax: The Locke Institute, 2009).

Sheng, Andrew, *From Asian to Global Financial Crisis: An Asian Regulator's View of Unfettered Finance in the 1990s and 2000s* (New York: Cambridge University Press, 2009).

Shirk, Susan L., *The Political Logic of Economic Reform in China* (Berkeley: University of California Press, 1993).

Whitfield, Andrew, *Hong Kong, Empire and the Anglo-American Alliance at War, 1941–1945* (Basingstoke: Palgrave, 2001).

Yeung Henry Wai-chung, *Transnational Corporations and Business Networks. Hong Kong firms in the Asian Region* (London: Routledge, 1998).

Youngson, A. J., *Hong Kong's Economic Growth and Policy* (Hong Kong: Oxford University Press, 1982).

Zhou, Kate Xiao, *How the Farmers Changed China: Power of the People* (Boulder: WestviewPress, 1996).

Articles, Essays and Working Papers

Alford, Duncan, 'The Influence of Hong Kong Banking Law on Banking Reform in the PRC', *East Asia Law Review*, Vol. 3, No. 1 (Summer 2008), 35–58.

Aliber, Robert Z., 'Financial Innovation and the Boundaries of Banking', *Managerial and Decision Economics*, Vol. 8, No. 1 (March 1987), 67–73.

Allen, Franklin and Douglas Gale, 'Competition and Financial Stability', *Journal of Money, Credit and Banking*, Vol. 36, No. 3, Part 2 (June 2004), 453–80.

Arner, Douglas W. et al., 'The Global Financial Crisis and the Future of Financial Regulation in Hong Kong', *AIIFL Working Paper No. 4* (February 2009), 1–97.

Barney, Solomon Smith, 'Fixed Income — Local Government ITIC Credits', 26 November 1998.

Barth, James R., Gerard Caprio, Jr. and Ross Levine, 'Bank Regulation and Supervision: What Works Best?', *National Bureau of Economic Research Working Paper Series, Working Paper 9323* (November 2002).

Baumol, William J., 'Entrepreneurship: Productive, Unproductive, and Destructive', *Journal of Political Economy*, Vol. 98, No. 5 (October 1990), 893–921.

Beltratti, Andrea and René M. Stulz, 'The Credit Crisis Around the Globe: Why Did Some Banks Perform Better?', *Dice Center WP 2010-05* (March 2010), 2–31.

———, 'Why Did Some Banks Perform Better during the Credit Crisis? A Cross-Country Study of the Impact of Governance and Regulation', *Dice Center WP 2009-12* (July 2009), 2–33.

Berndt, Antje and Anurag Gupta, 'Moral Hazard and Adverse Selection in the Originate-to-Distribute Model of Bank Credit' (November 2008) (URL: http://papers.ssrn.com/sol3/papers.cfm?abstract_id=1290312).

Blom, Jasper G. W., 'Governance pattern and market structure: the case of banking supervision under the Basel Capital Accords', *GARNET Working Paper No: 66/09* (June 2009), 2–28.

Caesar, Camille M., 'Capital-Based Regulation and U. S. Banking Reform', *Yale Law Journal*, Vol. 101, No. 7 (May 1992), 1525–49.

Calomiris, Charles W., 'The Political Lessons of Depression-Era Banking Reform' (April 2010), *Oxford Review of Economic Policy* (forthcoming), 1–37 (URL: http://www0.gsb.columbia.edu/faculty/ccalomiris/papers/CalomirisGreatDepressionBankRegulatoryReform2010.pdf).

Caprio, Gerard and Patrick Honohan, 'Restoring Banking Stability: Beyond Supervised Capital Requirements', *Journal of Economic Perspectives*, Vol. 13, No. 4 (Autumn 1999), 43–64.

Case, Karl E., Edward L. Glaeser and Jonathan A. Parker, 'Real Estate and the Macroeconomy', *Brookings Papers on Economic Activity*, Vol. 2000, No. 2 (2000), 119–62.

Cetina, Karin Knorr and Urs Bruegger, 'Global Microstructures: The Virtual Societies of Financial Markets', *American Journal of Sociology*, Vol. 107, No. 4 (January 2002), 905–50.

Chen, Charles J. P., Zengquan Li, Xijia Su and Zheng Sun, 'Rent-seeking incentives, corporate political connections, and the control structure of private firms: Chinese evidence', *Journal of Corporate. Finance* (2010), 1–15 (doi:10.1016/j.jcorpfin.2010.09.009).

Chen, Shimin, Zheng Sun, Song Tang and Donghui Wu, 'Government intervention and investment efficiency: Evidence from China', *Journal of Corporate Finance* (2010), 1–13 (doi:10.1016/j.jcorpfin.2010.08.004).

Cheng, Xiaoqiang and Patrick Van Cayseele, 'State Aid and Competition in Banking: The Case of China in the Late Nineties', *LICOS Discussion Paper 250/2009.*

Cheng, Wai-yan, Yan-leung Cheung and Yuen-ching Tse, 'The Impact on IPO Performance of More Stringent Listing Rules with a Pre-listing Earnings Requirement: Evidence from Hong Kong', *HKIMR Working Paper No. 17/2005* (October 2005).

Choi, Alex H., 'State-Business Relations and Industrial Restructuring', in Tak-Wing Ngo (ed.), *Hong Kong's History. State and society under colonial rule* (London: Routledge, 1999).

Choi, Eun Kyung and Kate Xiao Zhou, 'Entrepreneurs and Politics in the Chinese Transitional Economy: Political Connections and Rent-seeking', *China Review*, Vol. 1, No. 1 (Fall 2001), 111–35.

Corden, W. Max, 'Exchange Rate Regimes for Emerging Market Economies: Lessons from Asia', *Annals*, Vol. 579 (January 2002), 26–37.

Crawford, Darryl, 'Globalisation and Guanxi: The Ethos of Hong Kong Finance', *New Political Economy*, Vol. 6, No. 1 (2001), 45–65.

Davis, Gerald F. and Christopher Marquis, 'The Globalization of Stock Markets and Convergence in Corporate Governance', in Victor Nee and Richard Swedberg (eds.), *The Economic Sociology of Capitalism* (Princeton: Princeton University Press, 2005).

de Jonquières, Guy, 'China and the global economic crisis', *ECIPE Policy Briefs No. 02/2009*, 1–5.

Demyanyk, Yuliya S. and Otto Van Hemert, 'Understanding the Subprime Mortgage Crisis' (5 December 2008) (URL: http://papers.ssrn.com/sol3/papers.cfm?abstract_id=1020396).

Devane, Richard I., 'The United States and China: Claims and Assets', *Asian Survey*, Vol. 18, No. 12 (December 1978), 1267–79.

Doidge, Craig, G. Andrew Karolyi and René M. Stulz, 'Has New York become less competitive in global markets? Evaluating foreign listing choices over time', *Journal of Financial Economics*, Vol. 91, Issue No. 3 (March 2009), 253–77.

Fafanolli, Wojtek, 'A Brief Outline of China's Second Economy', in Stephen Feuchtwang, Athar Hussain and Thierry Pairault (eds.), *Transforming China's Economy in the Eighties,* Volume II (Boulder: Westview Press, 1988).

Firth, Michael, Chen Lin, Ping Liu and Sonia M. L. Wong, 'Inside the black box: Bank credit allocation in China's private sector', *Journal of Banking & Finance*, Vol. 33, Issue 6 (June 2009), 1144–55.

Flannery, Mark J., 'Using Market Information in Prudential Bank Supervision: A Review of the U.S. Empirical Evidence', *Journal of Money, Credit and Banking*, Vol. 30, No. 3, Part 1 (August 1998), 275–305.

Francis, Bill B., Iftekhar Hasana and Xian Sun, 'Political connections and the process of going public: Evidence from China', *Journal of International Money and Finance*, Vol. 28, Issue 4 (June 2009), 696–719.

Gaylord, Mark S., 'The Chinese Laundry: International Drug Trafficking and Hong Kong's Banking Industry', in Harold H. Traver and Mark S. Gaylord (eds.), *Drugs, Law and the State* (Hong Kong: Hong Kong University Press, 1992)

Goodhart, C. A. E., 'Why Do Banks Need a Central Bank?', *Oxford Economic Papers*, Vol. 39, No. 1 (March 1987), 75–89.

Goodstadt, Leo F., 'A Fragile Prosperity: Government Policy and the Management of Hong Kong's Economic and Social Development', *HKIMR Working Paper No. 1/2009* (January 2009).

———, 'China's Foreign Debts', *International Currency Review*, Vol. 10, No. 2 (May 1978), 55–60.

———, 'Control and Motivation of the Chinese Labour Force since the Cultural Revolution', in Lee Ngok and Leung Chi-keung (eds.), *China: Development and Challenge*. Proceedings of the Fifth Leverhulme Conference, Vol. 2 (Hong Kong: Centre of Asian Studies, 1979).

———, 'Dangerous Business Models: Bankers, Bureaucrats & Hong Kong's Economic Transformation, 1948–86', *HKIMR Working Paper No. 8/2006* (June 2006).

———, 'Fiscal Freedom and the Making of Hong Kong's Capitalist Society', *China Information*, Vol. 24, No. 3 (November 2010), 273–94.

———, 'Regulation and Financial Stability in Laissez-Faire Hong Kong: A Reassuring Record', in Greg N. Gregoriou (ed.), *The Banking Crisis Handbook* (London: CRC Press, 2010).

———, 'Taxation and Economic Modernization in Contemporary China', *Development and Change*, Vol. 10, No. 3 (July 1979), 403–21.

———, 'The Global Crisis: Fatal Decisions – Four Case Studies in Financial Regulation', *HKIMR Working Paper No. 33/2009*, November 2009.

———, 'The Global Crisis: Why Laisser-faire Hong Kong Prefers Regulation', *HKIMR Working Paper No. 01/2010*, January 2010.

———, 'The Global Crisis: Why Regulators Resist Reforms', *HKIMR Working Paper No. 32/2009*, November 2009.

Gore, Lance L. P., 'The Communist Legacy in Post-Mao Economic Growth', *China Journal*, No. 41 (January 1999), 25–54.

Gorton, Gary and Andrew Winton, 'Banking in Transition Economies: Does Efficiency Require Instability?', *Journal of Money, Credit and Banking*, Vol. 30, No. 3, Part 2 (August 1998), 621–50.

Greaves, Ida, 'The Character of British Colonial Trade', *Journal of Political Economy*, Vol. 62, No. 1 (February 1954), 1–11.

Guitián, Manuel, 'The Challenge of Managing Global Capital Flows', *Finance and Development*, Vol. 35, No. 2 (June 1998), 14–7.

Gunningham, Neil, 'Moving the Goalposts: Financial Market Regulation in Hong Kong and the Crash of October 1987', *Law & Social Inquiry*, Vol. 15, No. 1 (Winter, 1990), 1–48.

Hla Myint, 'Economic Theory and the Underdeveloped Countries', *Journal of Political Economy*, Vol. 73, No. 5 (October 1965), 477–91.

Hopkins, A. G., 'Back to the Future: From National History to Imperial History', *Past & Present*, No. 164 (August 1999), 198–243.

Huang, Hui, 'Institutional structure of financial regulation in China: Lessons from the global financial crisis', *Journal of Corporate Law Studies*, Vol. 10, Part 1 (April 2010), 219–54.

Hughes, Gordon A. et al., 'Protection and Developing Countries' Exports of Manufactures', *Economic Policy*, Vol. 1, No. 2 (April 1986), 409–53.

Hutchison, Michael M. and Ilan Noy, 'How Bad are Twins? Output Costs of Currency and Banking Crises', *Journal of Money, Credit, and Banking*, Vol. 37, No. 4 (August 2005), 725–52.

Jackson, Howell E., 'An American Perspective on the U.K. Financial Services Authority: Politics, Goals & Regulatory Intensity', *Harvard Law School Discussion Paper No. 522* (08/2005).

Jao, Y. C., 'Hong Kong as a Financial Centre of China and the World', in Lok Sang Ho and Robert Ash (eds.), *China, Hong Kong and the World Economy. Studies in Globalization* (New York: Palgrave Macmillan, 2006).

———, 'Monetary system and banking structure', in H. C. Y. Ho and L. C. Chau (eds.), *The Economic System of Hong Kong* (Hong Kong: Asian Research Service, 1988).

———, 'The Rise of Hong Kong as a Financial Centre', *Asian Survey*, Vol. 19, No. 7 (July 1979), 674–94.

Jensen, Michael C., 'The Modern Industrial Revolution, Exit, and the Failure of Internal Control Systems', *Journal of Finance*, Vol. 48, No. 3 (July 1993), 831–80.

Kapstein, Ethan B., 'Resolving the Regulator's Dilemma: International Coordination of Banking Regulations', *International Organization*, Vol. 43, No. 2 (Spring 1989), 323–47.

Karreman, Bas and Bert van der Knaap, 'The Financial Centres of Shanghai and Hong Kong: Competition or Complementarity?', *Erim Report Series Research In Management*, ERS-2007-062-ORG (September 2007), 1–28.

Kay, John, John Vickers, Colin Mayer and David Ulph, 'Regulatory reform in Britain', *Economic Policy*, Vol. 3, No. 7 (October 1988), 285–351.

Keys, Benjamin J., Tanmoy K. Mukherjee, Amit Seru and Vikrant Vig, 'Did Securitisation Lead to Lax Screening? Evidence from Subprime Loans', *EFA 2008 Athens Meetings Paper* (December 2008).

Kim, Harold Y. and Jianping Mei, 'Political Risk and Stock Returns: The Case of Hong Kong', *New York University Stern School of Business Finance Department Working Paper Series, 1994*, FD-94-39 (6 December 1994), 1–62.

King, Michael R. and Timothy J. Sinclair, 'Private Actors and Public Policy: A Requiem for the New Basel Capital Accord', *International Political Science Review/Revue internationale de science politique*, Vol. 24, No. 3 (July 2003), 345–62.

Knowles, Stephen and Arlene Garces-Ozanne, 'Government Intervention and Economic Performance in East Asia', *Economic Development and Cultural Change*, Vol. 51, No. 2 (January 2003), 451–77.

KPMG and Barents Group LLC, *Hong Kong Banking into the New Millennium*, Hong Kong Banking Sector Consultancy Study (December 1998) (URL: http://www.info.gov.hk/hkma/eng/public/index.htm — Reference Materials — Banking).

Kregel, J. A., 'Derivatives and global capital flows: applications to Asia', *Cambridge Journal of Economics*, Vol. 22, No. 6 (November 1998), 677–92.

Krueger, Anne O., 'Policy Lessons from Development Experience since the Second World War', in Jere Behrman and T. N. Srinivasan (eds.), *Development Economics*, Vol. IIIB (Amsterdam: Elsevier, 1995).

Lardy, Nicholas R., 'The case of China', in Chung H. Lee (ed.), *Financial Liberalization and the Economic Crisis in Asia* (London: Routledge Curzon, 2003).

Latter, Tony, 'Rules versus Discretion in Managing the Hong Kong dollar, 1983–2006', *HKIMR Working Paper No. 2/2007* (January 2007).

MacElderry, Andrea, 'Confucian Capitalism? Corporate Values in Republican Banking', *Modern China*, Vol. 12, No. 3 (July 1986), 401–16.

Mark, Chi-kwan, 'American "China Hands" in the 1950s', in Cindy Yik-yi Chu (ed.), *Foreign Communities in Hong Kong, 1940s–1950s* (New York: Palgrave Macmillan, 2005).

Miller, Geoffrey P., 'Banking Crises in Perspective: Two Causes and One Cure', in Gerard Caprio, Jr. et al. (eds.), *Preventing Bank Crises: Lessons from Recent Global Bank Failures* (Washington, DC: World Bank, 1998).

Parris, Kristen, 'The Rise of Private Business Interests', in Merle Goldman and Roderick MacFarquhar (eds.), *The Paradox of China's Post-Mao Reforms* (Cambridge, Mass.: Harvard University Press, 1999).

Philippon, Thomas and Ariell Reshef, 'Wages and Human Capital in the U.S. Financial Industry: 1909–2006' (December 2008) (URL: http://pages. stern.nyu.edu/~tphilipp/papers/pr_rev15.pdf).

Pistor, Katharina, 'Banking Reform in the Chinese Mirror', *Columbia Law and Economics Working Paper No. 354* (10 August 2009), 2–34.

Ranciere, Romain, Aaron Tornell and Frank Westermann, 'Decomposing the effects of financial liberalization: Crises vs. Growth', *National Bureau of Economic Research Working Paper 12806* (December 2006), 1–21.

Redak, Vanessa, 'Risks, Ratings and Regulation: Toward a Reorganization of Credit via Basel II?', in Peter Mooslechner et al. (eds.), *The Political Economy Of Financial Market Regulation: The Dynamics of Inclusion and Exclusion* (Cheltenham: Edward Elgar Publishing Ltd, 2006).

Redding, Gordon, 'Culture and Business in Hong Kong', in Wang Gangwu and Wong Siu Lun (eds.), *Dynamic Hong Kong: Business & Culture* (Hong Kong: Centre of Asian Studies, 1997).

Reed, Howard Curtis, 'The Ascent of Tokyo as an International Financial Center', *Journal of International Business Studies*, Vol. 11, No. 3 (Winter 1980), 19–35.

Rodrik, Dani, 'Goodbye Washington Consensus, Hello Washington Confusion? A Review of the World Bank's "Economic Growth in the 1990s: Learning from a Decade of Reform"', *Journal of Economic Literature*, Vol. 44, No. 4 (December 2006), 973–87.

Rogoff, Kenneth, 'International Institutions for Reducing Global Financial Instability', *Journal of Economic Perspectives*, Vol. 13, No. 4 (Autumn 1999), 21–42.

Rosas, Guillermo, 'Bagehot or Bailout? An Analysis of Government Responses to Banking Crises', *American Journal of Political Science*, Vol. 50, No. 1 (January 2006), 175–91.

Schenk, Catherine R., 'Banking and Exchange Rate Relations between Hong Kong and Mainland China in Historical Perspective: 1965–75', in Catherine R. Schenk (ed.), *Hong Kong SAR's Monetary and Exchange Rate Challenges: Historical Perspectives* (Basingstoke: Palgrave Macmillan, 2009).

———, 'The empire strikes back: Hong Kong and the decline of sterling', *Economic History Review*, Vol. LVII, No. 3 (August 2004), 551–80.

———, 'The origins of Anti-competitive Regulation: Was Hong Kong "Over-banked" in the 1960s?', *HKIMR Working Paper No. 9/2006* (July 2006).

Sheng, Andrew, 'Bank Restructuring revisited', in Gerard Caprio, Jr. et al. (eds.), *Preventing Bank Crises: Lessons from Recent Global Bank Failures* (Washington, DC: World Bank, 1998).

Simmons, Beth A., 'The International Politics of Harmonization: The Case of Capital Market Regulation', *International Organization*, Vol. 55, No. 3 (Summer 2001), 589–620.

——— and Zachary Elkins, 'The Globalization of Liberalization: Policy Diffusion in the International Political Economy', *American Political Science Review*, Vol. 98, No. 1 (February 2004), 171–89.

Singer, David Andrew, 'Capital Rules: The Domestic Politics of International Regulatory Harmonization', *International Organization*, Vol. 58, No. 3 (Summer 2004), 531–65.

Singer, H. W., 'The Distribution of Gains between Investing and Borrowing Countries', *American Economic Review*, Vol. 40, No. 2 (May 1950), 473–85.

Spero, Joan E., 'Guiding Global Finance', *Foreign Policy*, No. 73 (Winter 1988–89), 114–34.

Stulz, René M. and Rohan Williamson, 'Culture, openness, and finance', *Journal of Financial Economics*, Vol. 70 (2003), 313–49.

Tang Shu-hung, 'The Economy', in Joseph Y. S. Cheng and Sonny S. H. Lo (eds.), *From Colony to SAR: Hong Kong's Challenges Ahead* (Hong Kong: Chinese University Press, 1995)

Tarbert, Heath Price, 'Are International Capital Adequacy Rules Adequate? The Basle Accord and beyond', *University of Pennsylvania Law Review*, Vol. 148, No. 5 (May 2000), 1771–849.

Taube, Markus, 'Economic Relations between the PRC and the States of Europe', *China Quarterly*, No. 169 (March 2002), 78–107.

Thompson, Edmund R., 'Dangers of Differential Comprehensions of Hong Kong's Competitive Advantages: Evidence from Firms and Public Servants', *China Quarterly*, Vol. 167 (September 2001), 706–23.

Tobin, Damian, 'Austerity and Moral Compromise: Lessons from the Development of China's Banking System', *World Development* (2010),1-12. (doi:10.1016/j.worlddev.2010.10.002).

Turner, Matthew, 'Hong Kong Design and the Roots of Sino-American Trade Disputes', *Annals*, Vol. 547 (September 1999), 37–53.

Wang, JiangYu, 'Regulatory competition and cooperation between securities markets in Hong Kong and Mainland China', *Capital Markets Law Journal*, Vol. 4, No. 3 (July 2009), 383–404.

Williamson, John, 'The Years of Emerging Market Crises: A Review of Feldstein', *Journal of Economic Literature*, Vol. 42, No. 3 (September 2004), 822–37.

Wong, Christine P. W., 'Part One: People's Republic of China', in Pradumna B. Rana and Naved Hamid (eds.), *From Centrally Planned to Market Economies: The Asian Approach*, Vol. 2 (Hong Kong: Oxford University Press, 1996)

Wong, Y. C. Richard, 'Public Policies in the Hong Kong Economy: Emphasis on Manufacturing', in F. Gerard Adams and William E. James (eds.), *Public Policies in East Asian Development: Facing New Challenges* (Westport: Praeger Publishers, 1999).

Woo-Cumings, Meredith, 'Diverse Paths toward "the Right Institutions": Law, the State, and Economic Reform in East Asia', *ADB Institute Working Paper 18* (April 2001), 1–35.

Yao Yufang, Li Fuqiang and Wang Haiyan, 'China's Regional Economic Development: The Factor Analytic Approach', in Roger C. K. Chan, Tien-tung Hsueh and Chiu-ming Lok (eds.), *China's Regional Economic Development* (Hong Kong: Hong Kong Institute of Asia-Pacific Studies, 1996).

Yeh, Wen-Hsin, 'Corporate Space, Communal Time: Everyday Life in China's Bank of China', *American Historical Review*, Vol. 100, No. 1 (February 1995), 97–122.

Yeung, K. Y., Secretary for the Treasury, 'The Role of the Hong Kong Government in Industrial Development', in Edward K. Y. Chen et al. (eds.), *Industrial and Trade Development in Hong Kong* (Hong Kong: Centre of Asian Studies, 1991).

Yip, Leslie Sai-Ching and G. P. Walters, 'Wah Hoi Industrial Company', *Entrepreneurship: Theory and Practice*, Vol. 22, No. 3 (1998), 87–99.

Zhao, Zhijun, Yue Ma, Yak-yeow Kueh, Shu-ki Tsang, Matthew S. Yiu, and Shucheng Liu, 'Banking Deregulation and Macroeconomic Impact in China: A Theoretical Analysis and Implications of WTO Accession to the Mainland and Hong Kong', HKIMR Working Paper No.8/2002 (April 2002).

Official Publications

International Agencies

Ahn, Sanghoon and Philip Hemmings, 'Policy Influences on Economic Growth in OECD Countries: An Evaluation of the Evidence', *Economics Department Working Papers No. 246* (Paris: OECD, 2000).

Arora, Vivek and Athanasios Vamvakidis, 'China's Economic Growth: International Spillovers', *IMF Working Paper WP/10/165* (July 2010), 2–23.

Basel Committee on Banking Supervision, *A New Capital Adequacy Framework*, consultative paper (Basel: Bank for International Settlements, June 1999).

———, 'Supervisory lessons to be drawn from the Asian crisis', *Working Papers No. 2* (June 1999) (Basel: Bank for International Settlements, 1999), 3–59.

BIS, 'History of the Basel Committee and its Membership (August 2009)' (Basel Committee on Banking Supervision, 2009).

Blundell-Wignall, Adrian, Gert Wehinger and Patrick Slovik, 'The Elephant in the Room: The Need to Deal with What Banks Do', *OECD Journal: Financial Market Trends*, Vol. 2009, Issue 2, 2–27.

Borio, Claudio and Gianni Toniolo, 'One hundred and thirty years of central bank cooperation: a BIS perspective', *BIS Working Papers No. 197* (February 2006), 1–31.

Borio, Claudio and Ilhyock Shim, 'What can (macro-)prudential policy do to support monetary policy?', *BIS Working Papers No. 242* (December 2007), 1–38.

Caballero, Ricardo J., 'Sudden Financial Arrest', *IMF Economic Review*, Vol. 58, Issue 1 (August 2010), 6–36.

Claessens, Stijin and Simeon Djankov, 'Publicly-Listed East Asian Corporates: Growth, Financing and Risks', paper presented to the Regional Conference on Asian Corporate Recovery: Corporate Governance, Government Policy (World Bank, 15 March 1999).

——, Giovanni Dell'Ariccia, Deniz Igan and Luc Laeven, 'Lessons and Policy Implications from the Global Financial Crisis', *IMF Working Paper WP/10/44* (February 2010), 3–40.

Cooper, Richard N., 'Almost a century of central bank cooperation', *BIS Working Papers No. 198* (February 2006), 1–17.

Dabla-Norris, Era, 'Issues in Intergovernmental Fiscal Relations in China', *IMF Working Paper* WP/05/30 (February 2005), 3–28.

Feyzioglu, Tarhan, 'Does Good Financial Performance Mean Good Financial Intermediation in China?', *IMF Working Paper WP/09/170* (August 2009), 3–32.

Fonteyne, Wim, Wouter Bossu, Luis Cortavarria-Checkley, Alessandro Giustiniani, Alessandro Gullo, Daniel Hardy and Seán Kerr, 'Crisis Management and Resolution for a European Banking System', *IMF Working Paper WP/10/70* (March 2010), 6–98.

Horton, Mark et al., 'The State of Public Finances: A Cross-Country Fiscal Monitor', *IMF Staff Position Note SPN/09/21* (30 July 2009).

Iakova, Dora, 'How Hong Kong SAR Banks Survived the Asian Crisis', in Jahangir Aziz, Jeanne Gobat, Dora Iakova, William Lee and Peter Breuer, *People's Republic of China — Hong Kong Special Administrative Region Selected Issues and Statistical Appendix*, IMF Country Report No. 01/146 (August 2001), 23–31.

IMF, *Concluding Statement for the Article IV Consultation with the People's Republic of China in respect of the Hong Kong Special Administrative Region* (30 October 1998).

——, 'Cross-Cutting Themes in Economies with Large Banking Systems', (16 April 2010), 3–34.

——, *Global Financial Stability Report: Navigating the Financial Challenges Ahead October 2009* (Washington, DC: International Monetary Fund, 2009).

——, 'IMF Executive Board Concludes 2008 Article IV Consultation Discussions with People's Republic of China — Hong Kong Special Administrative Region', *Public Information Notice (PIN) No. 08/145* (8 December 2008), 1–5.

——, 'IMF Executive Board Concludes 2009 Article IV Consultation with the United Kingdom', *Public Information Notice (PIN) No. 09/84* (16 July 2009).

——, *People's Republic of China Staff Report for the 2010 Article IV Consultation* (9 July 2010).

Jones, Randall S., Robert E. King and Michael Klein, 'Economic Integration between Hong Kong. Taiwan and the Coastal Provinces of China', *OECD Economic Studies No. 20* (Spring 1993), 115–44.

Kodres, Laura and Aditya Narain, 'Redesigning the Contours of the Future Financial System', *IMF Staff Position Note SPN/10/10* (16 August 2010), 3–18.

Laeven, Luc and Fabian Valencia1, 'Resolution of Banking Crises: The Good, the Bad, and the Ugly', IMF Working Paper WP/10/146 (June 2010), 3–35.

Leung, Cynthia and Olaf Unteroberdoerster, 'Hong Kong SAR as a Financial Center for Asia: Trends and Implications', *IMF Working Paper WP/08/57* (March 2008), 1–18.

Mo, Y. K., 'A review of recent banking reforms in China', paper presented in Joint BIS/PBC Conference: 'Strengthening the banking system in China: issues and experience', *BIS Policy Papers No. 7* (October 1999), 90–105.

N'Diaye, Papa, 'Macroeconomic Implications for Hong Kong SAR of Accommodative U.S. Monetary Policy', IMF Working Paper WP/09/256 (November 2009), 1–15.

Strauss-Kahn, Dominique, IMF Managing Director, 'Beyond the Crisis: Sustainable Growth and a Stable International Monetary System', Sixth Annual Bundesbank Lecture (4 September 2009).

Sun, Tao and Xiaojing Zhang, 'Spillovers of the U.S. Subprime Financial Turmoil to Mainland China and Hong Kong SAR: Evidence from Stock Markets', IMF Working Paper WP/09/166 (August 2009), 3–42.

Tumpel-Gugerell, Gertrude, European Central Bank Executive Board Member, 'Business Models in Banking: Is There a Best Practice', paper presented in the CAREFIN Conference, Milan (21 September 2009).

Viñals, Jose and Jonathan Fiechter 'The Making of Good Supervision: Learning to Say "No"', *IMF Staff Position Note SPN/10/08* (18 May 2010), 4–19.

Wehinger, Gert, 'The Turmoil and the Financial Industry: Developments and Policy Responses', *OECD Financial Trends*, Issue 1 (2009).

World Bank, *Doing Business 2010: Reforming through Difficult Times* (Washington, DC: World Bank, 2009).

———, *Doing Business in 2006: Creating Jobs* (Washington, DC: World Bank, 2006).

———, *Managing Capital Inflows in East Asia* (Washington, DC: World Bank, 1995).

———, *The East Asian Miracle. Economic Growth and Public Policy* (New York: Oxford University Press, 1993).

———, Beijing, *Quarterly Update* (May 2007).

China

Cai Beihua, Shanghai Municipal People's Congress, 'Expectations for developing economic relations with Hong Kong', *Shehui Kexue,* No. 7 (15 July 1988), 11–13.

Cai Esheng, CBRC Vice Chairman, Speech at the China Financial Summit Meeting (19 May 2009) (URL: http://www.cbrc.gov.cn/english/home/jsp/docView.jsp?docID=2009071004058B1B7BBADA6DFFD29C0F11131100).

————, PBOC Assistant Governor, 'Financial supervision in China: framework, methods and current issues', paper presented in the Joint BIS/PBC Conference: 'Strengthening the banking system in China: issues and experience', *BIS Policy Papers No. 7* (October 1999), 167–72.

China Banking Regulatory Commission, *2008 Annual Report* (n.d., n.p.).

Contributing Commentator, 'Strive to develop industrial production, communications and transport with readjustment as the core', *Hongqi*, No. 8 (April 1981), 2–4, 8.

CBRC, 'List of foreign banks operating in China in 2010' (http://www.cbrc.gov.cn/chinese/home/jsp/docView.jsp?docID=2045).

Dai Xianglong, PBOC Governor, 'China's Financial Industry at the Threshold of the 21st Century', address at Stanford University (17 October 2000) (URL: http://www.pbc.gov.cn/publish/english/956/1937/19378/19378_.html).

Deng Xiaoping, *Fundamental Issues in Present-day China* (Beijing: Foreign Languages Press, 1987).

Feng Bangyan, 'The Role of Hong Kong in China's Modernisation Process', *Jingji Yanjiu*, No. 4 (20 April 1989), 64–70.

Hu Xiaolian, PBOC Deputy Governor, 'A Managed Floating Exchange Rate Regime is an Established Policy' (15 July 2010), 1–10 (URL: http://www.pbc.gov.cn/publish/english/956/2010/20100727144152118668062/20100727144152118668062_.html).

————, Speech at the 2008 Money and Banking Conference, Buenos Aires (1 September 2008) (URL: http://www.pbc.gov.cn/publish/english/956/1948/19481/19481_.html)

————, Speech at the Symposium on Judicial Interpretation of Law on Real Rights (31 May 2010) (URL: http://www.pbc.gov.cn/publish/english/956/2010/20100712145647328754806/20100712145647328754806_.html).

Hua Quan, 'Financial links between China's Mainland and Hong Kong', *Liaowang* (Overseas edition), No. 11 (17 March 1986), 2.

Jiang Dingzhi, CBRC Vice Chairman, 'Reform and development of China's banking industry in the past thirty years', speech at the CCISSR Forum, Peking University (10 April 2008) (URL: http://www.cbrc.gov.cn/english/home/jsp/docView.jsp?docID=2008042417574602F56CDDD2FF3D0F1898FBD800).

Li Qing and Lin Jianhan, 'A review of the use of foreign capital in the Xiamen Special Economic Zone', *Nanfang Jingji*, No. 6 (1986), 49–52.

Liu Mingkang, CBRC Chairman, Address at the third economic and financial situation briefing of CBRC (20 July 2010) (URL: http://www.cbrc.gov.cn/english/home/jsp/docView.jsp?docID=2010081369FB40E8533AAEBBFF3BDD3E98643100).

————, 'Chinese Bankers Carry Hopes for Future Balances', speech delivered in Hong Kong (20 January 2010) (URL: http://www.cbrc.gov.cn/english/home/jsp/docView.jsp?docID=2010012011DA7AE6925E5D48FF76107FF744C800).

————, 'Six Things that Make Us Concern[ed]', Keynote Speech at the 16th International Conference on Banking Supervision, Singapore (23

September 2010) (URL: http://www.cbrc.gov.cn/english/home/jsp/docView.jsp?docID=201010120E599F9AB245D490FF5BE7AD5A279B00).

——, 'Chairman LIU Mingkang attended on the 3rd economic and financial situation briefing', (20 July 2010) (URL: http://www.cbrc.gov.cn/english/home/jsp/docView.jsp?docID=2010081369FB40E8533AAEBBFF3BDD3E98643100).

National Audit Office, 'No. 6 Announcement of 2010: Audit Investigation Findings on Collection, Application and Management of Special Funds Earmarked for Land and Requisition and Transfer of Land in 40 Municipalities, Regions and Prefectures and 56 Counties and Districts under Their Jurisdiction', *Audit Reports* (17 September 2010) (URL: http://www.cnao.gov.cn/main/articleshow_ArtID_1092.htm).

Peng Naidian, 'Reflections on Deepening Economic and Trade Cooperation between Guangdong, Hong Kong, Macao', *Guoji Maoyi*, No. 6 (27 June 1988), 13–6.

People's Bank of China, *Annual Report 2008* (n.d., n.p.).

——, *China Financial Outlook 2000* (n.d., n.p.).

Qu Shunping, 'Policy Measures for the Utilisation of Foreign Capital in Guangdong', *Guoji Maoyi Wenti*, No. 1 (January–February 1986), 5–11.

Ren Tao, 'Consistency in Policies', in Su Wenning (ed.), *Modernization — the Chinese Way* (Beijing: Beijing Review, 1983).

State Statistical Bureau, *China Statistical Yearbook 1992* (Beijing: Statistical Information and Consultancy Service Centre).

State Statistical Bureau, *Statistical Yearbook of China 1984* (Hong Kong: Economic Information & Agency, 1984).

State Statistical Bureau, *Statistical Yearbook of China 1986* (Hong Kong: Economic Information & Agency, 1986).

Su Ning, PBOC Deputy Governor, 'Fostering Modern credit culture in China', speech at the International Conference on 'Publib Policy for Credit Reporting System' (28 September 2004), 1–4 (URL: http://www.pbc.gov.cn/publish/english/956/1941/19417/19417_.html).

——, 'Press ahead with Reform and Opening-up and Promote the Rapid and Healthy Development of the Financial Sector', speech at the Financial Summit Meeting (10 July 2006) (URL: http://www.pbc.gov.cn/publish/english/956/1945/19459/19459_.html).

Wang Hongzhang, PBOC Chief Disciplinary Officer, Speech at the National Teleconference on Corporate Cards Reform (30 January 2008), 1–5 (URL: http://www.pbc.gov.cn/publish/english/956/1947/19479/19479_.html).

Wang Huaqing, CBRC Vice Chairman, Speech at the 2010 Lujiazui Forum (26 June 2010) (URL: http://www.cbrc.gov.cn/english/home/jsp/docView.jsp?docID=201007210339137CBE126B75FFDDE305CD598400).

White Paper, *China's Efforts to Combat Corruption and Build a Clean Government* (Beijing: State Council Information Office 2010) (URL: http://english.gov.cn/official/2010-12/29/content_1775353.htm).

Wu Xiaoling, PBOC Deputy Governor, Remarks at the International Seminar on the Tenth Anniversary of the Asian Financial Crisis (21 June 2007), 1–6

(URL: http://www.pbc.gov.cn/publish/english/956/1946/19467/19467_.
html).

————, 'Strengthen China's Financial Industry in the Process of Opening
up' (14 February 2006), 1–6 (URL: http://www.pbc.gov.cn/publish/
english/956/1945/19452/19452_.html).

Xiang Junbo, PBOC Deputy Governor, 'Improve the Legal System to Prevent
Financial Risks', speech at the '2005 High-level Forum of China's Financial
Reform' (26 April 2005), 1–10 (URL: http://www.pbc.gov.cn/publish/
english/956/1942/19428/19428_.html).

Xu Dixin, 'On Hong Kong's economic relations with the Chinese Mainland',
Liaowang (Overseas edition), No. 1 (16 September 1985), 22–3.

Yang Peixin, 'Banking', in Yu Guangyuan (ed.), *China's Socialist Modernization*
(Beijing: Foreign Languages Press, 1984).

Yang Qinquan and Jiang Zhiyuan, 'Analysis of the results of Guangzhou's
foreign economic cooperation and future strategy', *Guangzhou Yanjiu*, No. 5
(September–October 1985), 35–7.

Yang Xin, 'Hong Kong's foreign banks energetically develop their China
business', *Gang Ao Jingji*, No. 3 (25 March 1985), 17–9.

Zhou Xiaochuan, PBOC Governor, Address at the Global Think-tank Summit (3
July 2009), 1–6 (URL: http://www.pbc.gov.cn/publish/english/956/2009/
20091229122954330948779/20091229122954330948779_.html).

————, 'Capital Return of State-owned Enterprises', speech at the 2005 Annual
Meeting of China Enterprises' Leaders (11 December 2005), 1–6 (URL:
http://www.pbc.gov.cn/publish/english/956/1944/19448/19448_.html)

————, 'Improve Corporate Governance and Develop Capital Market', speech at
the *Euromoney* 'China Forum: Capital Market and Corporate Governance',
Beijing (1 December 2004), 1–6 (URL: http://www.pbc.gov.cn/publish/
english/956/1942/19421/19421_.html).

————, 'Improve Legal System and Financial Ecology', speech at the 'Forum of
50 Chinese Economists' (2 December 2004), 1–15 (URL: http://www.pbc.
gov.cn/publish/english/956/1942/19422/19422_.html).

————, 'Instability and Evolution of the Financial System' (5 December 2007), 1–7
(URL: http://www.pbc.gov.cn/publish/english/956/1947/19476/19476_.
html).

————, 'Learn Lessons from the Past for the Benefit of Future Endeavour',
speech at the China Bond Market Development Summit, Beijing
(20 October 2005), 1–9 (URL: http://www.pbc.gov.cn/publish/
english/956/1943/19439/19439_.html).

————, 'Opening to the Outside World: Past Experience and Prospects',
speech at the conference to launch the *World Economic Development
Declaration* (10 November 2003) (URL: http://www.pbc.gov.cn/publish/
english/956/1939/19393/19393_.html).

————, 'Preventing Future Accumulation of Large NPLs by the Commercial
Banks after the Present Round of Reform', speech at the China Summit of
the 7th Beijing International Science Industry Expo (21 May 2004) (URL:
http://www.pbc.gov.cn/publish/english/956/1940/19408/19408_.html).

———, 'Reform of the internal control and internal incentive systems of the commercial banks', speech at the Beijing Finance Expo, Beijing (1 September 2005), 1–7 (URL: http://www.pbc.gov.cn/publish/english/956/1943/19435/19435_.html)

———, 'Some Issues Concerning the Reform of the State-owned Commercial Banks', speech at the IIF Spring Membership Conference, Shanghai (16 April 2004) (URL: http://www.pbc.gov.cn/publish/english/956/1940/19407/19407_.html).

———, 'Some Observations and Analyses on Savings Ratio', speech at the Bank Negara Malaysia High Level Conference, Kuala Lumpur (10 February 2009), 1–20 (URL: http://www.pbc.gov.cn/history_file/files/att_19482_1.pdf).

Hong Kong

A Policy Paper on Securities and Futures Markets Reform (Hong Kong: HKSARG, 1999).

Census and Statistics Department, *2003 Gross Domestic Product* (Hong Kong: Census and Statistics Department, 2004).

———, *Hong Kong Annual Digest of Statistics*, 1988 ed. (Hong Kong: Census and Statistics Department, 1988).

———, *Hong Kong Statistics 1947–1967* (Hong Kong: Government Printer, 1969).

———, *Report on Hong Kong Trade in Services Statistics for 2008* (Hong Kong: Census and Statistics Department, 2010).

Chan, Norman, HKMA Deputy Chief Executive, 'The Asian Financial Crisis: What have we Learnt?', speech to the Oxford University Asia-Pacific Affairs Society (7 June 1999).

He, Dong et al., 'Hong Kong's Financial Market Interactions with the US and Mainland China in Crisis and Tranquil Times', *Hong Kong Monetary Authority Working Paper 10/2009* (16 June 2009).

HKMA, 'Policy Response to the Banking Sector Consultancy Study', *HKMA* (June 1999).

Hong Kong Report for the Year 1969 (Hong Kong: Government Press, 1970).

Industry Development Branch, 'Memorandum to the Loans for Small Industry Committee', Department *of Commerce and Industry, IND 2/903* (4 November 1969), mimeo.

———, 'The Case for Improved Access to Loans for Re-equipment Purposes by Small Scale Industry', *Commerce and Industry Department, IND 2/903* (27 October 1969), mimeo.

Jiang, Guorong et al., 'Banking Sector Competition in Hong Kong — Measurement and Evolution Over Time', *Hong Kong Monetary Authority Research Memoranda* (20 April 2004).

Li, Charles, HKEx Chief Executive, 'Six Questions Regarding the Internationalisation of the Renminbi' (21 September 2010) (URL: http://www.hkex.com.hk/eng/newsconsul/speech/2010/sp100920.htm).

Nugée, John, 'A Brief History of the Exchange Fund', *Hong Kong Monetary Authority Quarterly Bulletin*, No. 3 (May 1995), 1–17.

Owen, Robert, 'Hong Kong Maintains Tradition of Light-Handed Regulation', in Securities and Futures Commission, *Securities Regulation in Hong Kong* (Hong Kong: Securities and Futures Commission, 2002).

Report of the Advisory Committee on Diversification 1979 (Hong Kong: Government Printer, 1979).

Report of the Commission … to Enquire into the Causes and Effects of the Present Trade Recession … (Hong Kong: Noronha & Co., 1935).

Securities and Futures Commission, 'Hong Kong as a Leading Financial Centre in Asia', *Supervision of Markets Division Research Department Research paper No. 33* (August 2006), 1–14.

Tomkins, H. J., *Report on the Hong Kong Banking System and Recommendations for the Replacement of the Banking Ordinance 1948* (Hong Kong: Government Printer, 1962).

Wong, Eric, Tom Fong, Ka-fai Li and Henry Choi, 'An assessment of the long-term economic impact of the new regulatory reform on Hong Kong', *Hong Kong Monetary Authority Research Note 05/2010* (9 November 2010).

Yam, Joseph, HKMA Chief Executive, 'Hong Kong — New Opportunities as an International Financial Centre', *HKMA*, 8 May 2007.

————, 'Hong Kong and Asia: Strategies for Recovery', *Far Eastern Economic Review* Conference, *HKMA*, 16 June 1999.

————, 'Issues in Monetary Policy', Hong Kong University Speech, *HKMA*, 19 January 2004.

————, 'Speech British Chamber of Commerce', *HKMA*, 20 October 2006.

————, 'The Lender of Last Resort', Hong Kong Association of Banks, *HKMA*, 29 June 1999.

————, 'The Political Process of Monetary Management', Hong Kong Management Association 13th Susan Yuen Memorial Lecture, *HKMA*, 20 October 1998.

————, 'Towards a Stronger Financial System', speech to the Hong Kong Society of Accountants, *HKMA*, 29 October 1999.

————, 'Viewpoint: Alan Greenspan and the Federal Reserve', *HKMA*, 1 February 2001.

————, 'Viewpoint: The roles of the HKMA', *HKMA*, 8 June 2000.

Yiu, Matthew S., Wai-Yip Alex Ho and Lu Jin, 'A measure of financial stress in Hong Kong financial market — The financial stress index', *Hong Kong Monetary Authority Research Note 02/2010* (3 March 2010).

Zhang, Zhiwei and Honglin Wang, 'What triggered China's economic slowdown in 2008? The role of commodity price volatilities', *Hong Kong Monetary Authority Research Note 01/2010* (9 February 2010).

Hong Kong Public Records Office (unpublished):

HKRS41-1-3044 'The Nam Sang Bank — 1. Application from … for a Banking Licence. 2. Balance Sheet of … 3. Cancellation of the Licence of … '.

HKRS41-1-6691 'Banking Operations Legislation for Control of … '.

HKRS163-1-305 'Retail Price & Wages Index. Preparation of … '.

HKRS163-1-402 'China Trade And Commerce — Aide Memoire re Closer Cooperation between China and Hong Kong in Connection with Trade and Exchange Control'.

HKRS163-1-403 'China Trade & Commerce — Aide Memoire re Closer Cooperation between China and Hong Kong in Connection with Trade and Exchange Control'.

HKRS163-1-442 'Import and Exchange Control in Hong Kong Proposed Visit of a H.K. Govt. Officer to the U.K. in Connection with … '.

HKRS163-1-634 'Public Utilities Companies Proposed Control of the Charges and Dividends Levied by … '.

HKRS163-1-679 'Banking Advisory Committee — 1. Minutes of the First Meeting held on 27.05.48 2. Banking Advisory Committee Circulars'.

HKRS163-1-2861 'Cotton Textiles Allocation of Quota to Restricted Markets'.

HKRS163-3-269 'Investment Guarantees by the United States Government'.

HKRS163-9-88 'Trade — Balance of Payment Statistics. Policy Regarding Preparation of … '.

HKRS163-9-217 '(A) Meeting of Senior Commonwealth Finance Officials 1970. Sterling Area Balance of Payments — Developments and Prospects to Mid-1971 (B) Overseas Sterling Area Countries Statistics'.

HKRS169-2-26 'Currency and Banking'.

HKRS169-2-53 'Rehabilitation of Business'.

HKRS170-1-307 'Banking Legislation — 1. General Supervision of Banking Concerns in Hong Kong 2. Appointment of a Committee in 1935 to Consider the Desirability of Specific Legislation for the Regulation of Banking Operations in the Colony 3. Report of the Committee 4. Appointment of a Committee in 1939 to Consider Further Action on This Question'.

HKRS270-5-44 'Commercial and Industrial Development — Major Policy'.

HKRS270-5-56 'Cotton Advisory Board. Minutes of Meeting'.

Ireland

Regling, Klaus and Max Watson, *A Preliminary Report on The Sources of Ireland's Banking Crisis* (Dublin: Government Publications, 2010).

The Irish Banking Crisis Regulatory and Financial Stability Policy 2003–2008. A Report to the Minister for Finance by the Governor of the Central Bank (31 May 2010), 16–7 (URL: http://www.bankinginquiry.gov.ie/The%20Irish%20 Banking%20Crisis%20Regulatory%20and%20Financial%20Stability%20 Policy%202003-2008.pdf).

United Kingdom

Bailey, Andrew, BofE Executive Director, 'Financial Reform', London (21 September 2010), 2-5. (URL: http://www.bankofengland.co.uk/ publications/speeches/2010/speech447.pdf).

Bean, Charles, BofE Deputy Governor, 'Measuring Recession and Recovery: An Economic Perspective', speech at the RSS Statistics User Forum Conference (27 October 2010), 2–10 (URL http://www.bankofengland.co.uk/ publications/speeches/2010/speech457.pdf).

———, 'Some Lessons for Monetary Policy from the Recent Financial Turmoil', remarks at the Conference on 'Globalisation, Inflation and Monetary Policy' (22 November 2008) (URL: http://www.bankofengland.co.uk/ publications/speeches/2008/speech368.pdf).

———, 'The Great Moderation, the Great Panic and the Great Contraction', Schumpeter Lecture of the Annual Congress of the European Economic

Association (25 August 2009) (URL: http://www.bankofengland.co.uk/ publications/speeches/2009/speech399.pdf).

———, and Matthias Paustian, Adrian Penalver and Tim Taylor, 'Monetary Policy after the Fall', paper presented at the Federal Reserve Bank of Kansas City Annual Conference (28 August 2010), 3–65 (URL: http://www. bankofengland.co.uk/publications/speeches/2010/speech444.pdf).

Blanchflower, David, BofE Monetary Policy Committee Member, 'The Future of Monetary Policy', Open Lecture at Cardiff University (24 March 2009) (URL: http://www.bankofengland.co.uk/publications/speeches/2009/ speech382.pdf).

Bond, Ian, BofE Financial Crisis Management Division Head, 'Managing a Bank-specific Crisis: A UK Perspective', BBA workshop on managing a bank-specific crisis (26 October 2006) (URL: http://www.bankofengland.co.uk/ publications/speeches/2006/presentation061026.pdf).

Clark, Alastair, BofE Executive Director, 'Accounting Standards and International Financial Markets', speech at the Institute of Chartered Accountants in Banking, Dublin (3 May 2000) (URL: http://www.bankofengland.co.uk/ publications/speeches/2000/speech84.htm).

Clementi, David, BofE Deputy Governor, 'Banks and Systemic Risk — Theory and Evidence', speech at the Bank of England Conference (23 May 2001) (URL: http://www.bankofengland.co.uk/publications/speeches/2001/ speech130.htm).

———, 'Crisis prevention and resolution — two aspects of financial stability', Inaugural Lecture at the South Bank University Centre for Monetary and Financial Economics (6 September 2000) (URL: http://www. bankofengland.co.uk/publications/speeches/2000/speech97.htm).

———, 'Property and the Economy', speech at the Chartered Surveyors Livery Company International Dinner (29 April 2002) (URL: http://www. bankofengland.co.uk/publications/speeches/2002/speech170.pdf).

FSA, 'Memorandum from the Financial Services Authority (FSA)', in House of Commons Treasury Committee, *Banking Crisis*, Vol. II. Written evidence (London: HMSO, HC 144-II, March 2009).

Gieve, John, BofE Deputy Governor, 'Financial System Risks in the UK — Issues and Challenges', speech at the Centre for the Study of Financial Innovation Roundtable (25 July 2006) (URL: http://www.bankofengland.co.uk/ publications/speeches/2006/speech280.pdf).

———, 'Seven lessons from the last three years' (19 February 2009) (URL: http://www.bankofengland.co.uk/publications/speeches/2009/ speech377.pdf).

———, 'The City's Growth: The Crest of a Wave or Swimming with the Stream?', speech to the London Society of Chartered Accountants (26 March 2007) (URL: http://www.bankofengland.co.uk/publications/speeches/2007/ speech306.pdf).

———, 'Uncertainty, policy and financial markets', speech at the Barbican Centre (24 July 2007) (URL: http://www.bankofengland.co.uk/ publications/speeches/2007/speech321.pdf).

Haldane, Andrew G., BofE Executive Director, 'Rethinking the Financial Network', speech at the Financial Students Association, Amsterdam (28 April 2009) (URL: http://www.bankofengland.co.uk/publications/speeches/2009/speech386.pdf).

——, 'Small Lessons from a Big Crisis', remarks at the Federal Reserve Bank of Chicago 45th Annual Conference (8 May 2009) (URL: http://www.bankofengland.co.uk/publications/speeches/2009/speech397.pdf).

——, 'The $100 Billion Dollar Question', comments given at the Institute of Regulation & Risk, Hong Kong (30 March 2010) (http://www.bankofengland.co.uk/publications/speeches/2010/speech433.pdf).

——, 'The Contribution of the Financial Sector: Miracle or Mirage?', speech at the Future of Finance Conference, London (14 July 2010) (URL: http://www.bankofengland.co.uk/publications/speeches/2010/speech442.pdf)

HMG, *Reforming financial markets* (London: HMSO, Cm 7667/2009).

Hogg, Ken, FSA Insurance Sector Director, 'Key priorities in regulation — outlining the FSA's strategy', speech at the Future of Life Assurance IEA Conference (19 May 2010) (URL: http://www.fsa.gov.uk/pages/Library/Communication/Speeches/2010/0519_kh.shtml).

House of Commons Treasury Committee, *Banking Crisis*, Vol. I Oral evidence (HMSO: HC 144–I, March 2009).

——, *Banking Crisis: regulation and supervision. Fourteenth Report of Session 2008–09* (London: HMSO, HC 767, 21 July 2009).

——, *Banking Reform Seventeenth Report of Session 2007–08* (London: HMSO, HC 1008, September 2008).

——, *Financial Stability and Transparency Sixth Report of Session 2007–08* (London: HMSO, HC 371, March 2008).

——, *Re-appointment of Mervyn King as Governor of the Bank of England Tenth Report of Session 2007–08*, Vol. I. Report together with formal minutes (London: HMSO, HC 524-I, April 2008).

——, *Re–appointment of Mervyn King as Governor of the Bank of England Tenth Report of Session 2007–08*, Vol. II. Oral and written evidence (London: HMSO, HC 524-II, June 2008).

——, *The run on the Rock Fifth Report of Session 2007–08*, Vol. I. (London: HMSO, HC56-I, January 2008).

Huertas, Thomas, FSA Banking Sector Director, 'Competition in Banking: The Role of Orderly Entry and Orderly Exit', speech at the Chatham House Conference, London (20 June 2008) (URL: http://www.fsa.gov.uk/pages/Library/Communication/Speeches/2008/0620_th.shtml).

——, 'The Outlook for Banking and Banking Regulation', speech at the ICFR Inaugural Summit, London (1 April 2009) (URL: http://www.fsa.gov.uk/pages/Library/Communication/Speeches/2009/0401_th.shtml).

Jenkinson, Nigel, BofE Executive Financial Stability Director, et al. 'Financial Innovation: What Have We Learnt?', Reserve Bank of Australia Conference on Lessons from the Financial Turmoil of 2007 and 2008 (14–15 July 2008) (URL: http://www.bankofengland.co.uk/publications/speeches/2008/speech351.pdf).

King, Mervyn, BofE Governor, Address to the 2010 Trades Union Congress, Manchester (15 September 2010), 2–7 (URL: http://www.bankofengland.co.uk/publications/speeches/2010/speech446.pdf)

———, 'Banking and the Bank of England', speech to the British Bankers Association, London (10 June 2008) (URL: www.bankofengland.co.uk/publications/speeches/2008/speech347.pdf).

———, 'Banking: From Bagehot to Basel, and Back Again', speech to the Buttonwood Gathering, New York (25 October 2010), 2–25 (URL: http://www.bankofengland.co.uk/publications/speeches/2010/speech455.pdf).

———, 'Finance: A Return from Risk', speech to the Worshipful Company of International Bankers (17 March 2009) (URL: http://www.bankofengland.co.uk/publications/speeches/2009/speech381.pdf).

———, Speech at the Civic Centre, Newcastle (25 January 2011), 1-8 (URL: http://www.bankofengland.co.uk/publications/speeches/2011/speech471.pdf).

———, Speech at the Lord Mayor's Banquet for Bankers and Merchants, London (16 June 2010), 2–8 (URL: http://www.bankofengland.co.uk/publications/speeches/2010/speech437.pdf).

Large, Andrew, BofE Deputy Governor, 'Basel II and Systemic Stability', British Bankers' Association — Basel II/Cad 3 Conference (13 March 2003), 2–9 (URL: http://www.bankofengland.co.uk/publications/speeches/2003/speech191.pdf).

———, 'Convergence in Insurance and Banking: Some Financial Stability Issues', speech at the Mandarin Oriental Hotel (12 June 2003) (URL: http://www.bankofengland.co.uk/publications/speeches/2003/speech196.pdf).

———, 'Financial Stability Oversight, Past & Present', speech at the London School of Economics (22 January 2004) (URL: http://www.bankofengland.co.uk/publications/speeches/2004/speech212.pdf).

Posen, Adam S., BoE Monetary Policy Committee External Member, 'The British Recovery in International Comparison', speech at the Society of Business Economists Annual Conference, London (30 June 2010), 2–24 (URL: http://www.bankofengland.co.uk/publications/speeches/2010/speech439.pdf).

Ross, Verena, FSA Director, 'Lessons from the Financial Crisis', speech at the Chatham House Conference on Global Financial Regulation (24 March 2009) (URL: http://www.fsa.gov.uk/pages/Library/Communication/Speeches/2009/0324_vr.shtml).

———, 'Risk management governance and controls and their importance in banking system and financial sector stability', speech at the Financial Stability Institute and Executives' meeting of East Asia-Pacific Central Banks (18 November 2008) (URL: http://www.fsa.gov.uk/pages/Library/Communication/Speeches/2008/1118_vr.shtml).

Sants, Hector, FSA Chief Executive, 'Do regulators have a role to play in judging culture and ethics?', speech at the Chartered Institute of Securities and Investments Conference (17 June 2010) (URL: http://www.fsa.gov.uk/pages/Library/Communication/Speeches/2010/0617_hs.shtml).

————, 'The challenges facing bank regulation', speech to the Association of Corporate Treasurers (14 May 2009) (URL: http://www.fsa.gov.uk/pages/Library/Communication/Speeches/2009/0514_hs.shtml).

————, and Mary Schapiro, SEC Chairman, 'FSA and SEC discuss approaches to global regulatory requirements', *FSA Press Release FSA/PN/124/2009 916* (16 September 2009) (URL: http://www.fsa.gov.uk/pages/Library/Communication/PR/2009/124.shtml).

Treaty Series No. 9 (1949), *Exchange of Notes … for the Prevention of Smuggling between Hong Kong and Chinese Ports,* (London: Cmd 7615/1949).

Tucker, Paul, BofE Deputy Governor, 'Financial Crisis and G20 Financial Regulatory Reform: An Overview', remarks at the FSB and Korean G20 Presidential Committee Conference, Korea (3 September 2010), 2–7 (URL: http://www.bankofengland.co.uk/publications/speeches/2010/speech460.pdf).

————, Remarks at the Institute of International Bankers Annual Breakfast Regulatory Dialogue, Washington, DC (11 October 2010), 2–8 (URL: http://www.bankofengland.co.uk/publications/speeches/2010/speech459.pdf).

————, Remarks at The Turner Review Conference (27 March 2009) (URL: http://www.bankofengland.co.uk/publications/speeches/2009/speech384.pdf).

Turner, Lord (Adair), FSA Chairman, Address to the IAIS Annual Conference, Dubai (27 October 2010) (URL: http://www.fsa.gov.uk/pages/Library/Communication/Speeches/2010/1027_at.shtml).

————, Annual Public Meeting Speech (23 July 2009) (URL: http://www.fsa.gov.uk/pages/Library/Communication/Speeches/2009/2307_at.shtml).

————, 'Banks are different: should accounting reflect that fact?', speech to The Institute of Chartered Accountants in England and Wales, London (21 January 2010) (URL: http://www.fsa.gov.uk/pages/Library/Communication/Speeches/2010/0121_at.shtml).

————, 'Building a more stable global banking system', speech at the Global Financial Forum, New York (27 April 2009) (URL: http://www.fsa.gov.uk/pages/Library/Communication/Speeches/2009/0427_at.shtml).

————, Mansion House Speech, London (21 September 2010) (URL: http://www.fsa.gov.uk/pages/Library/Communication/Speeches/2010/0921_at.shtml).

————, 'Priorities for the reform of global regulation — challenging past assumptions', speech at IOSCO 2009, Tel Aviv (11 June 2009) (URL: http://www.fsa.gov.uk/pages/Library/Communication/Speeches/2009/0611_at.shtml).

————, 'Protecting Consumers and Winning Trust', speech at the British Bankers' Association Conference (13 July 2010) (URL: http://www.fsa.gov.uk/pages/Library/Communication/Speeches/2010/0713_at.shtml).

————, 'Something old and something new: Novel and familiar drivers of the latest crisis', speech to the European Association of Banking and Financial History, Brussels (21 May 2010) (URL: http://www.fsa.gov.uk/pages/Library/Communication/Speeches/2010/0521_at.shtml).

———, Speech at The Turner Review Conference (27 March 2009) (URL: http://www.fsa.gov.uk/pages/Library/Communication/ Speeches/2009/0327_at.shtml).

———, 'The financial crisis and the future of financial regulation', The Economist's Inaugural City Lecture (21 January 2009) (URL: http://www.fsa. gov.uk/pages/Library/Communication/Speeches/2009/0121_at.shtml).

———, *The Turner Review. A regulatory response to the global banking crisis* (London: Financial Services Authority, March 2009).

———, 'What do banks do, what should they do and what public policies are needed to ensure best results for the real economy?', speech at the CASS Business School (17 March 2010), 1–31 (URL: http://www.fsa.gov.uk/ pages/library/communication/speeches/2010/0317_at.shtml).

United States

Bair, Sheila C., FDIC Chairman, 'Ending Too Big To Fail: The FDIC and Financial Reform', remarks at the 2010 Glauber Lecture at the John F. Kennedy Jr. Forum, Harvard University (20 October 2010) (URL: http://www.fdic.gov/ news/news/speeches/chairman/spoct2110.html).

———, Keynote Address to the 'Mortgages and the Future of Housing Finance' Symposium, Arlington (25 October 2010) (URL: http://www.fdic.gov/ news/news/speeches/chairman/spoct2510.html).

———, Remarks at the Bear Stearns Mortgage and Structured Product Conference, New York (17 January 2008) (URL: http://www.fdic.gov/ news/news/speeches/archives/2008/chairman/spjan1708.html).

———, Remarks to the Global Association of Risk Professionals, New York (25 February 2008) (URL: http://www.fdic.gov/news/news/speeches/ archives/2008/chairman/spfeb2508.html).

———, 'Restoring the Strength and Vitality of the U.S. Financial System', remarks before the Risk Management Association, Baltimore (18 October 2010) (URL: http://www.fdic.gov/news/news/speeches/chairman/ spoct1810.html).

———, Statement on Implementing the Dodd-Frank Wall Street Reform and Consumer Protection Act before the Senate Committee on Banking, Housing, and Urban Affairs (30 September 2010) (URL: http://www.fdic. gov/news/news/speeches/chairman/spsep3010.html).

———, Statement on the Causes and Current State of the Financial Crisis before the Financial Crisis Inquiry Commission (14 January 2010) (URL: http:// www.fdic.gov/news/news/speeches/chairman/spjan1410.html).

———, Testimony on Modernizing Bank Supervision and Regulation before the Senate Committee on Banking, Housing and Urban Affairs (19 March 2009) (URL: http://www.fdic.gov/news/news/speeches/archives/2009/ spmar0319.html).

———, Testimony on Regulatory Perspectives on Financial Regulatory Reform Proposals before the House of Representatives Financial Services Committee (24 July 2009) (URL: http://www.fdic.gov/news/news/ speeches/archives/2009/spjuly2409.html).

————, Testimony on the State of the Banking Industry before the Senate Committee on Banking, Housing and Urban Affairs (4 March 2008) (URL: http://www.fdic.gov/news/news/speeches/archives/2008/chairman/spmar0408.html).

Barr, Michael, US Treasury Assistant Secretary for Financial Institutions, Remarks on Regulatory Reform to the Exchequer Club, Washington, DC (15 July 2009) (URL: http://www.treasury.gov/press-center/press-releases/Pages/tg213.aspx).

Bernanke, Ben S., FRB Chairman, 'Central Bank Independence, Transparency, and Accountability', speech at the Institute for Monetary and Economic Studies International Conference, Tokyo (25 May 2010) (URL: http://www.federalreserve.gov/newsevents/speech/bernanke20100525a.htm).

————, 'Economic Challenges: Past, Present, and Future', speech at the Dallas Regional Chamber (7 April 2010).

————, 'Economic Policy: Lessons from History', speech at the 43rd Annual Alexander Hamilton Awards Dinner, Center for the Study of the Presidency and Congress, Washington, DC (8 April 2010) (http://www.federalreserve.gov/newsevents/speech/bernanke20100408a.htm).

————, 'Financial Innovation and Consumer Protection', speech at the Sixth Biennial Community Affairs Research Conference, Washington, DC (17 April 2009) (URL: http://www.federalreserve.gov/newsevents/speech/bernanke20090417a.htm).

————, 'Financial Reform to Address Systemic Risk', speech at the Council on Foreign Relations, Washington, DC (10 March 2009). (URL: http://www.federalreserve.gov/newsevents/speech/bernanke20090310a.htm).

————, 'Four Questions about the Financial Crisis', speech at the Morehouse College, Atlanta, Georgia (14 April 2009) (URL: http://www.federalreserve.gov/newsevents/speech/bernanke20090414a.htm).

————, 'Hedge Funds and Systemic Risk', speech at the Federal Reserve Bank of Atlanta's 2006 Financial Markets Conference, Georgia (16 May 2006) (URL: http://www.federalreserve.gov/newsevents/speech/bernanke20060516a.htm).

————, 'Implications of the Financial Crisis for Economics', speech at the Conference Co-sponsored by the Center for Economic Policy Studies and the Bendheim Center for Finance, Princeton University (24 September 2010) (URL: http://www.federalreserve.gov/newsevents/speech/bernanke20100924a.htm).

————, 'On Milton Friedman's Ninetieth Birthday', remarks at the Conference to Honor Milton Friedman, University of Chicago (8 November 2002) (URL: http://www.federalreserve.gov/boarddocs/speeches/2002/20021108/default.htm).

————, 'Regulatory restructuring', testimony before the House of Representatives Committee on Financial Services (24 July 2009) (URL: http://www.federalreserve.gov/newsevents/testimony/bernanke20090724a.htm).

————, Remarks at the Federal Reserve Bank of Dallas Conference on 'The Legacy of Milton and Rose Friedman's *Free to Choose*', Dallas (24

October 2003) (URL: http://www.federalreserve.gov/boarddocs/speeches/2003/20031024/default.htm).

———, 'The Transition from Academic to Policymaker', remarks at the Annual Meeting of the American Economic Association, Philadelphia (7 January 2005) (URL: http://www.federalreserve.gov/boarddocs/speeches/2005/20050107/default.htm).

Casey, Kathleen L., SEC Commissioner, Remarks at the Commission Open Meeting (3 December 2008) (URL: http://www.sec.gov/news/speech/2008/spch120308klc.htm).

Congressional Budget Office, *Report on the Troubled Asset Relief Program — November 2010* (Washington DC: CBO Report, 2010).

Cox, Christopher, SEC Chairman, Address to the Joint Meeting of the Exchequer Club and Women in Housing and Finance (4 December 2008) (URL: http://www.sec.gov/news/speech/2008/spch120408cc.htm).

Duke, Elizabeth A., FRB Governor, 'Consumer protection', testimony before the House of Representatives Subcommittee on Domestic Monetary Policy and Technology, Committee on Financial Services (16 July 2009) (URL: http://www.federalreserve.gov/newsevents/testimony/duke20090716a.htm).

———, 'Credit availability and prudent lending standards', testimony before the House of Representatives Committee on Financial Services (25 March 2009) (URL: http://www.federalreserve.gov/newsevents/testimony/duke20090325a.htm).

Ferguson, Roger W., Jr., FRB Vice Chairman, 'Financial Engineering and Financial Stability', remarks at the Annual Conference on the Securities Industry, American Institute of Certified Public Accountants and the Financial Management Division of the Securities Industry Association, New York (20 November 2002) (URL: http://www.federalreserve.gov/boarddocs/speeches/2002/20021120/default.htm).

Financial Crisis Inquiry Commission, *Final Report of the National Commission on the Causes of the Financial and Economic Crisis in the United States* (Official Government Edition, 21 January 2011) (URL: http://c0182732.cdn1.cloudfiles.rackspacecloud.com/fcic_final_report_full.pdf).

Geithner, Timothy F., U.S. Treasury Secretary, Speech at the Economic Club of Washington (21 April 2009) (URL: http://www.treasury.gov/press-center/press-releases/Pages/tg96.aspx).

Greenspan, Alan, FRB Chairman, Testimony before the House of Representatives, Committee on Banking and Financial Services (16 September 1998) (URL: http://commdocs.house.gov/committees/bank/hba51202.000/hba51202_2.HTM).

Schapiro, Mary L., SEC Chairman, Testimony concerning Regulation of Systemic Risk before the Senate Committee on Banking, Housing and Urban Affairs (23 July 2009) (URL: http://www.sec.gov/news/testimony/2009/ts072309mls.htm).

SEC, 'SEC Actions During Turmoil in Credit Markets' (22 January 2009) (URL: http://www.sec.gov/news/press/sec-actions.htm).

Special Inspector General for the Troubled Asset Relief Program, 'Extraordinary Financial Assistance Provided to Citigroup, Inc.', Washington DC (13

January 2011), 1-70. (URL: http://www.sigtarp.gov/reports/audit/2011/ Extraordinary%20Financial%20Assistance%20Provided%20to%20 Citigroup,%20Inc.pdf).

Spillenkothen, Richard, FRB Director, 'Oversight of investment banks' response to the lessons of Enron', testimony before the Senate Permanent Subcommittee on Investigations of the Committee on Governmental Affairs (11 December 2002) (URL: http://www.federalreserve.gov/boarddocs/ testimony/2002/20021211/default.htm).

Tafara, Ethiopis, SEC Director, 'A Few Observations Based on International Regulatory Conversations', speech at the CESR Conference, Paris (23 February 2009) (URL: http://www.sec.gov/news/speech/2009/ spch022309et.htm).

Tarullo, Daniel K., FRB Governor, 'Financial Regulatory Reform', speech at the U.S. Monetary Policy Forum, New York (26 February 2010) (URL: http:// www.federalreserve.gov/newsevents/speech/tarullo20100226a.htm).

————, 'Involving Markets and the Public in Financial Regulation', speech at the Council of Institutional Investors Meeting, Washington, DC (13 April 2010) (URL: http://www.bankofengland.co.uk/publications/speeches/2010/ speech433.pdf).

US Treasury, 'The Role of the Federal Reserve in Preserving Financial and Monetary Stability: Joint Statement by the Department of the Treasury and the Federal Reserve' (23 March 2009) (URL: http://www.treasury.gov/ press-center/press-releases/Pages/tg66.aspx).

Walter, Elisse B., SEC Commissioner, Testimony Concerning Securities Law Enforcement in the Current Financial Crisis before the House of Representatives Committee on Financial Services (20 March 2009) (URL: http://www.sec.gov/news/testimony/2009/ts032009ebw.htm).

Warsh, Kevin, FRB Governor, 'Regulation and Its Discontents', speech at the New York Association for Business Economics, New York (3 February 2010) (URL: http://www.federalreserve.gov/newsevents/speech/warsh20100203a.htm).

————, 'The Panic of 2008', speech at the Council of Institutional Investors 2009 Spring Meeting, Washington, DC (6 April 2009) (URL: http://www. federalreserve.gov/newsevents/speech/warsh20090406a.htm).

Index